the
narrative
voice

the narrative voice

Short Stories and Reflections
by Canadian Authors

Edited and with an Introduction by John Metcalf

McGraw-Hill Ryerson Limited
Toronto   Montreal   New York   London   Sydney
Johannesburg   Mexico   Panama   Düsseldorf
Singapore   Rio de Janeiro   Kuala Lumpur   New Delhi

the narrative voice

ISBN   0-07-092791-X

Library of Congress Catalog Card Number   79-38534

 2345678910   HR72   109876543

Printed and bound in Canada

Photo Credits
Pages 1, 131, 184: Courtesy Douglas S. Rollins, Fredericton.
Page 102: Courtesy Ashley & Crippen, Toronto.
Page 261: Courtesy Maclean-Hunter Studio.

Acknowledgements

By permission from Clark Blaise: "A North American Education" (as published in *Tamarack Review* No. 56, Toronto, 1971) and "Eyes" (as broadcast on CBC "Anthology" and published in *The Fiddlehead*, University of New Brunswick) © Clark Blaise, 1971; "Beginnings" © Clark Blaise, 1971. By permission from Shirley Faessler: "Henye" (as published in *Tamarack Review* No. 56, Toronto, 1971) © Shirley Faessler, 1971; "Maybe Later It Will Come Back to My Mind" (originally published in *The Atlantic Monthly*, April 1967) © Shirley Faessler, 1967; "The Poor Literatus" © Shirley Faessler, Toronto, 1971. Citations of H. L. Mencken from *Vintage Mencken*, ed. Alistair Cooke © Alfred Knopf, 1955, reprinted by permission of the publisher. By permission from David Helwig: "Presences," "Things That Happened Before You Were Born," and "Time in Fiction" © David Helwig, 1971. By permission from Hugh Hood: "Socks," "Boots," and "Sober Coloring: The Ontology of Super-realism" © Hugh Hood, Montreal, 1971. "The Loons" and "To Set Our House in Order" from *A Bird in the House* by Margaret Laurence, reprinted by permission of The Canadian Publishers, McClelland and Stewart Limited, Toronto. "Time and the Narrative Voice" reprinted by permission of John Cushman Associates Inc. Copyright © 1972 Margaret Laurence. "The Children Green and Golden" and "Robert, standing" by John Metcalf from *New Canadian Writing 1969*, © 1969 by Clarke, Irwin & Company Limited. Used by permission. "Soaping a Meditative Foot: Notes for a Young Writer" © John Metcalf, 1971. Quotes from *Lucky Jim* by Kingsley Amis, reprinted by permission of Victor Gollancz Ltd. Quotes from *The Doors of Perception* by Aldous Huxley by permission from Mrs. Laura Huxley and Chatto and Windus Ltd. Quotes from *Thank You, Jeeves* and *Jeeves and the Feudal Spirit* by P. G. Wodehouse reprinted by permission of the author and the author's agents, Scott Meredith Literary Agency, Inc., 580 Fifth Avenue, New York, N.Y. 10036. Quotes from *The Living Novel*, ed. Granville Hicks by permission of The Macmillan Company © 1957. By permission from Alice Munro: "Images" © Alice Munro, Toronto, 1968; "Dance of the Happy Shades" © Alice Munro, Toronto, 1968; "The Colonel's Hash Resettled" © Alice Munro, Toronto, 1971. "Peril" and "A Cynical Tale" © Ray Smith, 1969, previously published in *Cape Breton is the Thought Control Centre of Canada*, House of Anansi, Toronto, 1969, reprinted by permission of the author; "Dinosaur" © Ray Smith, Montreal, 1971. By permission from Kent Thompson: "Truancy" © Kent Thompson, Fredericton, 1971; "Because I Am Drunk" (first published in *Quarry*, v. 18, n. 3, Spring 1969, pp. 37-47) © Kent Thompson, 1969; "Academy Stuff" © Kent Thompson, Fredericton, 1971. By permission from Rudy Wiebe: "Millstone for the Sun's Day" (as published in *Tamarack Review*, Summer, 1967); "Where is the Voice Coming From?"; "Passage by Land" © Rudy Wiebe, 1971. "The Courtship of Edith Long" and "The Last Walk" from *The Short Happy Walks of Max MacPherson* by Harry Bruce, by permission of the author and The Macmillan Company of Canada Limited; "The Bad Samaritan down at the Railroad Station" by permission of the author and *Maclean's*; "Grub Street?" © Harry Bruce, 1971. Quotes from *Slouching Toward Bethlehem* by Joan Didion © 1968 reprinted by permission of the publishers Farrar, Straus & Giroux, Inc.

Contents

Introduction

This collection of stories and essays is not historical, thematic, chronological, or inclusive. It does not attempt to enshrine masterpieces. Such concerns are, rightly, academic. Rather, it attempts to present Canadian story-writing as a process.

Twelve of the stories were taken from individual collections, six from literary magazines, four were previously unpublished. The essays, which range from the personal and anecdotal to the argumentative and theoretical, allow the reader to share the concerns and prejudices of a group of working writers.

John Metcalf
Montreal 1971

Clark Blaise

"Clark Blaise, b. 1940, Fargo, N. Dakota, U.S.A.   B.A.
Denison, M.F.A. Iowa, since 1966 teaching at Sir George
Williams University, Montreal. Married to the Indian novelist
Bharati Mukherjee, two sons.

"Though born in the United States, both parents are
Canadian, and I feel my French heritage especially deeply,
as my story in this anthology, 'A North American Education,'
should reflect.

"For a number of years I have been writing a novel under
several titles that would express the totality of my experience
as North American outsider, set in Canada, in the suburbs
of the east coast American cities, and in the rural south.
Evidences have been published in various academic journals,
and in a full collection to appear in 1972."

Bibliography

" 'A North American Education' originally in *Tamarack Review*.

" 'The Salesman's Son Grows Older' in *Shenandoah*. I have published three other stories in this Virginia journal, only one of which is now readily available in book form: 'Notes Beyond a History' (in *New Canadian Writing 1968* and *Great Canadian Short Stories* edited by Alec Lucas), 'Relief' (1965) and 'Broward Dowdy' (1963).

" 'The Bridge' in *Florida Quarterly* (1971).

" 'Eyes' was first broadcast in CBC 'Anthology' and first published in *Fiddlehead*; 'Extractions and Contractions,' a story of Montreal, was broadcast on CBC after publication in *Tri-Quarterly* in 1969. That latter story is available in two anthologies: *Student's Choice*, ed. Kraus, and *The Story So Far* (Coach House, Toronto), ed. George Bowering.

" 'The Mayor' and its re-titled version, 'The Fabulous Eddie Brewster' was first published in *Tamarack Review* in 1967 and in *New Canadian Writing 1968* a year later. The other two stories that made up my contribution to that tripartite book were 'How I Became a Jew' and 'The Examination.' (Clarke, Irwin, Toronto, 1968).

" 'Thibidault et Fils,' my first effort with the French and English, Canadian and American themes: *Prism International*, 1965.

"There have been other stories published in Texas, California, Vermont, Colorado, Montana, Minnesota, totalling now nearly thirty. I've also done poems, translations, reviews and essays."

A collection of Clark Blaise's stories entitled *A North American Education* is to be published in 1972 by Doubleday Canada.

A North American Education

Eleven years after the death of Napoleon, in the presidency of Andrew Jackson, my grandfather, Boniface Thibidault, was born. For most of his life he was a *journalier,* a day-labourer, with a few years off for wars and buccaneering. Then at the age of fifty, a father and widower, he left Paris and came alone to the New World and settled in Sorel, a few miles down river from Montréal. He worked in the shipyards for a year or two and then married his young housekeeper, an eighteen-year-old named Lise Beaudette. Lise, my grandmother, had that resigned look of a Québec girl marked early for a nursing order if marriage couldn't catch her, by accident, first. In twenty-five years she bore fifteen children, eight of them boys, five of whom survived. The final child, a son, was named Jean-Louis and given at birth to the Church. As was the custom with the last boy, he was sent to the monastery as soon as he could walk, and remained with the Brothers for a dozen years, taking his meals and instructions as an apprentice.

It would have been fitting if Boniface Thibidault, then nearly eighty, had earned a fortune in Sorel—but he didn't. Or if a son had survived to pass on his stories—but none were listening. Or if Boniface himself had written something—but he was illiterate. Boniface was cut out for something different. One spring morning in 1912, the man who had seen two child-brides through menopause stood in the mud outside his cottage and defied Sorel's first horseless carriage to churn its way through the April muck to his door, and if by the Grace of God it did, to try going on while he, an old man, pushed it back downhill. Money was evenly divided on the man and the driver, whom Boniface also defamed for good measure. The driver was later acquitted of manslaughter in Sorel's first fatality and it was never ascertained if Boniface died of the bumping, the strain, or perhaps the shock of meeting his match. Jean-Louis wasn't there. He left the church five years later the only way, by walking out and never looking back. He was my father.

The death of Boniface was in keeping with the life, yet I think of my grandfather as someone special, a character from a well-packed novel who enters once and is never fully forgotten. I think of Flaubert's *Sentimental Education* and the *mousses* and *matelots* who littered the decks of the *Ville-de-Montereau* on the morning of September 15, 1840, when young Frédéric Moreau was about to sail. My grandfather was eight years old in 1840, a good age for cabinboys. But while Frédéric

3

was about to meet Arnoux and his grand passion, Boniface was content to pocket a tip and beat it, out of the novel and back into his *demi-monde*.

I have seen one picture of my grandfather, taken on a ferry between Québec and Lévis in 1895. He looks strangely like Sigmund Freud: bearded, straw-hatted, buttoned against the river breezes. It must have been a cold day—the vapour from the near-by horses steamed in the background. As a young man he must have been, briefly, extraordinary. I think of him as a face in a Gold Rush shot, the one face that seems both incidental and immortal, guarding a claim or watering a horse, the face that seems lifted from the crowd, from history, the face that could be dynastic.

And my father, Jean-Louis Thibidault, who became Gene and T. B. Doe—he too stands out in pictures. A handsome man, a contemporary man (and yet not even a man of this century; his original half-brothers back in France would now be 120 years old. He would be by now barely sixty-five); a salesman and a businessman. I still have many pictures, those my mother gave me. He is lounging on an old canvas chaise under a maple tree, long before aluminum furniture, long before I was born. A scene north of Montréal just after they were married. It is an impressive picture but for the legs, which barely reach the grass. Later he would grow into his shortness, would learn the vanities of the short and never again stretch out casually, like the tall. In another picture I am standing with him on a Florida beach. I am five, he is nearly forty. I am already the man I was destined to be; he is still the youth he always was. My mother must have taken the shot—I can tell, for I occupy the centre—and it is one of those embarrassing shots parents often take. I am in my wet transparent underpants and I've just been swimming in Daytona Beach. It is 1946, our first morning in Florida. It isn't a vacation; we've arrived to start again in the sun. The War is over, the border is open, the old black Packard is parked behind us. I wanted to swim but had no trunks; my father took me down in my underwear. But in the picture my face is worried, my cupped hands are reaching down to cover myself but I was late or the picture early—it seems instead that I am pointing to it, a fleshy little spot on my transparent pants. On the back of the picture my father had written:

Thibidault et fils,
Daytona, avr/46

We'd left Montréal four days before with snow still grey in the tenements' shadows, the trees black and budless over the dingy winter street. Our destination was a town named Hartley where my father had a friend from Montréal who'd started a lawn furniture factory. My father was to

4

become a travelling salesman for Laverdure's Lawn Laddies and I would begin my life as a salesman's son. My life as reader of back issues, as collector, as *retardataire,* like my father and grandfather before me. A collector of cancelled stamps (the inkier the better), a student and teacher of languages.

Thibidault et fils; Thibidault and son. After a week in Hartley I developed worms. My feet bled from itching and scratching. The worms were visible; I could prick them with pins. My mother took me to a clinic where the doctor sprayed my foot with a liquid freeze. Going on, the ice was pleasant, for Florida feet are always hot. Out on the bench I scraped my initials in the frost of my foot. It seemed right to me (before the pain of the thaw began); I was from Up North, the freezing was a friendly gesture for a Florida doctor. My mother held my foot between her hands and told me stories of her childhood: ice-skating for miles on the Battleford River in Saskatchewan, then riding home under fur rugs in a horse-drawn sleigh. Though she was the same age as my father, she was the eldest of six—somewhere between them were missing generations. Her youngest sister was still in college. The next morning the itching was worse and half a dozen new worms radiated from the ball of my foot. My mother then consulted her old *Canadian Doctor's Home Companion*—my grandfather Blankenship had been a doctor, active for years in curling circles, also in petitioning Ottawa for left-hand driving—and learned that footworms, etc., were unknown in Canada but sometimes afflicted Canadian travellers in Tropical Regions. Common to all hot climes, the book went on, due to poor sanitation and the unspeakable habits of the non-white peoples in the Gulf coast and Indian Territories of our southern neighbour. No known cure, but lack of attention could be fatal.

My mother called in a neighbour, our first contact with the slovenly woman who lived downstairs. She came up with a bottle of carbolic acid and another of alcohol, poured the acid over the worms, and told me to yell when it got too hot. Then with alcohol she wiped it off. The next morning my foot had peeled and the worms were gone. And I thought, inspecting my peeled brown foot, that in some small way I had become less Northern, less hateful to the kids around me though I still sounded strange and they shouted after me, 'Yankee, yankee!'

My father was already browned, already spoke with a passable Southern accent. When he wasn't on the road with Lawn Laddies, he walked around barefoot or in shower clogs. But he never got worms, and he was embarrassed that I had.

Thibidault and Son: he was a fisherman and I always fished at his side. Fished for what? I wonder now—he was too short and vain a man to really be a fisherman. He dressed too well, couldn't swim, despised the taste of fish, shunned the cold, the heat, the bugs, the rain. And yet we fished every Sunday, wherever we lived. Canada, Florida, the middle West, heedless as deer of crossing borders. The tackle box (oily childhood smell) creaked at our feet. The fir-lined shores and pink granite beaches of Ontario gleamed behind us. Every cast became a fresh hope, a trout or *doré* or even a muskie. But we never caught a muskie or a trout, just the snake-like fork-boned pike that we let go by cutting the line when the plug was deep. And in Florida with my father in his Harry Truman shirts and sharkskin pants, the warm baitwell sloshing with half-dead shiners, we waited for bass and channel cat in Okeechobee, Kissimmee and a dozen other bug-beclouded lakes. Gar-fish, those tropical pike, drifted by the boat; 'gators churned in a narrow channel and dragonflies lit on my cane pole tip. And as I grew older and we came back North (but not all the way), I remember our Sundays in Cincinnati standing shoulder-to-shoulder with a few hundred others around a clay-banked tub lighted with arc lamps. Scummy pay-lakes with a hot dog stand behind; a vision of hell for a Canadian or a Floridian, but we paid and we fished and we never caught a thing. Ten hours every Sunday from Memorial Day to Labor Day, an unquestioning ritual that would see me dress in my fishing khakis, race out early and buy the Sunday paper before we left (so I could check the baseball averages—what a normal kid I might have been!), then pack the tackle-box and portable radio (for the Cincinnati double-header) in the trunk. Then I would get my father up. He'd have his coffee and a few cigarettes then shout, 'Louise, Paul and I are going fishing!' She would be upstairs reading or sewing. We were still living in a duplex; a few months later my parents were to start their furniture store and we would never fish again. We walked out, my father and I, nodding to the neighbours (a few kids, younger than me, asked if they could go, a few young fathers would squint and ask, 'Not again, Gene?'), and silently we drove, and later, silently, we fished.

Then came a Sunday just before Labor Day when I was thirteen and we didn't go fishing. I was dressed for it and the car was packed as usual, but my father drove to the County Fair instead. Not the Hamilton County Fair in Cincinnati—we drove across the river into Boone County, Kentucky, where things were once again southern and shoddy.

I had known from the books and articles my mother was leaving in the bathroom, that I was supposed to be learning about sex. I'd read the books and figured out the anatomy for myself; I wondered only how to ask a girl for it and what to do once I got there. Sex was some-

6

thing like dancing, I supposed, too intricate and spontaneous for a boy like me. And so we toured the Fair Grounds that morning reviewing the prize sows and heifers, watching a stock-car race and a miniature rodeo. I could tell from my father's breathing, his coughing, his attempt to put his arm around me that this was the day he was going to talk to me about sex and the thought embarrassed him as much as it did me. I wanted to tell him to never mind, I didn't need it, it was something that selfish people did to one another.

He led me to a remote tent far off the fairway. There was a long male line outside, men with a few boys my age, joking loudly and smelling bad. My father looked away, silent. So this is the place, I thought, where I'm going to see it, going to learn something good and dirty, something they couldn't put on those Britannica Films and show in school. The sign over the entrance said only: *Princess Hi-Yalla. Shows Continuously.*

There was a smell over the heat, over the hundred men straining for a place, over the fumes of pigsties and stockyards. It was the smell of furtiveness, rural slaughter and unquenchable famine. The smell of boys' rooms in the high school. The smell of sex on the hoof. The 'Princess' on the runway wore not a stitch and she was lathered like a racehorse from her continuous dance. There'd been no avoiding the bright pink lower lips that she'd painted; no avoiding the shrinking, smiling, puckering, wrinkled labia. 'Kiss, baby?' she called out, and the men went wild. The lips smacked us softly. The Princess was more a dowager, and more black than yellow. She bent forward to watch herself, like a ventriloquist with a dummy. I couldn't turn away as my father had; it seemed less offensive to watch her wide flat breasts instead and to think of her as another native from the *National Geographic*. She asked a guard for a slice of gum then held it over the first row. 'Who gwina wet it up fo' baby?' And a farmer licked both sides while his friends made appreciative noises, then handed it back. The Princess inserted it slowly as though it hurt, spreading her legs like the bow-legged rodeo clown I'd seen a few minutes earlier. Her lower mouth chewed, her abdomen heaved, and she doubled forward to watch the progress. 'Blow a bubble!' the farmer called, his friends screamed with laughter; but a row of boys in overalls, my age, stared at the woman and didn't smile. Nothing would amaze them—they were waiting for a bubble. Then she cupped her hand underneath and gum came slithering out. 'Who wants this?' she called, holding it high, and men were whistling and throwing other things on the stage: key-rings, handkerchiefs, cigarettes. She threw the gum towards us—I remember ducking as it

7

came my way, but someone caught it. 'Now then,' she said, and her voice was as loud as a gospel singer's, 'baby's fixin to have herself a cig'rette.' She walked to the edge of the stage (I could see her moist footprints in the dust), her toes curled over the side. 'Which one of you mens out there is givin' baby a cig'rette?' Another farmer standing behind his fat adolescent son threw up two cigarettes. The boy, I remember, was in overalls and had the cretinous look of fat boys in overalls: big, sweating, red-cheeked, with eyes like calves' in a roping event. By the time I looked back on stage, the Princess had inserted the cigarette and thrust baby out over the runway and was asking for matches. She held the match herself. And the cigarette glowed, smoke came out, an ash formed. . . .

I heard moaning, long low moans, and I felt the eyes of a dozen farmers leap to the boy in overalls. He was jumping and whimpering and the men were laughing as he tried to dig into his sealed-up pants, forgetting the buttons at his shoulders; he was holding his crotch as though it burned. He was running in place, moaning, then screaming, 'Daddy!' and I forgot about the Princess. Men cleared a circle around him and began clapping and chanting, 'Whip it out boy!' and the boy was crying, 'Daddy, I cain't hold it back no more!'

My father grabbed me then by the elbow and said, 'Well, have you seen enough?' The farm boy had collapsed on the dirt floor, and was twitching on his back. A navy-blue stain that I thought was blood was spreading between his legs; I thought he'd managed to pull his penis off. My father led me out and he was mad at me for something—it was *me* who had brought him there, and his duties as my father—and just as we stepped from the tent I yelled, 'Wait—it's happening to me too.' I wanted to cry with embarrassment for I hadn't felt any urgency before entering the tent; it seemed like a sudden, irresistible need to urinate, something I couldn't hold back. But worse than water; something was ripping at my crotch. My light-coloured fishing khakis would turn brown in water, and the dark stain was already forming.

'Jesus Christ—are you sick? That was an old woman—how could *she* . . . how could *you* . . .' He jerked me forward by the elbow. 'Jesus God,' he muttered, pulling me along down the fairway then letting me go and walking so fast I had to run, both hands trying to cup the mess I had made. Thousands of people passed me, smiling, laughing. 'I don't know about you,' my father said. *'I think there's something wrong with you,'* and it was the worst thing my father could have said about me. We were in the car. I was crying in the back seat. 'Don't tell me someone didn't see you—didn't you think of that? Or what if a customer saw *me*

—but you didn't think of that either, did you? Here I take you to something I thought you'd like, something any *normal* boy would like, and—'

I'd been afraid to talk. The wetness was drying, a stain remained. 'You know Murray Lieberman?' my father asked a few minutes later.

'The salesman?'

'He has a kid your age and so we were talking—'

'I don't want to hear,' I said.

'Well, what in the name of God is wrong with two fathers getting together, eh? It was supposed to *show* you what it's like, about women, I mean. It's better than any drawing, isn't it? You want books all the time? You want to *read* about it, or do you want to see it? At least now you *know,* so go ahead and read. Tell your mother we were fishing today, O.K.? And *that*—that was a Coke you spilled, all right.'

And no other talk, man-to-man, or father-to-son, had ever taken place.

I think back to Boniface Thibidault—how would he, how *did* he, show his sons what to do and where to do it? He was a Frenchman, not a North American; he learned it in Paris, not a monastery as my father had. And I, partially at least, am a Frenchman too. My father should have taken me to a *cocotte,* to his own mistress perhaps, for the initiation, *la déniaisement.* And I in my own lovemaking would have forever honoured him. But this is North America and my father despite everything was in his silence a Québec Catholic of the nineteenth century. Sex, despite my dreams of something better, something nobler, still smells of the circus tent, of something raw and murderous. Other kinds of sex, the adjusted, contented, fulfilling sex of school and manual, seem insubstantial, wilfully ignorant of the depths.

My own sentimental education began that summer. At thirteen I was the oldest of eighty kids on the block, a thankless distinction, and my parents at forty-seven had a good twenty years on the next oldest, who happened to share our duplex.

There lived on that street, and I was beginning to notice in that summer before the sideshow at the county fair, several girl-brides and one or two maturely youthful wives. The brides, under twenty and with their first or second youngsters, were a sloppy crew who patrolled the street in cut-away shorts and bra-less elasticized halters that had to be pulled up every few steps. They set their hair so tightly in pin-curlers that the effect at a distance was of the mange. Barefoot they pushed their baby strollers, thighs sloshing as they walked, or sat on porch furniture reading movie magazines and holding tinted plastic baby

9

bottles between their knees. Though they sat in the sun all day they never tanned. They were spreading week by week while their husbands, hard athletic gas-pumpers, played touch-football on the street every Sunday.

But there were others; in particular, the wife next door, our two floors being mirror images of the other, everything back-to-back but otherwise identical. She was a fair woman, about thirty, with hair only lightly bleached and the kind of figure that one judges slightly too plump until something voluptuous in her, or you, makes you look again and you see that she is merely extraordinary; a full woman who had once been a lanky girl. She had three children, two of them girls who favoured the husband. Her name was Annette.

She was French; that had been a point of discussion once. Born in Maine, she would often chat with my father in what French she remembered while her husband played football or read inside. By that time I had forgotten most of my French. Her husband's name was Lance—Lance!—and he was dark, square-shouldered, with a severe crew-cut that sliced across an ample bald spot. He travelled a lot; I recall him sitting in a lawn chair on summer evenings, reading the paper and drinking a beer till the mosquitoes drove him in.

And that left Annette alone, and Annette had no friends on the block; she gave the impression, justified, of far out-distancing the neighbour girls. Perhaps she frightened them, being older and by comparison, a goddess. She would sit on a lawn chair in the front yard on those male-less afternoons of toddling children and cranky mothers and Annette in a modest sundress was so stunning that I would stay inside and peek at her through a hole I had cut in the curtains. Delivery trucks, forced to creep through the litter of kids and abandoned toys, lingered longer than they had to, just to look. At thirteen I could stare for hours, unconscious of peeping, unaware, really, of what I wanted or expected to see. It was almost like fishing, with patience and anticipation keeping me rooted. Those were the days with my parents at the new property cleaning it up for operation, that I was given three or four dollars a day for food and I'd spend fifty or sixty cents of it on meaty and starchy grease down at the shopping centre. I started getting fat. Every few days I carried a bulging pocketful of wadded bills down to the bank and cashed them for a ten or twenty. And the bills would accumulate in my wallet. I was too young to open an account without my parents finding out; the question was how to spend it. After a couple of weeks I'd go downtown and spend astounding sums, for a child, on stamps.

While I was in the shopping centre I began stealing magazines from the drugstore. The scandal mags, the Hollywood parties, the early *Playboy* and its imitators—I stole because I was too good to be seen buying them. I placed them between the pages of the *Sporting News,* which I also read cover-to-cover, then dropped a wadded five-dollar bill in the newspaper honour box, raced home, and feasted. Never one for risks, I burned the residue or threw them out in a neighbour's garbage can, my conscience clear for a month's more stealing and secret reading. There has never been a time in my life when sex was so palpable; when the very sight of any girl vaguely developed or any woman up to forty and still in trim could make my breath come short, make my crotch tingle under my baggy pants. In the super-market when young mothers dipped low to pick a carton of cokes from the bottom shelf, I dipped with them. When the counter girl at the drugstore plunged her dipper in the ice cream tub, I hung over the counter to catch a glimpse of her lacy bra; when the neighbour women hung out their clothes, I would take the stairs two at a time to watch from above. When those young wives hooked their thumbs under the knitted elastic halters and gave an upward tug, I let out a little whimper. How close it was to madness; how many other fat thirteen- and fourteen-year-olds with a drop more violence, provocation, self-pity or whatever, would plunge a knife sixty times into those bellies, just to run their fingers inside the shorts and peel the halter back, allowing the breasts to ooze aside? And especially living next to Annette whose figure made flimsy styles seem indecent and modest dresses maddening. Her body possessed the clothes too greedily, sucked the material to her flesh. She was the woman, I now realize, that Dostoyevski and Kazantzakis and even Faulkner knew; a Grushenka or the young village widow, a dormant body that kindled violence.

The duplexes were mirror images with only the staircases and bath-rooms adjoining. In the summer with Annette at home, her children out playing or taking a nap, her husband away or just at work, she took many baths. From wherever I sat in our duplex watching television or reading my magazines I could hear the drop of the drainplug in her bathroom, the splash of water rushing in, the quick expansion of the hot water pipes.

I could imagine the rest, exquisitely. First testing the water with her finger, then drying the finger on her shorts and then letting them drop. Testing the water again before unhooking the bra in a careless sweep and with another swipe peeling off her panties. The thought of Annette naked a foot away made the walls seem paper-thin, made the tiles grow warm. Ear against the tiles I could hear the waves she made as she settled back,

11

the squeaking of her heels on the bottom of the tub as she straightened her legs, the wringing of a face cloth, plunk of soap as it dropped. The scene as vivid, with my eyes closed and my hot ear on the warm tile, as murders on old radio shows. I thought of the childhood comic character who could shrink himself with magic sand; how for me that had always translated itself into watching the Hollywood starlets from their bathroom heating flues. But Annette was better or at least as good, and so available. If only there were a way, a shaft for midgets; it wasn't right to house strangers so intimately without providing a way to spy. I looked down to the tile floor—a crack? Something a bobby pin could be twisted in, just a modest, modest opening? And I saw the pipes under the sink, two slim swansnecks, one for hot, one for cold, that cut jaggedly through the tile wall—they had to connect! Then on my hands and knees I scraped away the plaster that held the chromium collar around the pipe. As I had hoped, the hole was a good quarter-inch wider than the pipes and all that blocked a straight-on view of the other bathroom were the collars on Annette's pipes. It would be nothing to punch my way through, slide the rings down, and lie on the tile floor in the comfort of my own bathroom and watch it all: Annette bathing! Ring level was below the tub, but given the distance the angle might correct itself. But detection would be unbearable; if caught I'd commit suicide. She was already out of the bath (but there'll be other days, I thought), she took ten-minute baths (how much more could a man bear?), the water was draining and now she was running the lavatory faucet which seemed just over my head. How long before she took another bath? It would seem, now that I had a plan, as long as the wait between issues of my favourite magazines.

I rested on the floor under the sink until Annette left her bathroom. Then I walked down to the shopping centre and had a coke to steady myself. I bought a nail-file. When I got back Annette was sitting in her yard wearing a striped housedress and looking, as usual, fresh from a bath. I said hello and she smiled very kindly. Then I turned my door handle and cried, 'Oh, no!'

'What is it, Paul?' she asked, getting up from her chair.

'I left my key inside.'

'Shall I call your father?'

'No,' I said, 'I think I can get in through the window. But could I use your bathroom first?'

'Of course.'

I checked upstairs for kids. Then I locked myself inside and with the new file scraped away the plaster and pulled one collar down. Careful as always, aware that I would make a good murderer or a good detective,

I cleaned up the plaster crumbs. I'd forgotten to leave our own bathroom light on but it seemed that I could see all the way through. Time would tell. *Take a bath*, I willed her, as I flushed the toilet. It reminded me of fishing as a child, trying to influence the fish to bite. *It's very hot, sticky, just right for a nice cool bath. . . .* My own flesh was stippled, I shivered as I stepped outside and saw her again. She'd soon be *mine*—something to do for the rest of the summer! My throat was so tense I couldn't even thank her. I climbed inside through the living room window that I had left open.

I took the stairs two at a time, stretched myself out under the sink to admire the job. I'd forgotten to leave *her* light on, but I thought I could see the white of her tub in the darkened bathroom, and even an empty tub was enough to sustain me.

How obvious was the pipe and collar? It suddenly seemed blatant, that she would enter the bathroom, undress, sit in the tub, turn to the wall, and scream. Do a peeper's eyes shine too brightly? In school I'd often been able to stare a kid into turning around—it was now an unwanted gift.

You're getting warm again, Annette. Very very hot. You want another bath. You're getting up from the chair, coming inside, up the stairs. . . . I kept on for hours till it was dark. I heard the kids taking baths and saw nothing. The white of the bathtub was another skin of plaster, no telling how thick. I'd been cheated.

Another day. There had to be another link—I had faith that the builders of duplexes were men who provided, out of guilt, certain amenities. Fans were in the ceiling. Windows opened on the opposite sides, the heating ducts were useless without a metal drill. Only the medicine cabinets were left. They had to be back-to-back. I opened ours, found the four corner screws, undid them, took out the medicines quietly (even my old Florida carbolic acid) then eased the chest from its plaster nest. It worked. I was facing the metal backing of Annette's medicine chest. Though the fit was tight and I could never take a chance of tampering with hers—what if I gave it a nudge when Lance was shaving and the whole thing came crashing down, revealing me leaning over my sink in the hole where our medicine chest had been?

The used-razor slot. A little slot in the middle. I popped the paper-coating with the nailfile. I darkened our own bathroom. If Annette opened her chest I'd see her. But would she open it with her clothes off? Was she tall enough to make it count? How many hours would I have to stand there stretched over the sink waiting, and could I, everyday, put the chest back up and take it down without some loud disaster? What if my father came home to shave, unexpectedly?

I waited all afternoon and all evening and when eight o'clock came I ended the vigil and put the chest back up. With a desire so urgent, there *had* to be a way of penetrating an inch and a half of tile and plaster. When she was in her bath I felt I could have devoured the walls between us. Anything *heard* so clearly had to yield to vision—that was another natural law—just as anything dreamt had to become real, eventually.

I became a baby-sitter; the oldest kid on the block, quiet and responsible. I watched television in nearly every duplex on the street, ignored the whimpers, filled bottles, and my pockets bulged with more unneeded cash. I poked around the young parents' bedrooms and medicine cabinets, only half-repelled by the clutter and unfamiliar odours, the stickiness, the grayness of young married life in a mid-west suburb. I found boxes of prophylactics in top drawers and learned to put one on and to walk around with it on until the lubrication stuck to my underwear. Sex books and nudist magazines showing pubic hair were stuffed in nightstands and in one or two homes I found piles of home-made snaps of the wife when she'd been slim and high-school young, sitting naked in the sun in a woods somewhere. She'd been posed in dozens of ways, legs wide apart, fingers on her pubic hair, tongue curled between her teeth. Others of her and of a neighbour woman on the same living-room sofa that I was sitting on: fatter now, her breasts resting on a roll of fat around her middle, her thighs shadowed where the skin had grown soft. *This is the girl I see every day*, pushing that carriage, looking like a fat girl at a high-school hang-out. Those bigger girls in my school in bright blue sweaters, earrings, black curly hair, bad skin, black corduroy jackets, smoking. They become like this; they *are* like this.

These were the weeks in August when my mother was leaving the articles around. Soon my father would take me to the county fair. There were no answers to the questions I asked myself holding those snapshots, looking again (by daylight) at the wife (in ragged shorts and elastic halter) who had consented to the pictures. They were like murder victims, the photos were like police shots in the scandal magazines, the women looked like mistresses of bandits. There was no place in the world for the life I wanted, for the pure woman I would someday, somehow, marry.

I baby-sat for Annette and Lance then for Annette alone and I worked again on the lavatory scheme, the used-razor slot, and discovered the slight deficiencies in the architecture that had thrown my calculations off.

14

I could see from their bathroom into ours much better than I could ever see into theirs. Annette kept a neat house and life with her, even I could appreciate, must have been a joy of lust and efficiency in surroundings as clean and attractive as a *Playboy* studio.

One evening she came over when my parents were working to ask me to baby-sit for a couple of hours. Lance wasn't in. Her children were never a problem and though it was a week night and school had begun, I agreed. She left me a slice of Lance's birthday cake and begged me to go to sleep in case she was late.

An hour later after some reading I used her bathroom, innocently. If only I lived here, with Annette over there! I opened her medicine chest to learn some more about her: a few interesting pills 'for pain', Tampax Super (naturally, I thought), gauze and adhesive, something for piles (for him, I hoped). And then I heard a noise from our bathroom. Our light snapped on. My parents must have come home early.

I knew from a cough that it wasn't my mother. The Thibidault medicine chest was opened. I peered through the razor slot and saw young fingers among our bottles, blond hair and a tanned forehead: Annette. She picked out a jar then closed the door. I fell to the floor and put my eye against the pipes. Bare golden legs. Then our light went out.

I looked into our bathroom for the next few seconds then ran to Annette's front bedroom where the youngest girl slept and pressed over her crib to look out the window. Annette was just stepping out and running to the station wagon of Thibidault Furniture, which had been parked across the street. She got in the far side and the car immediately, silently, backed away, with just its parking lights on. . . .

And that was all. For some reason, perhaps the shame of my complicity, I never asked my father why he had come home or why Annette had been in our bathroom. I didn't have to—I'd gotten a glimpse of Annette which was all I could handle anyway. I didn't understand the rest. Thibidault et fils, fishing again.

It was about that time that I retired from the world. About then I discovered my 'gifts' as the teachers would say—a good ear and tongue and memory for languages. A beginning with French and a curiosity for the rest. And I was interested in other antiquarian things like fossils and Indian mounds and history. I left my parents to their store and the store saw me through high school and college but all that is a different story. Also a different story that my father finally decided to marry again, to divorce, sell, divide, marry, and leave, which he did, and that lasted a year or two until she left him and he found another one and ended his days again in the South, again in Florida, selling furniture on the floor.

15

I once saw the place a year before he died: a large cinder-block shed with a lot of glass and potted plants, painted white and lewd with neon. A hell of a place to end one's days, I thought then, and he seemed to think so too. His widow opened a cocktail lounge with the insurance, bleached her hair and married a contractor. I'm tempted having come this far to supply some *meaning*, just as I was tempted at his funeral to have him removed from the Bridge of Sighs Cemetery in Venice, Florida, to a dingy plot in Sorel, Québec. I even wrote the *prêtre-vicaire*, but he turned it down.

I will close on a memory, an important one. A different Florida when Venice was still underwater. There was a day years earlier in Fort Lauderdale. As usual, a Sunday, shortly after we had moved there from Hartley. A hurricane was a hundred miles off-shore and due to strike Fort Lauderdale in the next six hours. We drove from our house down Las Olas to the beach (Fort Lauderdale was still an inland city then), and parked a half mile away safe from the paint-blasting sand. We could hear the breakers under the shriek of the wind shaking the wooden bridge we walked on. Then we watched them crash, brown with weeds and suspended sand. And we could see them miles off-shore rolling in forty feet high and flashing their foam like icebergs. A few men in swimming suits and woolen sweaters were standing in the crater pools pulling out the deep-sea fish that had been stunned by the trip and waves. Other fish littered the beach, their bellies blasted by the change in pressure. My mother's face was raw and her glasses webbed with salt. She went back to the car on her own. My father and I sat on the bench for another hour and I could see behind his crusty sunglasses. His eyes were moist and dancing, his hair stiff and matted. We sat on the bench until we were soaked and the municipal guards rounded us up. Then they barricaded the boulevards and we went back to the car, the best day of fishing we'd ever had, and we walked hand in hand for the last time, talking excitedly, dodging coconuts, power lines, and shattered glass, feeling brave and united in the face of the storm. My father and me; what a day it was, what a once-in-a-lifetime day it was.

Eyes

You jump into this business of a new country cautiously. First you choose a place where English is spoken, with doctors and buslines at hand, and a supermarket in a *centre d'achats* not too far away. You ease yourself into the city, approaching by car or bus down a single artery, aiming yourself along the boulevard that begins small and tree-lined in your suburb but broadens into the canyoned aorta of the city five miles beyond. And by that first winter when you know the routes and bridges, the standard congestions reported from the helicopter on your favorite radio station, you start to think of moving. What's the good of a place like this when two of your neighbors have come from Texas, and the French paper you've dutifully subscribed to arrives by mail two days late? These French are all around you, behind the counters at the shopping center, in a house or two on your block; why isn't your little boy learning French at least? Where's the nearest *maternelle*? Four miles away.

In the spring you move. You find an apartment on a small side-street where dogs outnumber children and the row houses resemble London's, divided equally between the run-down and remodelled. Your neighbors are the young personalities of French television who live on delivered chicken, or the old pensioners who shuffle down the summer sidewalks in pajamas and slippers in a state of endless recuperation. Your neighbors pay sixty a month for rent, or three hundred; you pay two-fifty for a two-bedroom flat where the walls have been replastered and new fixtures hung. The bugs *d'antan* remain, as well as the hulks of cars abandoned in the fire-alley behind, where downtown drunks sleep in the summer night.

Then comes the night in early October when your child is coughing badly, and you sit with him in the darkened nursery, calm in the bubbling of a cold-steam vaporiser while your wife mends a dress in the room next door. And from the dark, silently, as you peer into the ill-lit fire-alley, he comes. You cannot believe it at first, that a rheumy, pasty-faced Irishman in slate-gray jacket and rubber-soled shoes has come purposely to *your* small parking space, that he has been here before and he is not drunk (not now at least, but you know him as a panhandler on the main boulevard a block away), that he brings with him a crate that he sets on end under your bedroom window and raises himself to your window ledge and hangs there nose-high at a pencil of light from the ill-fitting blinds. And there you are, straining with him from the uncurtained

17

nursery, watching the man watching your wife, praying silently that she is sleeping under the blanket. The man is almost smiling, a leprechaun's face that sees what you cannot. You are about to lift the window and shout, but your wheezing child lies just under you; and what of your wife in the room next door? You could, perhaps, throw open the window and leap to the ground, tackle the man before he runs and smash his face into the bricks, beat him senseless then call the cops. . . . Or better, find the camera, afix the flash, rap once at the window and shoot when he turns. Do nothing and let him suffer. *He is at your mercy*, no one will ever again be so helpless—but what can you do? You know, somehow, he'll escape. If you hurt him, he can hurt you worse, later, viciously. He's been a regular at your window, he's watched the two of you when you prided yourself on being young and alone and masters of the city; he knows your child and the park he plays in, your wife and where she shops. He's a native of the place, a man who knows the city and maybe a dozen such windows, who knows the fire-escapes and alleys and roofs, knows the habits of the city's heedless young.

And briefly you remember yourself an adolescent in another country slithering through the mosquito-ridden grassy fields behind a housing development, peering into those houses where newlyweds had not yet put up drapes, how you could spend five hours in a motionless crouch for a myopic glimpse of a slender arm reaching from the dark to douse a light. Then you hear what the man cannot: the creaking of your bed in the far bedroom, the steps of your wife on her way to the bathroom, and you see her as you never have before: blond and tall and rangily-built, a north-European princess from a constitutional monarchy, sensuous mouth and prominent teeth, pale, tennis-ball breasts cupped in her hands as she stands in the bathroom's light.

"How's Kit?" she asks. "I'd give him a kiss except that there's no blind in there," and she dashes back to bed, nude, and the man bounces twice on the window ledge.

"You coming?"

You find yourself creeping from the nursery, turning left at the hall and then running to the kitchen telephone; you dial the police, then hang up. How will you prepare your wife, not for what is happening, but for what has already taken place?

"It's stuffy in here," you shout back, "I think I'll open the window a bit." You take your time, you stand before the blind blocking his view if he's still looking, then bravely you part the curtains. He is gone, the crate remains upright. "Do we have any masking tape?" you ask, lifting the window a crack.

And now you know the city a little better. A place where millions come each summer to take pictures and walk around must have its voyeurs too, and that place in all great cities where rich and poor co-exist is especially hard on the people in-between. It's health you've been seeking, not just beauty; a tough urban health that will save you money in the bargain, and when you hear of a place twice as large at half the rent, in a part of town free of Texans, English and French, free of young actors and stewardesses who deposit their garbage in pizza boxes, you move again.

It is, for you, a city of Greeks. In the summer you move you attend a movie at the corner cinema. The posters advertise a war movie, in Greek, but the uniforms are unfamiliar. Both sides wear moustaches, both sides handle machine-guns, both leave older women behind dressed in black. From the posters outside there is a promise of sex; blond women in slips, dark-eyed peasant girls. There will be rubble, executions against a wall. You can follow the story from the stills alone: moustached boy goes to war, embraces dark-eyed village girl. Black-draped mother and admiring young brother stand behind. Young soldier, moustache fuller, embraces blond prostitute on a tangled bed. Enter soldiers, boy hides under sheets. Final shot, back in village. Mother in black; dark-eyed village girl in black. Young brother marching to the front.

You go in, pay your ninety cents, pay a nickle in the lobby for a wedge of *halvah*-like sweets. You understand nothing, you resent their laughter and you even resent the picture they're running. Now you know the Greek for "Coming Attractions" for this is a gangster movie at least thirty years old. The eternal Mediterranean gangster movie set in Athens instead of Naples or Marseilles, with smaller cars and narrower roads, uglier women and more sinister killers. After an hour the movie flatters you. No one knows you're not a Greek, that you don't belong in this theater, or even this city. That like the Greeks, you're hanging on.

Outside the theater the evening is warm and the wide sidewalks are clogged with Greeks who nod as you come out. Like the *Ramblas* in Barcelona, with children out past midnight and families walking back and forth for a long city block, the men filling the coffee houses, the women left outside, chatting. Not a blond head on the side-walk, not a blond head for miles. Greek music pours from the coffee houses, flies stumble on the pastry, whole families munch their *torsades molles* as they walk. Dry goods sold at midnight from the sidewalks. You're wandering happily, glad that you moved, you've rediscovered the innocence of starting over.

Then you come on a scene directly from Spain. A slim blond girl in a floral top and white pleated skirt, tinted glasses, smoking, with bad skin, ignores a persistent young Greek in a shiny Salonika suit. "Whatsamatta?" he demands, slapping a ten-dollar bill on his open palm. And without looking back at him she drifts closer to the curb and a car makes a sudden squealing turn and lurches to a stop on the cross-street. Three men are inside, the back door opens and not a word is exchanged as she steps inside. How? you wonder; what refinement of gesture did we immigrants miss? You turn to the Greek boy in sympathy, you know just how he feels, but he's already heading across the street, shouting something to his friends outside a barbecue stand. You have a pocketful of bills and a Mediterranean soul, and money this evening means a woman, and blond means whore and you would spend it all on another blond with open pores; all this a block from your wife and tenement, and you hurry home.

Months later you know the place. You trust the Greeks in their stores, you fear their tempers at home. Eight bathrooms adjoin a central shaft, you hear the beatings of your son's friends, the thud of fist on bone after the slaps. Your child knows no French, but he plays cricket with Greeks and Jamaicans out in the alley behind Pascal's hardware. He brings home the oily tires from the Esso station, plays in the boxes behind the appliance store. You watch from a greasy back window, at last satisfied. None of his friends is like him, like you. He is becoming Greek, becoming Jamaican, becoming a part of this strange new land. His hair is nearly white; you can spot him a block away.

On Wednesdays the butcher quarters his meat. Calves arrive by refrigerator truck, still intact but for their split-open bellies and sawn-off hooves. The older of the three brothers skins the carcass with a small thin knife that seems all blade. A knife he could shave with. The hide rolls back in a continuous flap, the knife never pops the membrane over the fat.

Another brother serves. Like yours, his French is adequate. "Twa lif d'hamburger," you request, still watching the operation on the rickety saw-horse. Who could resist? It's a Levantine treat, the calf's stumpy legs high in the air, the hide draped over the edge and now in the sawdust, growing longer by the second.

The store is filling. The ladies shop on Wednesday, especially the old widows in black overcoats and scarves, shoes and stockings. Yellow, mangled fingernails. Wednesdays attract them with boxes in the window, and they call to the butcher as they enter, the brother answers, and the women dip their fingers in the boxes. The radio is loud overhead, music from the Greek station.

20

"Une et soixante, m'sieur. Du bacon, jambon?"

And you think, taking a few lamb chops but not their saltless bacon, how pleased you are to manage so well. It is a Byzantine moment with blood and widows and sides of dripping beef, contentment in a snowy slum at five below.

The older brother, having finished the skinning, straightens, curses, and puts away the tiny knife. A brother comes forward to pull the hide away, a perfect beginning for a game-room rug. Then, bending low at the rear of the glistening carcass, the legs spread high and stubby, the butcher digs in his hands, ripping hard where the scrotum is, and pulls on what seems to be a strand of rubber, until it snaps. He puts a single glistening prize in his mouth, pulls again and offers the other to his brother, and they suck.

The butcher is singing now, drying his lips and wiping his chin, and still he's chewing. The old black-draped widows with the parchment faces are also chewing. On leaving, you check the boxes in the window. Staring out are the heads of pigs and lambs, some with the eyes lifted out and a red socket exposed. A few are loose and the box is slowly dissolving from the blood, and the ice beneath.

The women have gathered around the body; little pieces are offered to them from the head and entrails. The pigs' heads are pink, perhaps they've been boiled, and hairless. The eyes are strangely blue. You remove your gloves and touch the skin, you brush against the grainy ear. How the eye attracts you! How you would like to lift one out, press its smoothness against your tongue, then crush it in your mouth. And you cannot. Already your finger is numb and the head, it seems, has shifted under you. And the eye, in panic, grows white as you finger approaches. You would take that last half inch but for the certainty, in this world you have made for yourself, that the eye would blink and your neighbors would turn upon you.

TO BEGIN, TO BEGIN

*"Endings are elusive, middles
are nowhere to be found, but
worst of all is to begin, to begin, to begin."*
           Donald Barthelme

The most interesting thing about a story is not its climax or dénouement —both dated terms—nor even its style and characterization. It is its beginning, its first paragraph, often its first sentence. More decisions are made on the basis of the first few sentences of a story than on any other part, and it would seem to me after having read thousands of stories, and beginning hundreds of my own (completing, I should add, only about fifty), that something more than luck accounts for the occasional success of the operation. What I propose is theoretical, yet rooted in the practice of writing and of reading-as-a-writer; good stories *can* start unpromisingly, and well-begun stories can obviously degenerate, but the observation generally holds: the story seeks its beginning, the story many times *is* its beginning, amplified.

The first sentence of a story is an act of faith—or astonishing bravado. A story screams for attention, as it must, for it breaks a silence. It removes the reader from the everyday (no such imperative attaches to the novel, for which the reader makes his own preparations). It is an act of perfect rhythmic balance, the single crisp gesture, the drop of the baton that gathers a hundred disparate forces into a single note. The first paragraph is a microcosm of the whole, but in a way that only the whole can reveal. If the story begins one sentence too soon, or a sentence too late, the balance is lost, the energy diffused.

It is in the first line that the story reveals its kinship to poetry. Not that the line is necessarily "beautiful," merely that it can exist utterly alone, and that its force draws a series of sentences behind it. The line doesn't have to "grab" or "hook" but it should be striking. Good examples I'll offer further on, but consider first some bad ones:

> *Catelli plunged the dagger deeper in her breast, the dark blood oozed like cherry syrup . . . .*
> *The President's procession would pass under the window at 12:03, and Slattery would be ready . . . .*

Such sentences can be wearying; they strike a note too heavily, too prematurely. They "start" where they should be ending. The advantages wrested will quickly dissipate. On the other hand, the "casual" opening can be just as damaging:

> When I saw Bob in the cafeteria he asked me to a party at his house that evening and since I wasn't doing much anyway I said sure, I wouldn't mind. Bob's kind of an ass, but his old man's loaded and there's always a lot of grass around . . . .

Or, *in medias res:*
> "Linda, toast is ready! Linda, are you awake?"

Now what's wrong with these sentences? The tone is right. The action is promising. They're real, they communicate. Yet no experienced reader would go past them. The last two start too early, (what the critics might call an imitative fallacy) and the real story is still imprisoned somewhere in the body.

Lesson One: as in poetry, a good first sentence of prose implies its opposite. If I describe a sunny morning in May (the buds, the wet-winged flies, the warm sun and cool breeze), I am also implying the perishing quality of a morning in May, and a good sensuous description of May sets up the possibility of a May disaster. It is the singular quality of that experience that counts. May follows from the sludge of April and leads to the drone of summer, and in a careful story the action will be mindful of May; it must be. May is unstable, treacherous, beguiling, seductive, and whatever experience follows from a first sentence will be, in essence, a story about the May-ness of human affairs.

What is it, for example, in this sentence from Hugh Hood's story "Fallings from Us, Vanishings" that hints so strongly at disappointment:

> Brandishing a cornucopia of daffodils, flowers for Gloria, in his right hand, Arthur Merlin crossed the dusky oak-panelled foyer of his apartment building and came into the welcoming sunlit avenue.

The name Merlin? The flourish of the opening clause, associations of the name Gloria? Here is a lover doomed to loneliness, yet a lover who seeks it, despite appearances. Nowhere, however, is it stated. Yet no one, I trust, would miss it.

Such openings are everywhere, at least in authors I admire:

> The girl stood with her back to the bar, slightly in everyone's way. (Frank Tuohy)

23

*The thick ticking of the tin clock stopped. Mendel, dozing, awoke
in fright.* (Bernard Malamud)

*I owe the discovery of Uqbar to the conjunction of a mirror and
an encyclopedia.* (Jorge Luis Borges)

*For a little while when Walter Henderson was nine years old, he
thought falling dead was the very zenith of romance, and so did a
number of his friends.* (Richard Yates)

Our group is against the war. But the war goes on. (Donald
Barthelme)

*The principal dish at dinner had been croquettes made of turnip
greens.* (Thomas Mann)

*The sky had been overcast since early morning; it was a still day,
not hot, but tedious, as it usually is when the weather is gray and
dull, when clouds have been hanging over the fields for a long time,
and you wait for the rain that does not come.* (Anton Chekhov)

I wanted terribly to own a dovecot when I was a child. (Isaac
Babel—and I didn't even know what a dovecot was when I started
reading.)

At least two or three times a day a story strikes me in the same way,
and I read it through. By then I don't care if the climax and dénouement
are elegantly turned—chances are they will be—I'm reading it because
the first paragraph gave me confidence in the power and vision of the
author.

Lesson Two: art wishes to begin, even more than end. Fashionable
criticism—much of it very intelligent—has emphasized the so-called
"apocalyptic impulse," the desire of fiction to bring the house down. I
can understand the interest in endings—it's easier to explain why things
end than how they began, for one thing. For another, the ending is a
contrivance—artistic and believable, yet in many ways predictable; the
beginning, however, is always a mystery. Criticism likes contrivances, and
has little to say of mysteries. My own experience, as a writer and
especially as a "working" reader is closer to genesis than apocalypse, and
I cherish openings more than endings. My memory of any given story is
likely to be its first few lines.

Lesson Three: art wishes to begin *again*. The impulse is not only to
finish, it is to capture. In the stories I admire, there is a sense of a con-
tinuum disrupted, then re-established, and both the disruption and re-
ordering are part of the *beginning* of a story. The first paragraph tells us,
in effect, that "this is how things have always been," or at least, how

they have been until the arrival of the story. It may summarize, as Faulkner does in "That Evening Sun":

> *Monday is no different from any other weekday in Jefferson now. The streets are paved now, and the telephone and electric companies are cutting down more and more of the shade trees. . . .*

or it may envelop a life in a single sentence, as Bernard Malamud's often do:

> *Manischevitz, a tailor, in his fifty-first year suffered many reverses and indignities.*

Whereupon Malamud embellishes the history, a few sentences more of indignities, aches, curses, until the fateful word that occurs in almost all stories, the simple terrifying adverb:
Then.
Then, which means to the reader: "I am ready." The moment of change is at hand, the story shifts gears and for the first time, *plot* intrudes on poetry. In Malamud's story, a Negro angel suddenly ("then") appears in the tailor's living room, reading a newspaper.

> *Suddenly there appeared . . .*
> *Then one morning . . .*
> *Then one evening she wasn't home to greet him . . .*

Or, in the chilling construction of Flannery O'Connor:

> *. . . there appeared at her door three young men . . . they walked single file, the middle one bent to the side carrying a black pig-shaped valise . . . .*

A pig-shaped valise! This is the apocalypse, if the reader needs one; whatever the plot may reveal a few pages later is really redundant. The mysterious part of the story—that which *is* poetic yet sets it (why not?) above poetry—is over. The rest of the story will be an attempt to draw out the inferences of that earlier upheaval. What is often meant by "climax" in the conventional short story is merely the moment that the *character* realizes the true, the devastating, meaning of "then." He will try to ignore it, he will try to start again (in my story "Eyes" the character thinks he can escape the voyeurs—himself, essentially—by moving to a rougher part of town); he can't of course.

25

Young readers, especially young readers who want to write, should forget what they're taught of "themes" and all the rest. Stories aren't written that way. Stories are delicate interplays of action and description; "character" is that force which tries to maintain balance between the two. "Action" I equate with danger, fear, apocalypse, life itself; "description" with quiescence, peace, death itself. And the purest part of a story, I think, is from its beginning to its "then." "Then" is the moment of the slightest tremor, the moment when the author is satisfied that all the forces are deployed, the unruffled surface perfectly cast, and the insertion, gross or delicate, can now take place. It is the cracking of the perfect, smug egg of possibility.

CLARK BLAISE

Shirley Faessler

Shirley Faessler wrote of herself, "Grade 8 (failed) is the extent of my academic education." The first story she ever wrote was accepted by the *Atlantic Monthly*. She is currently working on a long novel with a Toronto setting which will be published by McClelland and Stewart. She also plans a collection of short stories.

A particularly fine story, "A Basket of Apples," which also first appeared in the *Atlantic Monthly,* was reprinted in *Sixteen by Twelve.* (Ed. J. Metcalf, Ryerson Press, 1970.)

Shirley Faessler came to writing late but is quickly establishing herself as an important voice.

Henye

Fridays after school I used to get a nickel from Henye for going with her to the Out Patients Clinic at the Grace Street Hospital to speak English for her. I was ten years old and it was a terrible embarrassment for me to be seen on the street with her, she was so ugly.

Henye was a skinny little woman all bone, no flesh to her. Her hair which she wore in two braids around her head was the same colour as her skin, pallid. Her nose was long, her voice was hoarse, and on top of everything else she was bent over in the back.

She would hang on to my arm all the way to the clinic, pinching it now and then when she felt my attention was wandering from the recap she was giving me of her ailments, things to tell the doctor. We would take our place on the bench, Henye hunched forward with feet dangling free of the floor, her black stockings twisted and spiralled at the spindle-leg ankles, and wait for our number to be called. Our turn would come and I would give the doctor a rundown of her troubles, she all the while prompting me in Yiddish: *'Zog im, Soreh, zog im.'* She wanted me to tell him she had not moved her bowels in three days. I would sooner have died. 'I told him!' I would say to her in English. It was bad enough I was obliged to acknowledge before the gentile doctor that I understood the Yiddish she was speaking, let alone speak it in front of him.

Before the nickel was yielded up to me I would have to accompany her back to her house, even though she knew the way home. Not till we were in the house did she take from her pocket the knotted handkerchief in which she kept her change. Her husband, Yankev, who was my stepmother's uncle, would be home from his day's business when I returned his wife from the Out Patients. (Being Friday, Yankev saw to it that the day's business which consisted mainly of deliveries—he was a bootlegger—was done with and finished before *Erev Shabbus*.) 'Well?' he would say to me as Henye was unknotting the handkerchief. 'Did she get a little pinch from the doctor? A tickle, a little feel? She likes that, the old devil.'

Yankev, at that time in his late fifties, was a tall thickset handsome man with a bushy head of hair beginning to grey. He was a vigorous illiterate coarse-natured man with a ribald sense of humour. He loved a bit of mischief, a practical joke. Henye, a year younger than her husband but who looked old enough to be his mother, was a sobersides. Yankev and Henye made a striking pair; the contrast between husband and wife was something to see.

28

Yankev had a twin. His brother Yudah, whom (it was said) Yankev loved more than he did his own children. The twin brothers Yankev and Yudah were identical. In build, in countenance and voice they were one and the same. I never learned to tell them apart, nor could neighbours or friends distinguish between them. But my stepmother, who was their niece, could tell one from the other. And so could my father, who had no use for either of them, tell them apart . . . .

My mother died when my brother, my sister and I were very young and a year or so after her death my father, in search of a wife to make a home for his motherless children, met through the offices of a matchmaker the brothers Yankev and Yudah who were seeking a husband for their niece Chayele, whom they had brought over from the old country. The brothers, after the meeting took place, were not too keen on the match. They thought my father, a Rumanian immigrant who could speak English and could read and write, gave himself too many airs—for a poor man. On the other hand here was Chayele an old maid of thirty-five and altogether without prospects, so they gave in. But they never took to my father. Nor did he to my stepmother's family of Russian immigrants.

Yankev and Yudah were born in Chileshea, a village somewhere in the depths of Russia, Yankev the older of the pair by fifteen minutes. When the time came, they were married to wives picked for them by their father. Yankev in his twenty-first year and older than his brother by fifteen minutes, was the first to be betrothed. The father's choice for Yankev fell to the daughter of a landowner in Propoiske, a village a few miles from theirs. Yankev was informed by his father of the business and a week later he set out with his father by horse and cart for the seven mile journey to Propoiske to meet his wife-to-be, Henye.

The following, as was told (again and again) by Yankev himself, is an account of the meeting:

There was a bitter frost that night. It was black as pitch when we started out, not even a dog was to be seen on the road. We came to my beloved's house cold as stones. The landowner opened the door to us and we were conducted to a big room with a round table in it, a davenport, a carpet on the floor—very fine. He invited me to the stove to warm myself, giving me several glances. Then to my father he gave a nod. Satisfied.

Satisfied. Why would he not be satisfied? Warming himself at the stove stood a stunning youth—you should have seen me at twenty-one, I was like a tree. Tall, straight, a head of hair like a lion, a neck like a bull.

He took a few steps to the hall, my future father-in-law, and called for his wife. Right away a scrap of a woman came hurrying in. So fast I thought she was on wheels. A nothing of a woman, the size of a sitting dog. She gave me a dried hand, looking me up and down. 'Well, mamushka,' her husband said to her, 'are you pleased with your future son-in-law?' Her voice when it came out, was a croak. 'It is not for me to say. It's for Henyechke to say. If she is pleased with him I will be content.'

A second time the landowner went to the hall. 'Come, Henyechke,' he called to his daughter. 'We're waiting for you.'

The door opened and my beloved came to the room. One look and everything went black before my eyes. A duplicate of the mother! A chill fell on me. One minute I was cold, the next minute hot. She gave me her hand. 'Welcome to our house,' she said. The voice even was like the mother's. We were bidden to table and my sweetheart pouring out the tea did not take her eyes from me. Devouring me with her eyes. Meantime the mother—and this is something you would have to see with your own eyes to believe—was doling out the sugar. Breaking it off piece by piece from the sugar bowl which she kept in her lap between a pair of bony knees. Heed yourself, Yankev, an inner voice warned me. Heed yourself.

We drank a second glass of tea, we ate a stingy piece of cake, a spoonful of cherry jam, and it was time to go. My father took my hand and placed it in the hand of my future bride, and the pact was made. Unhappy ill-fated Yankev was now betrothed. It seemed to me I heard a howling of wolves. That witches were coupling, I knew for sure.

I whipped up the horse and we started for home. He talked and he talked and he talked, my father, so pleased was he with this night's business. The handsome dowry he had negotiated for his son, pitting his wits against the landowner's. I would not have to work like a horse to earn a bitter piece of bread as he at my age had done. I could go into business, or buy a piece of land. In a year or two I would be looked up to, respected. He kept on and on. Words piling up, every one of them a stone in my heart. The business of the dowry had not been as easy as I might think, he told me. I was not the only suitor. There was another candidate—'Who?' I said, speaking for the first time. 'The Devil?' 'Enough, Yankev!' he hollered. 'Enough!'

We were late getting home. My mother had gone to her bed, but not my brother Yudah to his. He was waiting to hear my news, I had left with such high hopes. I was a lusty youth at twenty-one—vital! One look at my face and he did not have to ask how I had fared. He signed to me behind my father's back and I followed him to the room we slept in together. I fell on his neck and poured out to him my bitter heart. He rocked me in his arms and hushed me like a baby, 'Shah, shah, shah.' He bade me to compose myself. He had a plan. 'Tomorrow in a quiet moment I will propose it to my father,' he said. What plan? I tried to worry it out of him but all I could get from him was, 'Rest easy, Yankev. Leave everything to me.' And as a condemned man with his head already in the noose clings foolishly to the hope of a reprieve, I was calmed by his words.

His plan? I heard it next morning. Keeping myself out of sight behind the kitchen door I heard the plan as he put it to my father.

'I beg you father, let me stand in my brother's place under the canopy. No one can tell us apart. Even you and my mother sometimes have to take a second look to make sure.' (True. The pranks we had played on shiksas in the fields—and even on respectable Jewish girls in our village.)

'Who put you up to this?' my father asked him. 'Your brother?'

'On my word, my brother knows nothing of this plan.'

'Why do you do it then?

My brother returned no answer.

I jumped from my hiding place. 'For pity!' I shouted. 'For pity, do you hear!'

My father lifted his hand as if to strike me. Which I deserved, raising my voice to my father.

'There will be no trickery,' he said. 'I gave my hand to the landowner, and Yankev gave his hand to the daughter. . . .'

In a month's time Yankev and Henye were man and wife.

The first child of the marriage, a boy, was born sickly. He lived only two weeks. The second child, again a boy, was a compact healthy child. He sickened and in six weeks was dead.

Henye, brooding, mourning the loss of her children, took a strange notion into her head. Two children one after the other had been snatched from her. A punishment, surely. A judgement. She had sinned, wronged, and was now being repaid . . . .

The night of the betrothal when Yankev's father on the way home from Propoiske told his son there was another candidate for the hand of the landowner's daughter, he was speaking the truth. Not the Devil, as Yankev conjectured, but a young man from Samatevitz who, prior to Yankev by a week or two, had been viewed and sent on his way after tea, a piece of cake and cherry jam, with a half-promise (which he took to be a firm commitment) that the dowry together with the landowner's daughter was as good as his. A week or two later when Henye clapped eyes on Yankev, all was up with the suitor from Samatevitz. The jilted suitor made a fuss. He demanded compensation. In rubles. The landowner peaced him off with soft words. The rejected suitor left in a dudgeon. Making an ominous pronouncement. 'God will repay me,' he said.

God will repay me—

These words came back to Henye, chilling her heart. Pregnant again and determined not to let this one slip away from her, she conceived a plan for holding on to her third child. To ensure the continuance of the child about to be born to her, she must solicit the pardon of her rejected lover. She was resolved that unless she petitioned his forgiveness no issue of hers would live to see the light of day.

Her third son was born and Henye, to ward off the Evil Eye, gave him the name Alter (Old One). Then as soon after the birth as she was able to, she put her plan into operation. She clothed the infant in old swaddling clothes, tatters, and journeyed with him by foot to the cemetery where her rejected suitor (who in the interim had died) lay buried. There, by his grave, she pleaded for pardon. Holding in her arms a ragamuffin whom no one on earth, or under, could conceivably covet, she begged forgiveness for the wrong she had done him.

Alter survived and thrived. At sixteen he was almost as tall as his father Yankev. Five more were born after him. The last born of the five, a girl. All persevered and held fast. Henye became shrunken and humped over in the back.

Yudah too had married and was fathering a family.

A few months after Yankev's marriage to Henye the father negotiated for Yudah a marriage with a girl called Lippa, a pretty girl from a nearby village. Yudah, as was the custom, brought his wife home after the marriage, and lodged her under the parental roof. With Lippa, the family consisted of seven. The old people, the twins, their wives, and Chayele, orphaned grandchild of the old people. (The child's mother, sister of the twins and older by a few years, was widowed early in marriage and died shortly after, leaving Chayele orphaned.)

Lippa over the years gave birth to four children; the first born a boy, and the other three, girls.

The old people died and the twin brothers in their forty-third year decided to emigrate to the new world. Yankev taking with him Alter, and Yudah taking his firstborn, the brothers set out. Their wives and remaining children to be sent for when they were settled. They set sail for the new world, all four, not a word of English among them. Their language was

32

Yiddish. To their work people and to the peasants in the field, they spoke Russian. Not one had been a greater distance than fifty miles (if that) from Chileshea. They brought food on board ship, not knowing for sure if they would be fed. They docked in Halifax, thinking they were in America.

They entrained for Toronto and were met at the station by a gang of people: *landsmen,* relatives, a junto of compatriots who had emigrated years before. The first few weeks were given over entirely to conviviality. Parties were given for them, dinners, suppers; days and nights were spent in nostalgic reminiscense. Their cousin Haskele (called behind his back Haskele the Shikker) toured the twins with their sons around the city in his car. He showed them Eaton's, Simpsons, the City Hall, Sunnyside, the Parliament Buildings, Casa Loma, the Jewish market on Kensington, and the McCaul Street synagogue.

Finally the business to hand—how to make a living—came up for consideration. The brothers were counselled, warned what to watch out for. Toronto was not Chileshea. Plenty of crooks on the lookout for a pair of greenhorns with money in their pocket. It was decided after a succession of councils and advisements that the best plan would be to start small. The name Chaim the *Schnorrer* (gone to his rest a few months since) came up at one of these sessions. He had started small and was rich as Croesus when he died. His investment? A few dollars for a peddler's licence, a few dollars for a pushcart—and the wealth he accumulated in six years!

'Who knew how rich he was getting, the fish peddling miser. He lived in a garret and slept on two chairs put together and ate *dreck.* We took pity on him. Only when he was dying in the Western Hospital from dried up guts that it came out how much money he had. He grabbed a hold of every doctor who put a nose even in the public ward, and begged them to save him. "Save me," he told them, "I've got money I can pay." He showed them bankbooks. A thousand in this bank, two thousand in another bank. In his shoes alone they found over four hundred dollars.'

The brothers obtained a fish peddling licence each, equipped themselves with carts and taking over Chaim the *Schnorrer's* circuit peddled their fish in the Jewish district, the area bounded by College and Spadina, Dundas and Bathurst streets, and beyond. And made a good thing of it. In less than three years they were able to provide passage for their families.

Henye arrived with their four sons, their daughter, and their niece

Chayele. Yudah, his wife Lippa having died a year after his departure, had only his three daughters to greet.

All this happened years before I was born. . . .

When Chayele came to us as stepmother I was six years old. We lived in rooms over the synagogue on Bellevue Avenue, and Yankev with his wife Henye and their daughter Malke, who was a dipper at Willard's Chocolates and engaged to be married to a druggist, lived around the corner from us on Augusta Avenue. Their youngest son, Pesach, lived with his wife, Lily, in the upstairs flat of his father's house. Their other four sons were domiciled with their wives and children around and about the city.

Yudah lived with a married daughter a few blocks from his brother's place.

Yankev was a social man. He loved company and almost every night of the week friends and relatives would gather at his house on Augusta Avenue. My stepmother too went there almost every night, and I used to tag along with her. I loved going to Yankev's, what a hullabaloo! No one spoke, everyone shouted, Yankev's voice rising above the hurly-burly. 'Henye!' he would call out when the full number was assembled. 'Where is she, my beauty?'

Henye would be sitting in a corner of the kitchen apart from the hubbub, and Yankev who knew exactly where she was located would make a great play of searching her out. Looking to the right of him, to the left of him, behind him, he would lift his head finally and craning it over the assembled company would direct his glance to her station.

'Ah there she is, my picture. What are you sitting there like a stump? People are in the house. Bring something to table. Fruit, a piece of cake. Make tea.'

Henye would rise to fill the kettle while Yankev, his eye on her, might mutter sotto voce: 'Crooked Back.'

Night after night they sat at Henye's table, friends and relatives, eating her food and laughing at Yankev's abuse of her. Now and then, not out of loyalty to her or compassion, but for the sake of mischief, for the sake of quickening the action, Henye would be prodded by one of the company to defend herself, to make some reply to her husband. 'Say something to him, Henye!'

Hunched over in a corner chair and blowing on her tea which she drank from a saucer, Henye would lift her shoulder in a shrug. 'Let him talk,' she would say, making her standard reply, her voice grating, harsh. 'As a dog howls so Yankev speaks. Does one dispute with a howling dog? Let him talk.'

One time I saw her go into a frenzied tantrum at Yankev's Crooked Back remark. Crooked Back was a commonplace in his vocabulary of insult. He had worse names for her. Old Devil, Witch, Scarecrow— these names went unheeded by Henye. Were passed over with a shrug from her, a spit on the floor. But this night for some unanswerable reason she was stung, inflamed by Yankev's 'Crooked Back' as she was filling the kettle. She went berserk. She stamped her feet like Rumpelstiltskin. Slammed the kettle, spilling water from the spout. With head thrust forward and bony arms bent at the elbow she busied herself with the back of her dress, unfastening it at the neck. Pulling at her undergarments till she had them far down enough to expose and lay bare her disfigurement, she turned her back to the company and displayed to them her dorsal hump.

'In his service,' she said in her rasp of a voice. 'In his service I have become crooked and bent. In my father's house my back was straight. In Yankev's service it became bent. Yankev has a right to insult me, I've earned it from him.'

She exhibited her twisted back, making sure everyone at her table had a good look. Like a mannequin displaying to a roomful of buyers some latter feature in haute couture, so Henye pirouetted and spun before them, pointing to the hump on her back.

The collection was titillated by this turnabout in the evening's advancement. They applauded her. She was given a handclap. 'Good for you, Henye! Give it to him!'

Yankev was stunned. Dumbfounded. But only momentarily. Quickly his surprise gave way to anger.

'Cover yourself!' he bellowed. 'Cover yourself you shameless old Jezebel! In my service!' he thundered. 'The gall of the woman—'

He rose to his feet and with shoulders back and handsome head lifted high he strutted a few steps in his kitchen like a cock. He squared himself against the wall, facing the company.

'I was a stunning youth! You should have seen me at twenty-one, I was like a tree! Tall, straight, a head of hair like a lion, a neck like a bull.' He pointed an accusing finger at Henye who was hooking herself up at the back. 'She became bent in my service? A lie! In her father's house she was straight? A lie! As you see her now so she was when I beheld her the first time. On my word my friends, no different. One look at this picture my father had picked for me and I was taken with the ague. One minute I was cold, the next minute hot—'

'Enough!' came Yudah's voice from the assembly. 'Enough, Yankev.'

Yankev turned an astonished face to his brother. 'You turn on me too? Is this Yudah, my second self, who speaks? Is this Yudah who volunteered out of pity for Yankev to stand in his place under the canopy?' Without another word, Yankev took his place again at the head of his table.

Henye, her own effrontery having gone to her head like wine, was not through with him yet. (Social ascendancy over Yankev was a potent draught.) Buttoned up now but unmindful of the kettle, she spoke up again.

'No need,' she said. 'There was no need for Yudah to step into Yankev's place, and there was no need for Yankev himself if I was so unpleasing to him, to take me for his wife. There were others,' she said, preening almost. 'One of my suitors died after I married Yankev, and left his curse on me for disappointment. I lost two children. I went to his grave after Alter was born, to beg his pardon—'

Yankev leapt to his feet, revivified. 'True! She went to beg his pardon. It's my pardon she should have begged, not his. He was lying undisturbed, unplagued—and she went to beg his pardon. He was liberated, *I* was in bondage—it's Yankev's pardon she should have asked. Yankev!' he cried bringing his fist to his chest and thumping himself like Tarzan.

Henye had had her brief moment. Now it was over and the company was restored to Yankev's sway.

When I knew the brothers, their fish peddling days were behind them. It was during Prohibition and they were making an easier dollar peddling illicit booze. The fish cart however was still in use. For deliveries. The topmost tray, concealing the bootleg booze in the interior of the cart, contained for the sake of camouflage a few scattered pickerel, a bit of pike, a piece of whitefish packed in ice. Yankev, to accommodate expanding trade, had a phone installed in the hall of his house and it rang at all hours, a customer at the other end asking for Jack. Their customers, for the most part gentile, could not get their tongues around Yankev so they called him Jack. Yudah was called Joe.

The brothers had acquired a bit of English, enough to see them through their business. Their inventory and records were kept in a lined exercise book, in Yiddish. Customers were designated by descriptive terms, nicknames: The Gimpy One on Bathurst, Long Nose on Lippincott. Using their fish carts mocked up with a scattering of moribund fish in the topmost tray they made their deliveries to Big Belly, Short Ass, The Murderer, Big Tits, The Pale One, The Goneff, The Twister, The Tank.

They operated a long time without running afoul of the law. But were apprehended eventually on a delivery run, and took a pinch. Which resulted in a fine. A sobering experience this, their first skirmish with the law, and despite loss of revenue and the clamouring of customers, the brothers lay low for a while. Then started up again. The fish cart, now that the cops were on to them, was held to be unserviceable, so the brothers bought a car and Yankev learned to drive it. Yudah, of a more nervous disposition than his brother, never learned to drive.

Again they went a good time unmolested by the law, and suddenly were fallen upon, nabbed by a pair of plainclothesmen as they were loading the car. The load was confiscated and the brothers in full view of neighbours who had come out to watch, were hustled into the squad car.

Henye was petrified. Frightened that she'd be hauled up too she scurried for a hiding place, hollering, 'Gevald!'

On the books a second time, the brothers drew a stiffer fine. Further, Yankev was prohibited from keeping so much as a single bottle of whisky on his premises, with a warning from the bench that a third offence would result in a jail sentence.

This gave the brothers a jolt. They were really shaken up. But it didn't stop them from selling. They kept to their course—but with more caution than before. Yudah with a few bottles stashed on his person would by foot or by streetcar, depending on his landing-place, make a discreet delivery. Yankev, equipped likewise, would take Henye for a ride in the car. Which she loved. 'In a car I could ride to Moskva,' she used to say. Yankev made a few stops en route, explaining he had to collect some money owing him, and with the motor running she sat quite content waiting for him. An unwitting shill, and terrified of the law, Henye accompanied her husband on his deliveries and never tumbled that she was fronting for him.

And so things went till one Friday with the brothers at Shul, and Henye at her pots, two plainclothesmen without a search warrant or even a knock on the door, came directly in and began taking the place apart, looking for booze. Henye hollered, 'Gevald! A pogrom!' and fainted. Her daughter-in-law Lily, screaming, came running down the stairs with Pesach close on her heels. The cops continued their search. Unearthing a couple of cases which they stored in their car, they sat themselves on the verandah awaiting the brothers' return.

The shame of it! People coming from synagogue and police on the verandah as if waiting for a pair of bandits. Henye banged her head on the wall. 'Let them wait inside!' she cried, and as Pesach went to fetch them she hid herself in the toilet. The brothers came in and before the law could put an arm on either of them, Pesach, youngest of the sons and quickest in the head, made a verbal deposition to the cops. He claimed the whisky was his. Which flummoxed the cops. Briefly. All three were taken to the station, all three booked, and Monday when the case came before the bench Pesach stepped forward and taking his oath on the Bible swore the whisky was his. And with the help of a lawyer, made the story stick. Pesach drew a fine for keeping on convicted premises declared by the law to be out of bounds.

The same night, and at Henye's behest, a family conclave made up of Yankev's five sons with their wives, Malke with her boyfriend the druggist, Yudah's four children with their partners, all talking at once exhorted the brothers to put an end to the business. Now that they were known to the law it was too risky. Both were well fixed with money in the bank, they were getting a good income from the two pieces of property they had bought, Yudah had only himself to provide for, Yankev with a paid up house was getting rent from Pesach, Malke was paying board. The brothers were reminded they were sick men, both. (They had become asthmatic in the last few years, with an advancing seriousness of chest congestion. A fright, a scare, the least bit of physical exertion brought on a fit of coughing, a whooping strangling seizure alarming to behold.)

The brothers gave up the booze. They were together all day as before, but now there was no occupation for them, nothing to do with their time. They played checkers by the hour, casino, and went oftener to the synagogue than before. In the spring of that year they sat on Yankev's verandah drinking a glass of tea sweetened with slices of peeled apple. I used to bring my homework to Yankev's verandah and would hear them talking nostalgically of the bootlegging days. They missed the action. 'The day is like a year,' said Yankev. 'But for that old devil of mine we'd still be in business.'

Augusta Avenue was a busy street and the brothers, to invent a bit of diversion for themselves, sat on the verandah making asides to each other about the passersby going to and coming from the market. Their eye one day was caught by a new nose in the neighbourhood, a big woman with an excessive bosom, her breasts under a cotton dress swinging free and unleashed. The brothers gawked. Yankev nudged Yudah: 'If one of those should fall on your foot God forbid—every bone would be crushed.' They fell over themselves, winded, short of breath from laughing. 'Och toch toch,' they gasped, gulping for breath, pummelling themselves on the chest. 'Och toch toch.'

Unperceived by the brothers, Henye had come out with a pot of fresh tea. In one wink she took in the scene. 'Shame on you. A pair of old men. Shame on you both,' she said, and spat.

Slowly, Yankev turned his head in her direction. 'To *look,* you old devil—is that forbidden too?' He snatched the tea pot from her hands. 'Get back in the house, I'll pour out myself.'

In the summer of that year, Yudah fell sick. Painfully congested and unable to speak, he lived only nine days. People came to the house of Shiva to comfort Yudah's children, the bereaved brother, and it was remarked by them that Yankev overnight had become an old man. When Shiva was over Yankev came every morning to the synagogue above which we had rooms to say Kaddish for his brother, and fell into the habit of coming upstairs after prayers to while away some time with his niece Chayele. He used the side door of the synagogue which gave secondary access to our place, a short climb, eighteen steps in all, but for Yankev a laborious ascent. You'd hear his 'och toch' as he paused every few steps.

One morning before sitting down to his tea he extracted from the inside pockets of his coat three bottles of whisky. 'A little favour, Chayele,' he said to my stepmother, 'to put away for a couple of days these few bottles.'

'With pleasure,' she responded, and hid them in the far end of the dark hall in an unused bunker filled with junk. He thanked his niece, and to me he gave ten cents not to say anything to my Pa.

Next morning he came as usual for his glass of tea and before leaving took a bottle from the bunker and put it in his pocket. In a few days the bunker, denuded of booze, was replenished. With six bottles. In a short while (the bunker unable to accommodate the increasing supply) whisky was being stored in the room my sister, my brother and I slept in. A few bottles under the bed I shared with my sister, a few bottles under my brother's bed.

Two or three times a day, except on the sabbath or a Jewish holiday —and never when my father was home—Yankev made his sorties to and from our place.

People remarked on the change in Yankev. They said he was becoming his old self again.

One day in the late Fall on a Jewish holiday with the synagogue packed out and a few members of the congregation standing out front in their prayer shawls taking a breather, a squad car drew up and two cops emerged, making straight for the outside door abutting the synagogue, which was the primary entrance to the stairs leading to our place.

A quick inspection uncovered bottles in the bunker and bottles under the beds. They began querying my stepmother, who didn't understand a word they were saying.

'Ask her what's all this whisky doing here,' they instructed me. 'Ask her who it belongs to.'

I put the question to my stepmother, then gave them her reply. 'She says she can't give you a straight answer because her head is spinning with fright. She wants you to take the whisky and go before my father comes home.'

They told me to ask her this, to ask her that, and as I was saying for the twentieth time, 'She would like you to take the whisky and go before my father comes home,' we heard his step on the stairs.

Without preamble, my father was taken over the hurdles. They told him right off they knew the whisky was not his. They knew who it belonged to, but that didn't absolve him from guilt. His place was being used as a drop. 'What do you get paid for keeping?' they asked him.

'I am not in a court of law,' said my father (showing off his English). 'In my own house I don't have to answer any questions.'

'Okay let's go,' they said, and my father, before going submissively downstairs with the cops, gave hell to my stepmother in Yiddish.

Doing my stepmother's bidding I ran to Yankev's house with the intelligence. Yankev and Henye with their daughter Malke and her boyfriend the druggist were at supper.

Yankev clapped a hand to his forehead. 'A *klog*!' he wailed, 'a *klog*!'

Henye set up a holler. 'He's been selling again! He wants to bury me, that *Poshe Yisroel*.'

Yankev beating his hands together lamented his fate. He was certain my father would open up, sell him down the river. A third conviction meant jail. Asthmatic as he was he would never survive even a short term in jail. He would die there like a dog. His life was in the hands of the Rumanian Beast (his name for my father behind his back). 'A frightening contemplation,' he moaned. 'Frightening.'

My stepmother came running. Pa had called from the station. From what she understood he never told on anybody. He took the blame on himself—but somebody had to go right away to the station with five hundred dollars. 'Bail,' she said. The word had been dinned into her head.

'Thank God!' said Yankev. 'The Almighty One has not forsaken me after all.'

And with my father cooling his heels in the pokey, Yankev sat down to finish his supper. 'Now another problem comes up,' he said drinking his second glass of tea. Who was to go to the station? He didn't dare put a nose in there. And neither did Pesach with a conviction against him. Malke's fiancé rose from his place. 'I'll go,' he said.

'Finish first,' said Yankev pointing to the druggist's dish of compote. 'The jail isn't on fire. He's not sitting there in a holocaust.'

My father was tried and because of the inside door of the synagogue giving secondary access to our rooms was convicted and fined for keeping whisky in a place held by the law to be public.

Yankev put up the money for the fine, and the same evening his four sons came to their father's house to upbraid and lecture him. They said they were surprised that their father, a man of principle, would go back on his word. And Yankev listened acquiescently, attended their words without demur. 'A mistake,' he conceded, 'a mistake.' Henye snorted. Next day friends and relatives came in their numbers and Yankev, constrained to give an ear to them too, acknowledged he was ashamed of having gone back on his word. Henye, filling the kettle, gave out a short derisive laugh. Except for a muttered 'Gazlan!' as she set her husband's glass of tea before him, she had nothing to say.

In the following months Yankev became soft as butter. Henye's days became easier; he had stopped belabouring her. He let up on her altogether. When company came she still kept to her corner chair, but she could open her mouth now without being jumped on.

In January Yankev fell ill and was taken by ambulance to hospital. First day, he was allowed no visitors. Second day only his wife was permitted in the sick-room. Henye sat by his bed peering at him through the oxygen tent, and crying.

'Don't mourn me, I'm still alive,' said Yankev, and signed to her to go.

His third day in hospital his children were allowed in two at a time, and on the fourth day (Saturday) it was given out to them by the doctor that their father was very low. Saturday noon we had a hysterical call from Pesach. His father was dying, he said, and requested of my stepmother that I be sent right away to fetch Henye. Yankev was asking for her.

When I came to Henye with my tidings she was sitting at the kitchen table drinking tea from a saucer. I told her I had come to take her to the hospital. 'Yankev wants to see you,' I said. She put her saucer down and with hands clasped loosely in her lap studied my face. 'Yankev sent for me?' she said in her harsh voice. I waited for her to get ready but she continued at table rocking back and forth and muttering to herself. I caught the words 'mechilah betten.'* She rose abruptly from her chair and a minute later returned in her coat and shawl.

*To beg forgiveness.

We trudged through the snow, Henye with shawled head thrust forward holding on to my arm and keeping up a hoarse monologue on our way to the hospital.

'So the time of reckoning has come and Yankev sends for his wife. *Mechilah betten,*' she said, nodding her bent head. 'What is there to forgive? Everything—and nothing. Without Yankev I'll be alone. Alone like a stone. I have children—God give them health—but children are one thing and a husband is another. A husband is a friend, my dear. So Yankev hollered at me, called me names—that's nothing, it's soon forgotten. Like last year's snow. I had my faults too. Yankev was an open handed man and I was a—' she gave me a sideways glance—'I know people called me a stingy,' she said, using one of the few English words in her vocabulary. 'And also other faults. Sinful faults nobody knows about except Henye. Jealous, jealous, jealous. All my life jealous,' she said with a rueful shake of her head. 'People liked Yankev, I was jealous. My sister-in-law Lippa was pretty, I was jealous. People said Lippa is like a little doll, I ate my heart out. Least little thing, I laid the blame on Lippa. Yankev loved his brother Yudah, again jealous. I tried many times to come between them—'

She stopped to kick snow from her shoes, then passed under her dripping nose the handkerchief she used on the Sabbath bound around her wrist like a bandage, and we continued.

'People said Yankev doesn't like his wife—what do people know? You're a young child so you won't understand,' she said, (I was fourteen) 'but if a woman is disliked by her husband, uninviting to him, she cannot give him even one child—let alone eight children. I was very sick when Malke was born and who looked after me? Not my sister and not my mother. Yankev. Who fed me from a spoon like a baby? Yankev. He went two miles by foot to buy me an orange.'

We came in sight of the hospital; she stopped to take a dab at her eyes with the back of her handkerchief-bandaged wrist. Being the Sabbath Henye would not ride the elevator so we walked the four flights to Yankev's room. She searched the faces of her children who were standing in the corridor, then opened the door to her husband's room. She stood by his bed looking at him; he appeared to be asleep.

He opened his eyes, and motioned her to sit down. 'Henye,' he said, 'I have a request—'

Henye leaned forward. 'No need, Yankev. All is forgiven—'

'Good,' he said nodding his head. 'Good.'

'And I beg your forgiveness,' she continued. 'I beg your forgiveness for—'

42

'What *is* this?' he said looking at her in puzzlement. 'I'm not dying yet. You'll have plenty of time to ask for my forgiveness.'

'The children said you sent for me? I thought, God forbid—'

He laughed. 'Och toch toch,' he gasped, pummelling his chest. Henye handed him his glass of water. 'Don't worry I'll climb out. My time isn't up yet,' he said, sipping water from his glass. 'I sent for you to tell you something—but I don't want the children to know, you hear?' He paused to summon breath. 'The last few weeks I took a little order here, a little order there—'

Henye gaped.

'In the summer kitchen behind the new bag of potatoes,' he continued, 'you'll find a few bottles—' he paused for breath—'so if a customer phones—'

Henye didn't wait to hear the rest. With Yankev still talking she rose to her feet and the next minute she was out of the room.

'Come,' she said taking hold of my arm. And to her children clustered outside their father's door, 'He'll live,' she said.

Holding on to my arm Henye sped along the snow covered streets, I had to run to keep pace with her. She opened the door to her house, and beckoned me to follow. Speeding through hall, through kitchen, she proceeded to the back of the house lean-to, which they called the summer kitchen. This small area used as a store-house contained the Passover pots and pans and dishes, jars of preserves, bushel baskets of apples, onions, carrots, and in a corner of the summer kitchen two burlap bags of potatoes; the one in use easy of access, the unopened one wedged in the corner and barricaded behind several earthenware crocks containing pickled cucumbers, beet borscht and kvass.

Seizing hold of it by its neck, Henye lifted the foremost bag of potatoes, thrust it aside, then stooped to the earthenware crocks (which had to be shifted in order to gain access to the hindmost bag of potatoes). I watched Henye, a little gnome with black shawl sweeping the floor, grappling with the unwieldy crocks.

'You try,' she said. 'Young hands are stronger.'

Tilting the crocks and rolling them on their rims I managed, with Henye clearing space for them, to open a passage wide enough to admit a burlap bag of potatoes. Together, we pulled the bag from its lodging and there, as Yankev said she would, Henye found a few bottles. Four. She took two bottles and bade me to take the other two. 'Come,' she said, and I followed her to the kitchen.

She pulled the shawl from her head and took off her coat. 'Open up a bottle,' she directed me. She took the bottle to the sink. 'Here's a customer for you, Yankev,' she said, and emptied it down the drain. She told me to uncap another one. 'Here's another customer,' she said, and that too went down the drain. A third bottle was emptied. Draining the last one down the sink, she turned her head to me. 'When it comes to whisky Henye is not a Stingy,' she said slyly.

'I would give you something,' she said thanking me, 'but Shabbus I don't carry money.' Then as I made to go, she called me back. She pulled open a drawer in which she kept odds and ends, her pills, her medicines and the knotted handkerchief with its nickels and dimes. 'Take ten cents,' she said pointing to the knotted handkerchief. I took hold of the knot and applying the technique I had seen her use so many times—a tug, a twist, a pull, a pluck—went to work on it. I couldn't even loosen the knot, let alone untie it. I returned the handkerchief to the drawer. 'You'll pay me tomorrow.'

Three days later Yankev came home.

Company came the same night to welcome him home. Henye bustled and scurried about. Unbidden, she brought fruit to table, cake, and made tea. 'What an escape,' said Yankev, shaking his head. 'To scramble out of their hands—a deliverance, my friends', he said solemnly. 'A deliverance.'

With Yankev home, the phone began ringing again. One night at supper the phone rang, and Henye went to it. The call was for Jack. 'Jeck?' she said. 'Jeck not home. In Hallyefacks,' she said and hung up.

For the first time since coming home, Yankev showed anger. 'Don't make a fool of me, Henye!' he said as she resumed her place. 'Attend to your business and leave my business to me—'

'*His* business,' she said. 'It's my business too. You took me in for a partner, you forgot? Last Saturday in the hospital when you sent for me—you don't remember? You told me where the whisky was, you told me to attend—and I did. When I came home a customer was waiting so I gave him the whisky.'

Yankev stared. 'A customer was here? In the house?'

Henye pointed to the sink. 'That customer.'

Yankev rose and made his way to the summer kitchen. He returned and without a word took his place at table. Henye, undisturbed, continued with her food. She poured him a glass of tea and dropped into it a heaping spoonful of cherry conserve. 'You saw for yourself there's no more whisky?' she said. He made no reply. She poured some tea from her glass into her saucer. 'We're out of business, Mister Jeck,' she said bringing her saucer to her lips—and Yankev despite himself began to laugh. 'Och toch toch,' he gasped, and signaled her to get him some water. 'You old devil,' he said, his breath restored, 'you'll be the death of me yet.'

'Don't worry, Yankev,' she returned, 'you'll bury me.'

Henye's words were prophetic; two months later she died in her sleep.

I went with my stepmother to Henye's funeral. With the service at the open grave concluded, Yankev took hold of the shovel. 'So swift, Henye, so fast,' he said shovelling earth on the coffin. 'You left in such a hurry there was no time for me to ask your forgiveness. I ask it now. Intercede for me, Henye,' he said, then handed the shovel to his oldest son Alter.

People came all week to the house of Shiva to comfort Henye's children and her bereaved husband. Henye was lauded, praised to the skies. Her children, concurring, wept at every mention of their mother's name while Yankev, obsessed with the speed of Henye's departure, talked of it without beginning and without end.

'So fast,' he said. 'Like a whirlwind. We ate supper, we talked of Malke's wedding next month, how much will it cost for the hall, how much for the music—' Malke began to cry. Her father gave her a baleful look, and continued. 'All of a sudden she said "I feel like to go to bed." Henye to go to bed before twelve, one o'clock? Henye to leave dishes on the table? I went up myself to bed an hour later, maybe two hours later— who can remember—and she was asleep. Of *that* I'm sure. She turned around when I put on the light. In the morning she was cold.' He struck his forehead with the palm of his hand. 'When did she die? Of what? And without a word!'

Six months after Henye's death Malke was married to her druggist. With Malke gone, Yankev sat at Pesach's table Friday after Shul for the Sabbath meal. Now and then Lily's mother, an active widow, a big woman who drove her own car, spoke English and lived in an apartment, made a fourth at Pesach's table for Friday night supper—and it was observed by Pesach that his father seemed more animated the nights the widow came for supper.

Before long it was put about that Yankev was going to remarry.

One afternoon we heard the familiar 'och toch toch' on the stairs giving notice of Yankev's approach. Without any waste of time he told my stepmother what was on his mind. 'The truth, Chayele, will I be making a fool of myself?' 'Why a fool?' my stepmother replied. 'People will laugh,' he said. 'Yankev a *chossin* in his old age—' 'Let them laugh,' said my stepmother. 'What kind of life is it to be alone?'

In March, a year to the month of Henye's death, Yankev was married and went to live with his new wife in her apartment. Three months went by, and not a word from Yankev. My stepmother began to worry. She handed me a scrap of paper with Yankev's new phone number. 'Phone,' she said. His wife answered the phone. 'Yankev went for a stroll,' she said in English. 'Tell your mother I'll be going to the market tomorrow and I'll drop him off at your place.'

Next morning we heard Yankev making his ascent. He came to the kitchen spruced up in a navy blue suit. 'Och toch toch,' he gasped, fanning himself with a panama hat. 'I'm not used any more to steps—in the building we have an elevator.'

My stepmother fussed over him. She made tea, complimented him on his attire, his looks—'You lost a little weight, Yankev?' 'Lost a little weight,' he repeated. 'She put me on a diet. Gives me grass to eat.' (His word for lettuce.) He pointed to his glass, indicating it was to be filled again. 'It's good to drink tea again from a glass,' he said. 'She gives me tea in a cup. What taste is there to a glass of tea in a cup? Chayele, Chayele, Chayele,' he said shaking his head and sighing. My stepmother was disturbed. 'You're not happy?' 'Happy,' he echoed. 'It's like you said —what kind of life is it to be alone?'

All at once he was his old self again. He smiled at my stepmother, a look of mischief coming to his face. 'She bought me a pair of pyjamas,' he said. 'Yankev sleeps now in pyjamas, and his missus like a man sleeps also in pyjamas. First thing in the morning she opens up a window, and makes exercises. First of all she stretches,' he said, demonstrating with his arms aloft. 'Then she bends down and puts her ass in the air. And that's some ass to put in the air, believe me. And all day, busy. Busy, busy, busy. With what? To make supper takes five minutes. Soup from a can, compote from a can—it has my *boba*'s flavour. A piece of herring? This you never see on the table, she doesn't like the smell. A woman comes in to clean—with what is she busy, you'll ask? With gin rummy. True, gin rummy. They come in three or four times a week her friends, to play gin rummy. They cackle like geese, they smoke like men. Dear, my wife says to me, bring some ginger ale from the frig, the girls are thirsty—she hasn't got time to leave the cards. Girls, she calls them. Widows! Not one of them without a husband buried in the ground,' he said with sudden indignation. 'Dear, she calls me, nu? Before me there was another Dear and she buried *him*. Once in a while without thinking, I call her Henye. She gets so mad, oh ho ho. So I make a mistake sometimes, it's natural? How does a man live with a woman all his life and blot out from his memory her name—'

He rose suddenly from his chair, took a handkerchief from his pocket and blowing his nose in it went to the mirror over the sink and peered in it, dabbing at his eyes. 'Cholera take it,' he said, 'there's something in my eye.' My stepmother looked away; next minute we heard the sound of a horn. Yankev went to the window. 'There she is, my prima donna.' He embraced his niece. 'Drives a car like a man,' he muttered, and took his leave.

Maybe Later It Will Come Back to My Mind

'Lady! Lady!' An old man in a wheelchair at the far end of the corridor was beckoning me. I was standing at the elevator preoccupied with thoughts of my father, whom I was visiting at the Jewish Home for the Aged, and had not noticed the old man before. I took my finger from the UP button and went to him.

'Good morning,' he said, adjusting his yarmulka. 'You got somebody here?'

'My father,' I said.

'Where is he?'

'On the fifth floor.'

'That's in the hospital part, no?'

'Yes. He's recovering from an operation. And I've only got time for a short visit with him,' I added warily. I had been trapped so often before. I had been prevailed on to make calls to delinquent sons, daughters, grand-children; I had made trips to the kitchen with complaints about the menu; I had been asked to rustle up a doctor for somebody, a nurse, an orderly —and I was bound this morning not to become involved as I had only a short time to spend with my father.

The elevator came to the door. 'Excuse me,' I said. 'My father's waiting for me.'

'So he'll wait a little minute,' he said. 'I want you should do me a little favour first.'

'If I can, and providing it doesn't take too long.'

Instead of saying what he wanted of me, he kept me waiting—quite deliberately, I could tell. He kept me waiting while he searched his pockets, brought out a match, struck it on his chair, and held the flame to his stump of a cigar. Even after he got it going, he sat puffing away and slapping at the ashes on his vest.

A second elevator came to the floor. I was disposed to leave him, and took a few steps toward it.

'Wait a minute,' he said. 'What are you in such a hurry? Your father wouldn't run away. All I want is you shall take me out in the garden.' He cocked an eye at me. 'Easy, no?'

I looked at the old man, taking him into account for the first time. During visits to my father I had encountered dozens of old men in wheelchairs, also old ladies in wheelchairs. I had spent the time of day with them in hallways, in sitting-rooms, and had done errands for many of them. I had been thanked, excessively so, for a trifling service like addressing an envelope. For making a telephone call I had been blessed. But this man—there was something odd about him. I had never been addressed with such peremptoriness, such lack of regard for my own affairs. There was something about him that took me back. Where had I seen him? I looked at the old man, studying him. Broad face, heavy-lidded eyes, hooked nose, thick torso, and short legs, his feet barely reaching the footrest of his chair.

'What are you looking?' he said, bringing me up short. 'You never saw an old man before? Go behind better, and give me a little push,' he said in Yiddish. 'The Messiah will come first before I'll come out in the garden.'

Ah, now I had it! Now I knew who he was!

'Is your name Layevsky? Myer Layevsky?'

He closed an eye at me. 'How did you know?'

'I used to work for you. A long time ago, about thirty years ago. I was your office lady; my name was Miss Rotstein. I worked for you nine months, and you fired me. Do you remember me?'

He wagged his big head. 'From this I shall remember you? God willing I shall have so many years left how many girls I fired. So I fired you. On this account you wouldn't take me out in the garden?'

'Oh, don't be—' I was about to say don't be silly. Fancy saying don't be silly to Myer Layevsky.

I wheeled him to the lobby, and once outside the glass portals, carefully down the ramp.

'How's your son?' I asked.

He turned full face to me. 'My Israel? A very important man,' he said, giving equal emphasis to each word. 'A very big doctor in the States.'

'And Mrs. Layevsky, how's she?'

He turned, facing front. 'Dead. A healthy woman crippled by arthritis.

Ten years younger than me. I always had in my mind the *Molochamovis* will come for me first, but it turned out different. Take me over there by the big tree.'

I settled him by the big tree. 'And you don't remember me? I was only sixteen, and now I'm a married woman with two grown children, so I must have changed a lot. But you should remember me. You gave me a week's holiday; I took an extra few days, and when I came back, you had another girl in my place. Now do you remember?'

'Ask me riddles,' he said, again in Yiddish. 'Do me a favour and go to your father,' he said, using the familiar thou instead of the formal you, with which he had first addressed me. 'Maybe later it will come back to my mind.'

My father was in the armchair beside his bed, reading a newspaper. 'Pa! You'll never guess who I saw downstairs. Remember Myer Layevsky, the man I used to work for?'

My father removed his eyeglasses. 'I remember him very well. And also how you hid under the bed from him when he came to find out why you didn't come in to work one morning. Correct?'

My father had it wrong. He was confusing Myer Layevsky with Mr. Teitlbaum, the comforter manufacturer, from whom I *had* hidden under the bed.

'You've got it wrong, Pa,' I said. 'You're thinking of Teitlbaum, the comforter manufacturer. But how did you know I hid under the bed? Ma swore she wouldn't tell you.'

'Maybe a little bird told me,' he said. 'Now I remember. It seems to me you got another job that summer. Correct?'

'That's right. For a toy factory, remember? Three days after I quit Imperial Comforters I went to work for a toy factory, in the Kewpie doll section. I wanted to stay on, but you wouldn't let me. You made me go back to commercial school. But I went only six weeks of my second term, and you let me quit. *Then* I went to work for Layevsky, the man I saw downstairs—'

'I let you quit Commercial? This I don't remember, but if you say so, maybe you remember better.' He sighed reminiscently. 'You always had your own way with me. Whatever you wanted you accomplished.'

Like fun I'd always had my own way with him. For one thing, I never wanted to go to Commercial. My plan, after being passed out of Grade VIII, King Edward School, was to go with my best girlfriend, Lizzie Stitsky, to Harbord Collegiate, but my father wouldn't cough up the money for books. So I had to go instead to commercial school, where the books were free and the course took only two years. I loathed the sight of that dismal building, the dreary classroom, the drabs I was thrown in with, and went every morning five days a week with a resentful, heavy heart, and my lunch in a paper bag.

Sure, he let me quit Commercial after only six weeks of my second term, but not through any understanding on his part, or sympathy: I swung him around through a trick, a bit of chicanery.

Everything had gone wrong for me that Monday of my seventh week. I had gone to bed the night before with a bag of hot salt pressed against my cheek to ease a toothache, and Monday morning after a troubled night's sleep my cheek was inflamed, and the brassière I had washed the night before was still wet. When the noon bell rang, I was as miserable as I had ever been in my life. When I tried to get at my lunch, my desk drawer was jammed. Propping my feet against the legs of the desk, I gave the drawer a terrific yank. It shot out suddenly, knocking me back and landing overturned in my lap. Everything spilled to the floor, pencils, pads, erasers, books. I scrabbled around collecting my things, and returning them to the drawer, noticed a man's handkerchief, dirty, clotted, and stuck in the right-hand corner. I had never got the drawer more than partially open before, so it must have been there all these weeks side by side with my lunch. My tooth began to ache again. I fled the room, and that night at supper, screwed up enough courage to tell my father I would not be returning to Commercial.

He reared. 'Why?' he wanted to know.

'Because I found something in my desk.'

'What did you find?'

I made no answer; I knew under cross-examination my case would be lost. He insisted on knowing; he kept badgering me. 'A dead mouse?'

'Worse.'

'What worse?' he persisted, getting angry.

'Don't ask me, Pa.' On the inspiration of the moment, I turned my inflamed cheek to him and said, 'I'm ashamed to talk about it.'

And my father, sensing that the object had something to do with sex, stopped questioning me. I had won. I knew he'd never let me quit on account of a dirty hankie in my desk.

A week later, through an ad in the paper reading *Girl Wanted, Easy Work, Easy Hours, Good Pay*, I went to work for Myer Layevsky. Myer Layevsky was sitting in a swivel chair at a cluttered roll-top desk in his two-by-four office when I came to be interviewed for the job. His hat was on the back of his head, and in his mouth a dead cigar. He swivelled around, and closing one eye, inspected me with the open one.

50

'You're a Jewish girl, no?'

'Yes.'

'I had already a few people looking for the job, but I didn't made up my mind yet.' He pointed to a beat-up typewriter. 'You know how to typewrite?'

'Yes.'

'So if I'll give you a letter, you'll be able to take down?' He rooted around the desk and came up with several lots of file cards, each bound with a rubber band. 'Customers,' he said. 'I sell goods on time. You heard about that joke a dollar down and a dollar when you ketch me? This is my business.'

He extracted one lot of cards and put them aside. 'Deadbeats,' he said, screwing both eyes shut and shaking his head. 'Deadbeats. From this bunch nobody comes in to pay. I have to collect myself. Sometimes I even have to go and pull back the goods, so this bunch you can forget about.' He went on to the other cards. 'This bunch is something difference,' he said fondly. 'Good customers, honest people which they come in regular with a payment. So this is what you shall do. A customer comes in the office with a payment? First you'll take the money. Next you'll find out the name. Then you'll make a receipt, mark down on the card the payment, and keep up to date the balance.' He struck a match on the desk and put it to his cigar. 'Easy, no?'

'Another thing which I didn't mention it yet,' he said. 'Sometimes it happens a cash customer calls in the office for a pair sheets, a pair towels, a little rug, a lace panel, something—so come in the back, I'll show you my stockroom.'

I was taken by surprise when he stood up, to see how short he was. Sitting, he looked like a giant of a man. But the bulk of him was all in his torso; his legs were short and bowed, and he stood barely over five feet, and loping in baggy pants to the stockroom he looked like a comic mimicking someone's walk.

Except for a conglomeration of stuff piled in a corner of the stockroom, everything was in order, price-tagged, and easy to get at.

'This mishmush,' he said, indicating the heaped-up pile, 'is pulled goods from deadbeats which they didn't pay. So if a poor woman comes in the office with cash money for a pair secondhand sheets, a pair secondhand towels, a lace panel, something, let her pick out and give her for lest than regular price. Give her for half. A really poor woman, give her for a little lest than half.'

Right away I panicked. 'How will I know a real poor woman from only a poor one?'

51

'You got a pair eyes, no?' He snapped off the overhead light. 'So that's all. You'll come in tomorrow half past eight.'

'An office job,' said Ma when I gave her my news. 'Wait till Pa hears.'

When Pa heard, the first thing he said was, 'How much a week?'

'I forgot to ask, Pa.'

'Very smart. The first thing you do,' he lectured me, 'is to ask how much. If he mentions a figure not satisfactory, you ask for more. The way you handled, you'll have to take whatever he gives. But it's not too late yet. You didn't sign no contract, so tomorrow before you'll even sit down or take off your coat, you'll ask him.'

You'd think, to hear my father, that he was the cagey one, the astute bargainer. All his years a loyal slavey he had worked his heart out for peanuts, protecting the boss's interest, saving him a dollar—and only the year before he had been slugged holding off two armed thugs to keep them from getting at the boss's safe. My father had been out of work, and things were so desperate in the house with no money for food or rent that he went finally (and at the cost of his pride) to Iscovitz, one of his rich Rumanian connections who owned a tobacco factory. Iscovitz had nothing to offer my father except a job as night watchman.

'I've got a man already, an old *cukker* half blind, half deaf. I'll let him go, Avrom Mendl, and give you the job.'

My father refused; he wouldn't take another man's job; but Iscovitz argued he needed a younger man, would have to let the old man go eventually—so my father came in as second night watchman. The old man ducked for cover when the heist took place, but not my father. Unarmed, he stood up to the thugs, and was cracked over the head for it.

He lay in bed three weeks with a bandaged head and fractured shoulder.

A few days after the foiled stickup a basket of fruit came to the house with a card from Iscovitz, and one night the millionaire Iscovitz himself came to visit. It was a hot night and the millionaire sat by my father's bed a few minutes fanning himself with a folded newspaper. 'Take your time, Avrom Mendl, and don't worry. I don't want to see you in my place till you're better,' he admonished my father, then came to the kitchen seeking my mother.

'He's a wonderful man,' he said in Yiddish, and slipped her an envelope with a month's pay in it.

When I came to work, Myer Layevsky was out front loading his car. He blinked an eye at me, and I passed through to the office. Doing my father's bidding, I stood without removing my coat or sitting down. It took him a while to complete loading, and lugging goods through the office to the car he passed me several times, never once looking at me. This made me very nervous. Finally the car was loaded, and Layevsky came back. He straightened his hat and put a match to his cigar. 'So I'll go now. You didn't brought a lunch?'

'I thought I'd go home,' I said. 'I live only ten minutes from here.'

'Next time bring something to eat. I don't like the office shall be left alone. A customer comes in to pay and they find a closed office, they have an excuse to put off. Even a good customer will take advantage. Take off your coat and come in the back; I'll show you a hanger.'

He was back at the door, and I hadn't got up nerve to ask about my pay. 'Mr. Layevsky? I forgot to ask you yesterday. We haven't settled yet—'

'I had in my mind to pay ten,' he said, 'but I need a Jewish girl in my business, so you I'll give twelve.'

It was late in October when I came to work for Layevsky, and during the winter months I had to keep my coat on, it was so cold in the office. There was a hot-air register behind the door at the entrance to the stockroom, with hardly any heat coming through, and I used to stand on it stamping my feet, which were icy by midday.

'I'll tell a few words to the janitor,' Layevsky kept promising, and one morning before the day's peddling, he did go down to the basement. There was a great rumbling below, and in a few minutes a rush of smoke came shooting through the register. Layevsky came back and stood over the register, rubbing his hands.

'You wouldn't be so cold no more,' he said. 'Comes up a little bit heat now, no?'

'You mean smoke,' I said.

He blinked an eye at me. 'So she *has* a little sense,' he said in Yiddish.

There wasn't enough work to keep me busy, and in the beginning I sat banging away at the old typewriter, getting up speed against the day he'd give me dictation. But I soon got bored with that, and one morning came to work with a book.

Layevsky spotted it immediately. 'No, no, no,' he said, wagging his head. 'Don't bring no more a book to the office. It's not nice a customer comes in and the girl sits with a book.'

'But there isn't enough work here to keep me busy,' I protested.

'Who said? In an office you can always find something to do. Check over the cards; it wouldn't hurt.' I took my coat to the stockroom, smouldering.

'Come here, my book lady,' he called.

Hunched over the desk with knees bent and arms locked behind his back, he was peering at some cards he had fanned out, his nose almost touching, ashes dropping all over the place.

'Pick out Mrs. Oxenberg's card,' he said.

I pointed to it.

'Pick it up, it wouldn't bite you. Now take a look.'

I knew the cards were in order, but to satisfy him I glimpsed it briefly and returned it to the desk. 'There's nothing wrong with this card.'

'Look again,' he said, thrusting it under my nose.

I resisted an impulse to slap it out of his hand, and turned my head away instead.

'Mrs. Oxenberg,' he mused, 'a good customer. I only wish I had more customers like that.' Suddenly he slapped the card down, and with his nicotined finger, pointed to the last entry on it. 'When did she made the last payment?'

'October twelfth,' I said, 'but that's before I was here.'

'And today is already middle November, no? You can't see from the card that up till now she came in regular every week with a payment, and now it's a whole month she didn't come in? This you didn't notice? Maybe she's sick. Maybe she died, God forbid. Pick up the phone, find out. Attend better to my business, and you wouldn't find time to read a book in the office.'

The first three weeks I worked for Layevsky he used to come back from the day's peddling before five. I would vacate the swivel chair, and he would sit down to check the day's take. No matter how much the amount varied, 'That's all you took in today?' he'd ask. I took it as a joke at first, a pleasantry between us, but when I got to dislike the man, I resented it. 'As if I were a salesgirl,' I muttered once. 'Or even a thief.'

'What did you said?'

'Nothing.' I had a feeling as I went to the door that he was laughing at me, but I did not look back to see.

After I'd been there a month he started coming back later each day; it was seldom before six now when he returned, and I'd stand peering through the office window looking for the car.

One night he didn't get back till seven, nor had he telephoned. Cold and hungry, I was standing on the register, and through the half-open stockroom door, saw him as he came in. He took a one-eyed look around. Lights on, no one in the office. He came loping to the stockroom.

'You're still here?'

I was incensed, indignant to the point of tears. 'You speak as if I'm

54

a guest who's overstayed her welcome.' I swept by him; he followed me to the office.

'I speak like a what?'

I took my handbag from the desk. He followed me to the door.

'No, earnest,' he said in Yiddish. 'I speak like a *what*? Tell me.' His manner was concerned, solicitous even, but I felt he was mocking me.

'Never mind,' I said. This time I did look back, and saw him laughing at me.

One day a month was given over to repossessing merchandise from deadbeats. 'Today I am pulling,' he would say grimly; 'give me the deadbeats.' Deadbeat— the word was anathema to him. He couldn't say it without screwing both eyes shut. He would return at day's end, and through the office window I'd see him yanking piece by piece from the car, loading his shoulders. Draped like an Eastern merchant escaped from a bazaar holocaust, he loped from office to stockroom, muttering. 'Deadbeat. You can't afford? Don't buy. I don't go in with a gun to nobody. *Chutzpah*. When it comes to take advantage, everyone knows where to find Myer Layevsky.'

One day he was muttering, mulling this over, the injustice of it, the grievance to himself, when the telephone rang. I took the phone. It was Mrs. Greenberg, a good customer, an honest woman. Where's that tablecloth? she wanted to know, the one she ordered three days ago.

'It's Mrs. Greenberg,' I said, my hand over the mouthpiece. 'About that tablecloth, style 902 with the lace border? I told you about it—' He took the receiver from me. 'Hello. Who? Oh, Mrs. Greenberg, what can I do for the lady? What tablecloth, when tablecloth? Who did you gave the message? Oh, my office lady,' he said, swivelling around so that his back was to me. 'You'll have to excuse. She's a young girl, she thinks about boys. Next time if you need something in a hurry, better speak to me.'

I wanted to knock his hat off, grab the cigar from his mouth, and jump on it.

Despite having been forbidden to bring books to the office, I kept sneaking them in under my coat, and one morning, caught up in *Of Human Bondage,* I didn't hear the door. I jumped as if I'd been surprised in a criminal act; I put the book out of sight as if it were a bottle. Standing before me was a blond young man, tall, thin, with a pointed nose and white eyelashes. An albino.

'Is my dad here?' he asked. 'I'm Israel Layevsky, Mr. Layevsky's son.'

I told him his father would not be back before five, and loping like his old man, he went to the door. 'Tell my dad I was here. And also that I came first in my class.'

'Your son was here.' I reported to Layevsky. 'He asked me to tell you he came first in his class.'

A smile came over Layevsky's face, breaking it wide open. All of a sudden he jumped up, clicked his heels together, and in baggy pants began a little dance in the office, clapping his hands. For a minute I thought he was going to ask me to partner him. He left off as suddenly as he began, and sank to the swivel chair puffing, fanning himself with his hat. 'Twenty years old and going through for a doctor already since seventeen. So better don't make eyes on him,' he said, wagging a roguish finger at me, 'because it wouldn't help you nothing. I'm looking for a rich daughter-in-law.'

One Friday, the second week in July, Myer Layevsky said, 'How long do you work here now, nine months, no?'

About that, I said.

He blinked an eye at me. 'You feel you're entitled to a holiday?' He handed me a roll of single dollar bills. 'Count over, you'll find two weeks' pay. You don't work so hard in my place you need a holiday, but I close up anyway the office a week in July to take my missus to the country.'

A holiday! The idea was thrilling. Except for day excursions to Hanlan's Point or Centre Island with Lizzie Stitsky, I had never been anywhere.

'So where will you go?' my father asked when I told him about the holiday.

'I don't know, Pa. I'll look in the paper under Summer Resorts.'

'Don't look in the paper because I wouldn't let you go just anyplace, a young girl, and fall in the wrong hands.'

I began boo-hooing, the disappointment was so keen, and ran to the room I shared with my sister, Gertie, slamming the door shut. I heard him in the kitchen talking it over with Ma, but as to what was being said, nothing. I heard him go to the telephone in the hall, but he spoke into the mouthpiece, keeping his voice down. He then came to the door. 'Come out, my prima donna, and we'll talk about the holiday.'

'Don't bother,' I said, 'I'm not interested any more.'

'So what did I spend money on a long distance call to Mrs. Rycus?'

Mrs. Rycus, another one of my father's Rumanian connections, was a widow who had a small hotel in Huntsville and took lodgers during the summer months, mostly Rumanians.

56

'Poor woman,' Pa said anytime he spoke of her. 'Lived like a duchess in Focsani; now it's all she can do to keep a head over water.'

My sister Gertie came home from work. She went to the kitchen, then came to the room we shared. 'Pa says you're going to Huntsville? Mrs. Rycus says she can take you, but you'll have to share a room with the cook and maybe help out in the kitchen.'

'That's great,' I said.

'Why, what's wrong with that?' my sister said. 'At least you'll be out in the country, and that's something, isn't it?'

'Have you got a bathing suit?' my father asked me at supper. 'Mrs. Rycus said you'll need one.'

'You mean an apron,' I said, and my father flared up.

'Don't be so smart. I can still phone Mrs. Rycus and cancel.'

My mother winked at me to keep quiet and not ruin my chance of a holiday.

First thing Saturday morning I went to Eaton's, and in the bargain basement equipped myself with a few assorted summer items, including a bathing suit, and Monday morning my father put me on the train for Huntsville. He fussed about securing me a window seat, then fussed again about whether it would be best to put my case on the rack or at my feet. The conductor called *All Aboard!* and my father unexpectedly leaned down to kiss me. His kiss, embarrassing both of us, landed on my ear. Through the window I saw him on the platform.

'Don't forget what I told you,' he was saying.

I was to be met by Mrs. Rycus's truck driver, Bill Thompson. 'You'll wait till a man approaches you. Don't you mention the name first,' my father had warned me. 'If he says Bill Thompson, you'll get in the truck with him. Have a good time,' my father called, and as we pulled out, he raised his hat to me!

The station emptied quickly at Huntsville. I waited ten minutes, and the only living soul to show up was a good-looking boy, about twenty, who positioned himself inside the door, giving me the once-over. Could this be Bill Thompson? I was expecting an old man. Forgetting my father's warning, I jumped from the bench. 'Is your name Bill Thompson?' 'That's right,' he said, and I got in the truck with him. We drove four miles to the hotel, the truck driver all the while stealing flirtatious glances at me as I sat puffing away on the cigarette he had given me. My father, fearful I might fall into wrong hands under Summer Resorts, should have seen this!

Mrs. Rycus, a lot shorter and greyer than I remembered, was on the hotel veranda to greet me. 'Sura Rivka.' She smiled, giving me my Jewish name, and stubbing out her cigarette, came slowly forward on swollen legs to embrace me. 'Come, we'll go in the garden for tea,' she said in an accent as thick as my father's. 'Bill, take her suitcase up to Mrs. Schwartz's room,' and the truck driver, picking it up, gave me a wink.

Sitting at café tables in the garden were about a dozen ladies, all in brightly coloured dresses, some with straw hats on their heads, others with kerchiefs.

Mrs. Rycus clapped for attention. 'I have a surprise for you,' she said, putting her arm around my waist. 'This lovely girl is Avrom Mendl's daughter.'

A fluster and flurry ensued at all tables. There were cries of *No! I don't believe it! So big!*

Mrs. Rycus whispered, 'Don't be shy, darling. These are all Daddy's friends.' Piloted by Mrs. Rycus, I was taken from table to table, each lady in turn kissing and complimenting me. I had never been called darling or kissed so much in my life. One lady, a Mrs. Ionescu, wouldn't let go of me. 'Sit by me, darling,' she coaxed, as the tea trolley was wheeled in by a maid. The trolley contained such a variety of things, I couldn't take them all in at a glance. Sandwiches, small sausages, black olives, fruit, iced cakes, cream buns. I pointed to a cream bun, and the maid put it on my plate.

'Tea or coffee?' she asked.

'Tea, please.'

'Milk or lemon?'

'Milk, please.'

Wasn't this thrilling! I was with real quality now, classier by far than anything I had read about in books. I wondered if I should have said please to the maid. I had said it twice—maybe even once was infra dig?

'What grade are you in school?' I was asked by a Mrs. Kayserling.

'I'm not in school any more. I'm working.'

'Clever girl,' she said. 'What kind of work?'

I had got over my initial shyness and felt at ease now, on top of everything. Incorrigible show-off, I rattled away like one o'clock. 'Oh, at a sort of bookkeeping job. I work for a Myer Layevsky, a very funny man. He sells goods on time.'

'Goods?' another lady asked.

'Yes. Sheets, towels, blankets, Axminster rugs, and lace panels. He calls it goods.'

'On time?' another lady asked.

58

'Yes. To poor people,' I said, offhandedly dismissing the poor as if my only connection with them was through my job. 'It's a dollar down and a dollar when you ketch me.' I loped across the lawn imitating Myer Layevsky. I blinked an eye at the assembled company. 'That's all the money you took in today?' And they fell about.

After tea the ladies retired for a siesta, and I went up to the cook's room to unpack. Dinner was not till eight, and it was now only six—was I expected to help? I went downstairs and located the kitchen. Mrs. Rycus was at the stove beside a fat lady in an apron, a waitress was putting hors d'oeuvres on a tray, and Bill, in a far corner of the kitchen, was emptying a garbage container.

'Mrs. Schwartz, this is Sura Rivka, the daughter of a very dear friend, and for the next week your room companion,' said Mrs. Rycus, introducing me to the fat lady in an apron. She then introduced me to Leona, the waitress.

'What can I do?' I asked Mrs. Rycus. 'My father said I was to give you a hand in the kitchen—'

'Certainly not,' she said. 'That was Daddy's suggestion, not mine.' Nothing was expected of me except I come to the kitchen in the morning and get my own breakfast. 'The dining-room does not open till one,' she said. 'The ladies don't come down to breakfast; they take a cup of hot chocolate and a biscuit or something like that in their rooms. I'm short a waitress, so if you don't mind to give Leona a hand with the trays, I would appreciate it. But only if you like, darling; otherwise, Leona can manage herself. Meantime, go for a little walk to the beach, it's very pretty there. Bill, take the garbage to the incinerator, then show her where the beach is.'

It was a fifteen-minute walk to the beach, Bill flirting with me all the way, and by the time we got there I was in love with the good-looking truck driver, head over heels.

At dinner that night I was seated with Mrs. Kayserling and her husband, Aaron, who had come for a few days in the country. I came to the dining-room hungry as a bear, but when I saw the array of silver at my place I was dismayed, appalled, my appetite left me. 'When I was your age I could eat an ox,' Mrs. Kayserling chided me. I made out that I had a very small appetite, so small it caused my father worry sometimes. After dinner we went to the lounge for coffee, and I sat listening to nostalgic talk of Rumania. Wonderful stories, and told for my benefit, I expect, as my father was featured in most of them. Tales of escapades, derring-do. My father? Fabulous stories, fascinating to listen to—but in the end they had the effect of sending me to bed unhappy, depressed.

In Focsani my father had been on easy terms with these people, on equal footing with them. What a contrast now between their way of living and ours. He, so far as I knew, was the only failure of the Focsani émigrés, the only pauper.

But I was up early next morning, happy again, restored. What was the matter with me? I was holidaying in the country, *and* in love. After breakfast I helped Leona with the trays, then went to the beach in my new bathing suit. I had not been there ten minutes when Bill Thompson arrived. 'Mrs. Rycus sent me. I'm supposed to keep an eye on you,' he said, ogling me. On the way back I let him kiss me, and remembering my first kiss, could not for the rest of the day fix my attention on anything.

Wednesday morning at trays Leona was not at all friendly. Was she in love with Bill too? Later in the day I went to market with Bill and the cook, and sat between them in the cab, thrilled at the truck driver's proximity. Thursday morning Bill told me he and Leona were going to town that night for a movie. 'See if Mrs. Rycus will let you come too,' he said.

'Go, darling,' Mrs. Rycus said, 'there is nothing here for you to do.'

Bill sat between us, and in the dark of the cinema, held my hand all through *Catherine the Great* with Elizabeth Bergner.

What a wonderful week. The excitement of being in love, the secrecy, the preoccupation, the thralldom of it. The ruses I contrived to meet my love at the incinerator for a few minutes before dinner, and again after dinner for walks along the country road. . . . But the inevitable Sunday arrived. The holiday was over. I was to leave by the six o'clock train. I took my things from the cook's closet, snuffling over my open case. To go back to my dreary home, my miserable job, and never again to see Bill. He had said something about getting work in Toronto, but I knew for sure I'd lose him to Leona, who was prettier than me, and older.

Mrs. Rycus came to the room. 'I shall miss you, darling. It's such a pity you have to go back to the hot city. Wait,' she said, 'I have an idea. Leave everything. Go down and phone your Mr. Layevsky. Ask him to let you stay another week. It won't cost him anything; you'll stay as my guest.'

I was so nervous when Layevsky's voice came over the long distance wire I had to make my request a second time before he understood me.

'It won't cost you anything, Mr. Layevsky. I don't expect to get paid.'

'So what can I complain? Stay long as you like,' he said, and hung up. That worried me, I didn't like the sound of it, but surely that was

60

only Layevsky's way? He would have ordered me back if he didn't want me to stay.

I managed to get word to Bill. I told him at the incinerator I was staying another week, and again that night after dinner I excused myself from the lounge on the pretence of going up to bed, then sneaked down the back staircase to meet him.

Monday morning Leona handed me Mrs. Rycus's tray. 'She wants you to bring it,' she said.

I knocked, Mrs. Rycus called 'Come,' and I brought the tray to her.

'Sit down a minute, Sura Rivka,' Mrs. Rycus said, and I took the chair beside her bed. She put her cigarette in a holder, smiled at me, and began. 'You're a big girl, a young lady now, and I would not presume to lecture you, but as I am such a close friend to Daddy you won't take offence? Bill is a nice boy, but just a boy from the village. Common. He is not for you, darling, and I don't like for you to be so much with him. You understand what I mean?'

I wanted the floor to open up. I wanted to drop out of sight never again to be seen by Mrs. Rycus. I reached forward almost toppling the hot chocolate in her lap.

'Yes, of course I understand. You don't want me to go to the market with him any more—'

'To the market is all right, and to the pictures if Leona goes too is all right. But at night alone with him for a walk? No, darling, this worries me.'

So she had known all along. I could die for shame. Talking so cleverly in front of the ladies, then sneaking down the back staircase for hugs and kisses with the truck driver.

I went to the cook's room and stayed there, ignoring the one o'clock signal for lunch. Mrs. Rycus came up to fetch me.

'I want to go home,' I bawled.

'Darling,' she said, embracing me. 'I could bite my tongue. You must excuse an old lady. Come down to lunch. Please, for my sake.'

Next morning at her usual time she came to the kitchen with instructions for the cook. 'Sura Rivka,' she said, handing me a list. 'If you don't mind to do me a favour, go with Bill to town. I need a few things from the drugstore, and he will not be able to attend everything.'

Bill, instead of continuing on the main road, turned sharply off onto a side road. 'How come you stood me up last night? Are you playing hard to get?' He made a grab for me, and tried some fancy stuff. I slapped his hand. He lit a cigarette and backed the truck onto the main road again. 'You Jewish girls are all alike,' he said. 'There's only one thing you're after, that wedding band.'

Through the corner of my eye I studied his face as he drove sullenly to town. His head had assumed peculiar contours; it looked flat on top, something I had not noticed before. I was out of love. Leona was welcome to him. I had a longing suddenly to go home. To see my father, who had raised his hat to me in the station, to see my mother, and even my sister Gertie. After lunch I sought out Mrs. Rycus. 'Please, I want to go home on the six o'clock train. Not because of anything you said yesterday, honestly. It's just that I'm homesick.'

'Darling,' she said, 'I understand what it is to be homesick.'

Oh, I was glad to be on my way. I wouldn't have to think up funny stories to amuse the ladies at tea-time. At home I didn't have to sing for my supper; I could be as glum as I pleased. My father might call me prima donna, my mother might ask if I'd got up on the wrong side of the bed.

Pa was at the station to meet me. 'You had enough of the country?' he said, and we boarded a streetcar.

Next morning, apprehensive of my encounter with Layevsky, I put off going to work till nine o'clock. By nine he'd be on his way for the day's drumming, and I could let myself in with the office key. I arrived ten past nine and through the office window saw a girl sitting at the desk. She swivelled around as I entered. She was blonde, with buckteeth and eyeglasses. Definitely not a Jewish girl. I stammered, 'Are you —is this—'

'This is Supreme Housefurnishings,' she said briskly. 'Did you want to see some merchandise?'

'No, no,' I said, collecting my wits. 'I used to work here, but I've got another job now.' I put the key on the desk. 'I always meant to return this, but with one thing and another—'

'Thank you,' she said, and turned to the cards, dismissing me.

Deposed! Supplanted! It hit me like a stone to see her swivelling about in my chair. . . .

My father had dozed off again. I roused him. 'Pa!'

He excused himself again. 'I had some pills this morning, it makes me very sleepy. We were talking about something—that man you saw downstairs.'

'That's right. Myer Layevsky. He's the one that gave me a week's holiday, and I went to Mrs. Rycus in Huntsville, remember?'

'Oh, yes,' said my father. 'She was a wonderful woman, Mrs. Rycus.

You know we grew up together in Focsani? In Rumania she lived like a duchess, but here she had a hard time to keep a head over water.'

'I'll go now, Pa, and see you tomorrow.'

My father held his hand out, and as was our custom except for the time he kissed me on the train, we shook hands on leave-taking.

Myer Layevsky was still under the big tree where I had settled him. He beckoned me, and I cut across the lawn.

'Didn't I told you maybe later it will come back to my mind?'

'Then you *do* remember,' I said, exhilarated beyond all reason.

'I gave you a week off, but that wasn't enough for you. You made me a long distance call, no?'

'That's right. You know why I didn't want to come back? I fell in love that summer. With a *shaygitz,*' I added mischievously.

That stopped him. He cocked an eye at me. 'Did you married him?'

'No, I married a nice Jewish boy.'

'Better,' he said, nodding his head and chewing his dead cigar. 'Better.'

I had, in fact, married a nice gentile boy—but there was no need for Myer Layevsky to know that.

THE POOR LITERATUS

"If only I could write, my life story would make a book—"

We've heard this said many times, if not in the exact words then in essence. And it is true that anybody's story if he could write it would make a book. *My* life story if only I could write would make a best-seller novel; and that in a nutshell is the story of writing. The things one could get down on paper if only one could write.

I never thought to be a writer. Like most kids I as a child had diverse and variegated ambitions to become in the eyes of my family and the populace in general a very special person. But winning for myself acclaim and admiration through the written word was not one of them. Congenitally atonal and incapable of carrying a tune, I longed to be a singer. At public school during singing lessons in class, and at end of term concerts in the auditorium, I was always enjoined and instructed by the singing teacher to "Just mouth the words, don't sing." In fantasy daydreams I saw myself grown-up, dressed in a red velvet gown and singing like Jenny Lind to an audience of a thousand or more who at the end of the concert applauded me to an echo. That sustained me for a while. At twelve I wanted to be a nurse, at thirteen an actress, at fourteen my desire of distinction had narrowed itself down to a single and defined aspiration: to be popular with boys.

I was married very young, and before I was nineteen was the mother of a child. The raising of a child was for a start an engrossing and satisfying business. Before long, however, the novelty of scrubbing diapers ran its course and I began to cast about for something to do, something to relieve the tedium of a locked-in domesticity.

I heard about an all but forgotten girlfriend of mine who had got herself (with no background or experience) a job writing freelance features for *The Star Weekly*. I presented myself at the offices of the Features Editor of *The Weekly*, talked myself up as a writer, and was given an assignment: I was to interview by telephone about a dozen women for a piece entitled *I Don't Like Men Because*. "Get a few prominent women," the editor told me, "names that are known in the city." I telephoned society ladies, political ladies, ladies in the arts, ladies in sports, and came up with the bona fide beefs of three or four ladies well known in the city; to make up the full quota I invented some names and wrote the copy. A while later and there it was, an almost-full page spread on the inside pages of *The Weekly* with author's name in print that looked to me like seventy-two-point-type. What a thrill, what a pleasure to the eye! I spent hours on the phone hustling friends to buy *The Star Weekly*.

I was given four or five more assignments, and it came to me one day as I was interviewing a paraplegic chess player in Long Branch what a fraud I was. I didn't know anything about chess, what was I doing here being so brisk and bright with a crippled chess player? When the interview was over he wanted to know what I'd put down and I was so flustered I couldn't make head or tail of what I'd written. His wife saw me to the door. "You should learn your homework," she said, and I blushed on the way home to remember that less than a week ago I had put myself down on the voters' list as Writer-Reporter.

When I began to think seriously of writing I was advised by a friend who had had some experience in the business to read Sherwood Anderson and study him. Read Hemingway, study him. Read Katherine Mansfield, study her. I read Anderson, Hemingway, Mansfield, de Maupassant, Chekhov, Sholem Aleichem; later it was Isaac Babel, Malamud, Bellow, Updike, Cheever, Flannery O'Connor; I didn't do any writing, I just never stopped reading. And always the nagging thought at the back of my mind—if I'm going to be a writer I'd better stop reading and start writing. The easiest way, I thought, and also good practice, might be to begin by writing a love story for the pulps. It was easy, and fun to do, but the fun derived from that exercise was quickly dissipated by a fast rejection slip.

All those years though, the years I was caught up in a total absorption in the works of writers I admired, I had a feeling, an awareness of an exhilarating germination going on in me, shaping and moulding itself into a beneficent repository, a well-spring I would be able, when the time came, to draw upon. I felt confident that when the time came a story would (like Athena from the head of Zeus) spring full-blown from my head.

My first story ("Maybe Later It Will Come Back to My Mind") came out of my head alright, but did not spring from it full-blown; it was hard work. After two rejections it was accepted by *The Atlantic*. No use trying to describe the pride, the excitement of selling your first story. . . . In a few days however an ebbing, a falling away of excitement, and in place of pride a worry and fret that the first story had been a flash in the pan. The self-confidence I'd had—before selling— was suddenly gone, vanished. Working on a second story, I despaired of every line. A complimentary copy of *The Atlantic* comes through the mail, and I'm restored. The conceit at seeing my story in print! How beautiful it reads. I'm confident again; the second one will be even better.

This business is like malaria; one minute the fever is on you, the next minute it's off.

That was four years ago. To date I've published four short stories, with a fifth soon to be published in *The Atlantic*. On hand I have two completed ones waiting for a rewrite; a third, a good story badly written, wants a total overhaul. But I've been engaged the last year and a half in the writing of a novel.

My first story, "Maybe Later It Will Come Back to My Mind," was not, despite the vividness of my memory of the (now dead) man I call Myer Layevsky, as easy to write as I thought it would be. The first try was easy enough, but I sensed at the conclusion of it that what I had written was not a short story but a literal diatribe, a harangue against the man whom I at sixteen had held to be a villain. It took several rewrites to establish the character, to achieve an artistic balance between Layevsky the villain, and myself the victim.

By chance I encountered the son of Layevsky, an orthopedic surgeon of some distinction. I told him I'd written a story about his father, and he was amused. "What's there to write about my old man?" he said.

My fourth story, "Henye," started out by being a story of the twin brothers Yankev and Yudah, its title, "A Time of Reckoning." As the writing of the story progressed, Henye, of whom I had made in the beginning a subsidiary character, took over, and it became apparent during rewrites that she was the central character, the person about whom I had a story to tell. (That happened also in "A Basket of Apples": the story I meant to be about my father turned out to be a story of my stepmother. I'm fairly certain now that if I start out with a story about Chaim it will turn out to be a story about Moses.) As a child I loved the brothers Yankev and Yudah; Henye, I detested. Where then does the compassion for her as a human being come from? What is the difference between the real person and the literary creation? All my characters are based on real people but somewhere along the line a transmuting occurs. I disliked the man who was Myer Layevsky, but he is not a dislikable figure in the story. Neither, I think, is Henye. What process occurs? I can't answer that.

More than anything, what interests and engages me is character, and the interrelation of character. Like most writers I have a good recall for the events of my childhood. In my Jewish background there were many unusual, out-of-the-way characters, vital people, outspoken, outrageous—I was ashamed to be connected with them. But the back-

66

ground I was in my early years ashamed of and tried to put behind me by marrying a gentile, now pulls me back, as any writer is drawn back into what he knows. The world I rejected in my early years is the world that sustains me in my writing. I start writing a story in which the chief character is a gentile and the ubiquitous Jew crops up, lurking somewhere there in the background.

I try to avoid as much as I can (if they are put in just for the sake of display) the use of Yiddish expressions; instead of *shadchin* I write marriage broker. On the other hand I could not write rag in place of *shmata* because for me it is *shmata* and *shmata* only that conveys the flavour, the essence and the true meaning of rag, shred, tatter, patch, clout.

I read and study the writers I admire, but I don't try to emulate or copy them. Unless I were to plagiarize word for word how could I hope, for example, to reproduce an approximation even of the brilliance of Malamud's stories in *Idiots First,* Flannery O'Connor's in *A Good Man Is Hard to Find.* If you are serious about writing, you must read, study, absorb, but what comes out in your writing has got to be you. You can write only out of your own experience, out of your own head and heart.

I do pick up a few tips here and there. In the *Paris Review's* series, "Writers at Work," this and that writer says the keeping of notes is indispensable; so I start keeping notes, pages of them in a notebook which after a few days can't be located, doesn't show up again. The ones I've written on scraps and snippets of paper do show up; they show up after a wash (illegible from having been soaked and mangled and spun dry) in the pocket of a dressing gown, a shirtwaist, a house-coat. What works for one writer doesn't work for another; I stop keeping notes.

"Do you like writing?" I am asked.

"I hate it. I mistrust it. I'm scared of it, it frightens me."

"No one's forcing you to write, why don't you give it up?"

"Because I love it. I can't keep away from it, I'm hooked."

H.L. Mencken says, apropos of writing being the lonely business it is, "If authors could work in large, well-ventilated factories, like cigar-makers or garments workers, with plenty of their mates about them and a flow of lively professional gossip to entertain them, their labour would be immensely lighter," but since they have to be "continuously and inescapably" in the presence of themselves, "the horrors of loneliness are added to stenosis and their other professional infirmities." This makes him (the author) a hypochondriac: "every time a vagrant regret or sorrow assails him, it has him instantly by the ear, and every time a wandering ache runs down his leg it shakes him like the bite of a tiger." Mencken says, "The poor literatus encounters them"—these ailments—"every time he enters his work-room and spits on his hands. The moment the door bangs he begins a depressing, and losing struggle with his body and his mind." He goes on, "Why then do rational men and women engage in so barbarous and exhausting a vocation," and decides that an author, "like any other so-called artist is a man in whom the normal vanity of all men is so vastly exaggerated that he finds it a sheer impossibility to hold it in. His overpowering impulse is to gyrate before his fellow men, flapping his wings and emitting defiant yells." These being forbidden by the police and the authorities, "he takes it out by putting his yells on paper. Such is the thing called self-expression."

From time to time I am asked by friends who are genuinely interested in my progress, "Are you still working on that novel! When are you going to finish it?"

Am I still working on that novel—I go out of my mind! I can't begin to explain, nor do I want to, the difficulty I'm having with the *time* development of it. The novel begins with a couple, divorced after twenty years of marriage, sitting at a kitchen table drinking whiskey and talking, without rancour or bitterness, of times gone by. From there it goes back in time to when they met, fell in love, and got married. . . .

William Styron in *Lie Down In Darkness* used a wonderful expedient for taking the reader back into time. The engine of the hearse bearing the daughter Peyton to the cemetery breaks down again and again; the driver gets out to tinker with it and while the engine is being repaired Styron takes you back into time. As soon as the engine is repaired you move forward again (with the hearse) to the present time.

Margaret Laurence in *The Stone Angel* brilliantly and with great skill moves her gorgeous Hagar Shipley back and forth in time.

But I'm stuck with a static situation. Every time I pull the reader from the past back into the present, my two people are still sitting at the kitchen table drinking whiskey. . . .

Ah to be a singer in a red velvet gown with the voice of a Maureen Forrester.

SHIRLEY FAESSLER

David Helwig

David Helwig was born in Toronto in 1938 and was brought up there and in Niagara-on-the-Lake. He went to university in Toronto and Liverpool, England, and for the past several years has lived in Kingston where he teaches English at Queen's University. He was one of the founding editors of *Quarry* magazine.

His short stories and poems have been widely published in Canadian literary magazines. One of his stories was anthologized in Robert Weaver's *Canadian Short Stories* (Second Series) Oxford University Press, Toronto, 1968.

Bibliography

Figures In a Landscape. Oberon Press, Ottawa, 1968. (Poems and plays)
    Out of print
The Streets of Summer. Oberon Press, Ottawa, 1969. (Stories)
The Sign of the Gunman. Oberon Press, Ottawa, 1969. (Poems)
The Day Before Tomorrow. Oberon Press, Ottawa, 1971. (Novel)
Fourteen Stories High. Oberon Press, Ottawa, 1971. (A short story
    anthology edited by David Helwig and Tom Marshall.)

Presences

"I never wanted to be a butcher," Tom would say.

We would be standing around with nothing important to do, Tom and I talking a bit, old Jack McGrath sometimes part of the conversation, more often not.

The store where we worked was almost like two stores, the meat and vegetables on our side, and beyond an archway, almost cut off from us, the grocery store, with an office and store rooms out behind it. There was something isolated, almost private, about our half of the store, even though its plate glass windows faced the wide main street of the town.

When I remember it now, it seems to me that I heard Tom's story often, but perhaps it was just the kind of story that had that sound because the man had told it over so many times, to himself, and to a few of the customers who were his friends, some who had been coming to the store for twenty years, who knew him from before the war and his time in the army.

He would have liked to be a gardener and had some vague, half-formed plan that someday he would leave the butcher shop and work with flowers, growing things. I can't remember how or where this was to happen, but that hardly mattered, for the story was told for comfort, something to help him through the day by day of work he hated.

We did not have a lot of time to talk most days, but I worked in the store part-time for several years, summers, weekends, sometimes after school, so that the spare seconds and minutes mounted up to hours of conversation. I remember Tom, leaning his big body against the back of the meat counter and looking, not at me, but past me, with mild eyes, the sweet clean slow manner of Jersey cattle, and telling me things, telling me things, a bit here, a bit there, that added up to his steady self.

His car was a 1935 Packard that he was still driving in the early fifties, a big square car that took him to work in the morning and home at night, and every Wednesday evening could be seen parked in front of the town movie, and in summer took its longest excursion, six or seven miles (each Sunday) to a park where there was a weekly band concert.

The car did not last forever, not even the short forever of the years that I worked there. Looking back, it seems to me that one day Tom went out and got in the car, and it would not start, and like an old horse that will not get up, it was taken away and replaced by a year-old green Pontiac. Perhaps it didn't happen that way, but the car was replaced, and the green Pontiac appeared in all the places where the old Packard had been seen.

It must have been about that time that the girl came to work there, for in my memory she is connected with the new car.

There was Tom's brother too, a presence on a bicycle here and there on the streets of the town. He had no steady work, but he did odd jobs here and there. He may have been slow or a bit mad, but he was a presence in Tom's life, not a family skeleton exactly (no kind of skeleton at all but like his brother a slow, fat man), but I imagined him lying down a great deal, smiling, not exactly seeing Tom enter the house and leave it, but aware, as a presence is aware of the person it is presenting itself to.

"I never wanted to be a butcher," Tom would say and tell the story of how, when he was perhaps thirteen, his father decided he must be set to work and took him to a butcher shop (because it was the closest place perhaps, there was never a reason given) and told them to make a butcher of him.

"I always thought that was wrong," he said, not so much as a grievance as a statement of principle, one that had taken him some time to be sure of, one that he was humble enough not to force on you, but a statement of principle all the same.

What Tom liked best, in this job he didn't like, was waiting on the customers, passing the time of day, giving the best cuts, the leanest hamburg to those he liked, proud that the store sold only the best quality meat, that we did not grind the hamburg in advance so it was always fresh, and everyone could see it was not adulterated.

My jobs were various. The earliest were slicing bacon and cutting up scraps for hamburg, and these remained occasional responsibilities, but as I learned more, I took up new jobs, putting up orders, serving a few customers, even such exotic activities as trying to drive the wild cat out of the basement or making a new crock of brine for the preparation of corned beef.

The crock of corned beef was more important to the butcher shop than anything so seldom used would seem, for it was a matter of occasional angry disagreement between Tom and old Jack McGrath, but then everything was at one time or another, for their disagreement was like God whose centre is everywhere and circumference nowhere. It had probably been that way for years. Soon after my arrival in the butcher shop, I became a territory up for grabs, for I was hired by the manager who supervised the whole of the double store, hired on the assumption that they could use somebody young and cheap, and I started on neutral ground working at the vegetable counter, but when my work was finished there, there were bitter disputes about whether I should help Jack cut hamburg or help Tom prepare the orders for delivery, but after a while I got settled into a sequence of duties, and somehow everything got done.

Old Jack had his stories too, of course. He was old enough and (we suspected) rich enough to retire, but he liked the work and liked the money and showed no signs of being close to the day when he would stop liking either.

("Those others," Jack would say under his breath to me, "they're not butchers, not real butchers. They've never killed an animal. They're just meat cutters."

"What if a customer saw him doing that?" Tom would say to me after Jack had blown from his nose a great cascade of mucus, snapping it down between his fingers to the sawdust floor of the meat cooler.)

Jack had a metal plate in his head that foretold the coming of rain. It did this by causing him pain and making his temper, which was never good, worse than ever. At some time in the past, he had owned his own store, but a horse had run wild in a local show, and he had been thrown from a carriage and fallen on his head. He had sold his store and been unable to work for some time, finally going to work in someone else's store, his ability to foretell the weather (of which he was publicly proud) a small and painful compensation for what he had lost.

He too had a car, and its path, like that of Tom's car, was regular. We would see it only on Saturday nights when the store stayed open until nine o'clock. The other days of the week, Jack arrived by bus in the morning and left by bus when the store closed, but on Saturday night his wife would come for him in a big black Buick which she would park outside the plate glass windows of the butcher shop. She would wait there for Jack to come out, and I never once saw her get out of the car and come into the store.

Jack liked to tell me about his wife's driving. She drove, he always said, exactly fifty miles an hour, not one mile over and not one mile under. I'd think of that as I watched the black car taking Jack away somewhere each Saturday night.

Old Jack was a shorter, even fatter man than Tom, and his very belly was aggressive, and especially on days when his head was bad, he would walk, quick and angry, down the narrow alley behind the meat counter with a large chunk of beef and a butcher knife resting on that big belly and defying anyone to step in front of him. He did not dare run into Tom, but no-one else was safe, and hours of muttering followed each collision.

72

Then there was the morning of the rat: I was often a few minutes late for work, and when I walked in that morning, I could hear Tom speaking angrily in the back corner by our sink and see Jack in his bloody apron working in aggressive isolation on the wooden chopping block. I put on my apron and walked back to the sink. Tom told me what had happened. A rat had been caught by the tail in one of the traps I had set, and Jack, who found it, had dealt with the thing by holding it on the chopping block where the meat was cut and chopping off its head with a meat cleaver. Now Tom was furiously disinfecting everything in the store.

Angry rumbling went on, the rat one day, something else the next, some days cheerful enough until there would be an exchange over the hamburger, Tom picking out the leanest pieces and leaving Jack to sell the fat (which he objected to on principle, but was happy enough to do in practice, for he would be greedy not just on his own behalf, but on behalf of the store as well).

Then the girl came, to work part-time on the vegetable counter. I was not fond of her, but we got on well enough. She was a member of the evangelical Mennonite Brethren. I had seen them once on a Sunday morning baptising adults at the public beach, the minister's black gown floating out around him as he stood waist deep in the water. This girl had the bright hypocritical sunniness and the unctuous solicitude that can go with a certain kind of evangelical piety. She was small and neatly enough put together that if someone else had lived in her body I might have found it attractive. As it was, it provoked only a cold curiosity.

But she was there, day after day, like all of us, like the store fixtures, something the customers, passing like time, passed by.

I remember a kind of tableau from the days after she came: Tom leaning heavily on the vegetable counter near the girl, he dressed all in white, jacket and huge apron, she in a dress or skirt and blouse (sometimes a short sleeved blouse so that when she reached up I could see the brown hair under her arm) and a white apron over it, Jack facing away from the two of them, behind the meat counter, cutting away at a chunk of meat, his fat face blank and furious.

Tom told the girl all his stories. He carried out the heavy crates of vegetables for her. He drove her home sometimes when the weather was bad or on Saturday nights after we had worked late.

In the tableau in my memory, the two of them are always there in that corner, and the girl smiles at Tom, and he tells her all his stories.

Jack had often said that he did more than his share of work in the butcher shop, and after the girl came and Tom began to spend his time talking to her, Jack's anger increased, crowding his pained head with storms.

I missed the final fight. One day I came up from cleaning the basement, and there was no-one behind the meat counter but the store manager. Everyone was working with ominous concentration, and it was a few minutes until I learned that Tom and Jack were out in the back store-room with the owner. Neither one appeared as the afternoon went on, ended, and we closed the store.

The next morning Jack was not at work, and everyone knew, without a word said, that he would not be back, and it was possible to miss him, crude and vicious and blundering as he was. His absence had, at first, some of the force of his presence.

No doubt Tom talked to the girl a little less often, for a while at least. He had won, but he never said a word to me to suggest that he rejoiced in his victory which anyway only lasted for a few weeks until the arrival of the new butcher.

He too was fat, this new butcher, fat and loud and effeminate and crude, poking, prodding, laughing, and every five minutes, it seemed, going away for a long conference with the owner and the manager. Later, the owner and the manager would talk with Tom.

Soon, the big meat cooler held the dark meat of an old bull, and pieces were added to our hamburg to give it more colour, make it look leaner. We ground the hamburg ahead of time now and scooped out a handful to weigh to the customer's request. We got a machine that could turn almost anything into minute steak, chopping the meat apart and patching it together all in one operation. Things happened fast now and kept happening. Tom complained a bit, but this was part of his victory, and he had to live with it.

Sometime during all this, the girl got engaged. Her boyfriend began to meet her after work, and we all got to know him, but Tom especially, for Tom was her friend. When she married, Tom was the only one from the store who was at the wedding.

She married and left, and soon I left too. Tom, of course stayed, wait-ing for the day when he too would learn to leave. I moved to the city, but when I was back in town, I'd drop in at the store, and Tom and I would talk a bit, old friends who no longer had anything to say.

It was in the city that I met the girl again, just once, on a city street, and we said hello, and hello, and how are you, and how are you, and were almost ready to walk away, when the girl asked if I had heard about Tom, and I said I hadn't.

Tom was dead, she told me, had suffered a heart attack, but lingered

74

on in hospital for several weeks and then died. Yes, it was too bad, wasn't it. And added from the book of her small wisdoms that he hadn't really wanted to get well, hadn't cared that much about living.

I listened and nodded and walked away down the city street. As I walked I gave Tom a careful thought and reflected that, in a better century, it would have been a prayer for his soul.

Things That Happened Before You Were Born

I know I'm always the one to mention age. I know that you don't care how old I am, but I notice, I have to notice when I look at you, that you are young, so young, and then I remember that I've somehow used up half of the old Biblical allotment, and then I mention it, and you say, "I don't care, I really don't care," and smile, and I feel that underneath that smile you're annoyed with me again, for picking at you and for reminding you of something that might be true.

Fifteen years I have to deal with somehow. If only I could write you everything that happened in those fifteen years that I lived before you were born. When you came back (if you do, how I hope you do), you could read this. Then would we be the same age? As if I could take away those years, empty myself of them, give them to you, and you could take them and ingest them through eyes or fingertips.

It's late afternoon outside my window, and I just went and poured a drink to prime my memory. Maybe it's the time of year that started me, that and the time of day. There's something about a November afternoon that makes one soulful. Is that the word? Anyway, quick to remember. And I visited my children this morning. Cindy is twelve now and beginning to be a woman. I think she'll drive men mad. She has a kind of overwhelming vitality that makes her irresistible. Yet she's so gentle, so feminine. I wonder if she'll suffer. I suppose everyone does.

Remember, remember. I was standing with my father in the doorway of a store, a drugstore I think, and there were enormous hailstones falling on the street in front of us. You might have a memory just the same of yourself at three, and yet it wouldn't be the same, for all the things I can't consciously remember, the details of the drugstore windows, the clothes that everyone wore, all these things shape the feeling of the memory and make it a memory of 1938 and different from a memory of

75

1953. I could never prove that, but remember the night we saw Paul Muni in "I Am a Fugitive from a Chain Gang," you laughed so much more than I did, and I said it was because of the clothes. I thought I could remember them, even though I couldn't remember that I remembered them.

How angry I was that night. We stood in the cold by the door of my car, and you would not see the point of what I was saying, and as you refused me, stood there with your mouth, your lovely odd mouth almost pinched, I thought you looked like a crone, and all your laughter in the movies seemed to have been directed at me. As I opened the door for you, I said something angry and bitter, and you turned away from me and began to walk home. I shouted after you, my shout absurd in the snow-silence, but you didn't slow or turn, and I got into the car and drove halfway to my apartment then had to turn back. I drove to your place. And we fought our way back to love.

I just checked the Muni film in a reference book. 1932, and I was born in 1935.

Yet I do feel that I remember the Depression somehow, not as incidents, but as a state of mind, almost as if it were a state of light and space. And then the war came, and the light and space changed.

Imagine fifteen years with you not there, when I can't ask myself where you might have been at that moment. I always want to know where you are when I'm away from you, or where you were at times when I'd never met you. Like the day of my marriage. You were seven years old, living somewhere in the suburbs of Toronto while I was getting married in a little church in Etobicoke and preparing to fly to New York for a week's honeymoon. I like to know that, you see, I like to know where you were. Where are you now? I wish I knew. I wish you were here.

I've just made myself another drink and then reminded myself that I shouldn't have it, that I should cut down on my drinking, cut down on my smoking, so many things, so many things.

You never think in those terms. You still trust your body so entirely. I'm not so very old, but I'm losing that trust in my body. Maybe I never had it, never was really young. Maybe that's one of the things that happened before you were born, that I got old, suddenly, wrongly, grew up old.

Not true. I distort everything, why? When I was twenty, playing in that dance band, playing all those old songs that you laugh about now when

I mention them, "In the Mood," "Moonlight in Vermont," "Blue Moon," songs that can still move me to remember them, I'd stay up all night and all day, playing, talking, chasing the girls that came to the dancehall.

Waking on the beach wrapped in a blanket, seeing the water, calm, pale, endless water. Did I ever tell you?

You were five years old then, perhaps on holiday at that summer cottage you told me about, where the water was too weedy to swim in.

But before you were born, that magic time, what then? The years from 1935 to 1950, that much history to think through. I see it that way too, as history. Because of the war I suppose. That was the time that created history for me, made real events occur in my imagination until it seemed that I had a map of Europe tattooed on my brain. And you weren't there, not anywhere, not born. Perhaps never to be born. Sometimes you were impossible.

I remember the silence of the house in those years, when my father was away, an odd silence just behind my back as if I could turn around quickly and find the man I hardly remembered looking down at me.

"L for Lanky." That was a radio program about the crew of a Lancaster bomber. I listened to it every week and thought of my father flying over Germany. I'd listen to the Air Force March that ended the program and go into their room (*her* room now) and look at the picture of my father in his Air Force uniform, his face serious, the eyebrows drawn in a bit toward the nose, his hair brushed straight across his forehead. He was 30 when the picture was taken in 1941. I have that picture here in my desk. Years later when he had come back safely and there were other pictures of him in the house, I asked my mother for that one, and she gave it to me.

Why is it that since I met you, since I've been close to the reality of the future, that I think more and more of the past?

Today, sitting here drinking, terrified that you'll never come back, once again I start to remember things.

It has something to do with saying goodbye. I'm afraid that in writing this, that's what I'm doing, and that makes me remember the other times, Jane, my wife, and I start a process of going backward and end up staring at myself in that hailstorm and asking how that child came to be me, where that child failed so that he could never build anything to last but over and over again must say goodbye and resume the discipline of imagining death, imagining dying alone somewhere.

But maybe that won't happen. Maybe you'll come back, will love me enough to come back, risk everything for me. For me.

I see you at the bus terminal, sitting at the window, smiling and waving, as if you were what? My daughter going to stay with a favourite aunt. Something like that, so simple. How could you smile so easily, as if nothing mattered?

I took a break from this and made a sandwich. As I was making it, I saw the photograph tacked on the wall, a picture of the two of us skiing last year, the first time we ever went anywhere together, during the week of term when you were supposed to be studying and I was meant to be catching up on my marking.

As I stood there I tried to remember what I was thinking when the photograph was taken. At first I was tempted to sentimentalize the memory, but then I got it clear and remembered that I'd felt a cold hatred for you at that moment, for you'd asked another skier to take the picture, and I thought, as I often did then, that you were collecting keepsakes of our relationship, not living in it.

I called you the Snow Queen, to myself, angrily, and described you in Voltaire's patronizing phrase about this country, "*quelques arpents de neige.*" But later, in bed, in the cabin I'd borrowed from a friend, your face was silver, and I hated myself for my suspicion of you.

It's nearly dark now, only 24 hours until you're due back.

VE Day, the end of the war. I heard the announcement at school, and we were given the day off. I rushed home and ran into the house, feeling that the greatest thing in the world had happened, that we had defeated the devil Hitler. But the house was still silent, and today the silence seemed ominous in the middle of the official rejoicing. I walked down the hall and into the kitchen, and suddenly I felt sure that my father was dead.

At first I was afraid to ask my mother. I went away and came back and finally asked her.

He was alive. She had received a telegram from him that day.

It's night. I've been reading Heracleitus. Why could I never convince you of the beauty of his aphorisms?

Time is a child moving counters in a game, the royal power is a child's.

The sequence of my goodbyes, the things I spoiled, are perhaps only the accidents of a childish fate.

Not true, of course. If you don't come back, I'll know the reason. Always the same reason that somehow I surround and destroy what I love, that I can't leave anyone alone. That I want to be in your body, in

78

your brain. And when I can't I attack you, tear at you, blame you for my failure.

It was the same with Jane, with my wife, but I didn't recognize it then. You taught me, you who seem little more than a child, with so many childish habits, your odd phrases, your keepsakes, superstitions. You taught me what I am, by being so insistently yourself, young, foolish in ways, but always yourself, making me know that I wanted you not to be that, that I wanted to wound you, destroy you, make you part of me.

I was fifteen years old, in 1950, and on New Year's Eve I sat alone, except for my baby brother asleep upstairs and read in the new issue of *Life* a pictorial history of the half century that was ending and even then, even then, *you weren't born.* You were a foetus, growing in your mother's belly.

I ask myself now why I sent you to Toronto, drove you out, wanting you to make a decision, to commit yourself to me or leave me. Why couldn't I live with what I had?

It would not be better if things happened to men just as they wish.

Wise Heracleitus. I love your sayings but I learn nothing from them.

Where are you now? Somewhere in Toronto, at a movie maybe. With Paul (is that his name?) your old friend there. Will he ask you to stay? I wish you could know that now, right now, I'm thinking about you. I wish that knowledge could explode in your brain and wreck it.

Once on a November evening a man of thirty-five wrote a long letter to his youthful mistress in the hope that she would return to read it.

Once on a winter evening more than thirty years earlier, a small boy stood with his father in the doorway of a drugstore and watched the unexpected, large, extraordinary hailstones fall to the ground.

TIME IN FICTION

Imagine you are in love. You are in central Canada, lonely, depressed; the one you love is in England. So you decide to phone. It's eleven at night by the time you reach the decision. You phone. In England it's four in the morning. Your lover is slow-witted, sleepy, not as sympathetic as you wish.

Imagine yourself not in love any more.

That's a very simple example of the whole problem of time and how it mocks us. Of course it's the same time at both ends of the phone—how else could you carry on a conversation? But in another way, judged by the location of the sun, by the conventional, even biological patterns of people's lives, it's a different time.

Our lives, our loves, all the things we care about are dependent on continuation through time. Even those who claim to live for the moment can't really cut down their perspective to less than a few hours. You don't want enduring love? Still, you have to keep track of your partner for long enough to find a bed.

And memory: what we are, perhaps, is an accumulation of memories, conscious and unconscious. At the lowest level, the chemical memory in the cells of our bodies causes them to produce the pattern of our being again and again, so that even when all the cells in the body have been replaced, we remain the same person. And our minds seem to remain the same minds, even though they go through a lifetime's variety of experience.

Each day our bodies live through a certain metabolic cycle, sleep, waking, hunger, satisfaction. and we live this cycle over and over again. Yet each day seems to us different from the one before, always unique. Heracleitus says, "You cannot step into the same river twice."

We have a body clock and a mind clock, and the two of them may work together or apart. And neither works like a machine.

Remembering the failures of the past, we plan the successes of the future.

How long is now? When does it happen?

The short story writer is perhaps especially aware of time, for he attempts to give a sense of life, of the distances of time, in a few pages, a few minutes' reading. Not quite William Blake's "world in a grain of sand," but something on the way to it.

In writing a story, the author places words one after another, in sequence, an arrangement of impulses in time. The words themselves move the reader's thoughts forward at a certain real, literal speed. Yet the reference of the words may be to events of the story's past, present or future, any of these at any moment.

In reading a story, you feel the movement in time as the eye or voice moves forward over the page, and even in the simplest story, the speed of this movement will not be the same as the speed of the events described. Sometimes the author may take a page to describe a few moments, sometimes pass over a year in a single phrase. You get one impression (of many possible ones) of how time worked for one person or group during one set of events.

But that is only the simplest case. The story may refer to the past but make it part of the present by showing its occurrence in a character's mind. Or it may show what he does remember and what he doesn't.

The hunger for my next meal can interrupt me as I recall my childhood in an attempt to explain the way I behaved last night to the woman who will perhaps sit with me while I eat the meal I'm now hungry for. And to tell that, I will have to make many choices about the length of time given to creating the imaginative reality of each part of the sequence.

It isn't simple. In fact it seems to me that perhaps time is the ultimate mystery of our lives.

"Presences" is a story that deals with a man talking about events in his past. In a way they aren't crucial events for him. They didn't cause him to make any important decisions about his life. Yet they are somehow important.

I could have made the events into a dramatic little sketch with a simple conflict and resolution. Then it would have been a story about the two butchers. But as it is, the story is about "presences," about the way the past endures in the mind of the narrator, the way its events occur not only as a causal series, each step leading toward a conclusion, but also as a series of tableaux, icons, moments that are built by the imagination out of a confusion of related memories, something much more complex than cause and effect.

The two butchers and the girl didn't greatly change the narrator's life, but they endure in him. They are part of him. Or perhaps he is part of them. At any rate, the movement of the story is the movement of his mind through a selection of memories, searching for meaning, not an explicit, abstract meaning, but the shape, the feeling, the true rhythm of the past.

"Things That Happened Before You Were Born" is also a story about a man looking back to the past, but here there are more complexities in the pattern of time. His life has a time dimension, one pattern of actions and memories, changes and continuations; the girl's life has a different pattern. But the two patterns have intersected, and the narrator is now wondering if this sharing of time will continue. He's also concerned with the fact that the girl is young, still developing, that time is her friend, while he is older, perhaps past developing, the victim of time's rush, the prisoner of his past.

Yet this isn't a Freudian or psychoanalytic story. There is no reason in his memories for what he is, what he has become. Still, those memories are a part of him. Sometimes it seems to him that everything is random, all meaningless chance. "Time is a child. . . ." Yet once the events have happened, it seems that they had to happen that way. Sometimes, before the girl was born, her birth would have been nearly impossible on a statistical basis, but of course the impossible happens every moment, and once it happens it has some kind of inevitability.

Heracleitus, whose sayings I've quoted twice in the story, is perhaps my favourite philosopher; he shows a world of change and movement shot through with glimpses of meaning, truth, God, what you will. And is himself a perfect sign of this world, for all that remains of his work is fragments.

Everything changes; we are always losing. Yet we remember, imagine, foresee, endure. We know ourselves, remain.

Only the imagination can grasp time without turning it into death.

Imagine you are in time.

Imagine you are in love.

Imagine you are.

Imagine.

DAVID HELWIG

Hugh Hood

Hugh Hood was born in Toronto in 1928. He was educated in the parochial and high schools of that city, and at the University of Toronto from which he received a Ph.D. degree in 1955. Mr. Hood married Noreen Mallory, a painter and theatrical costume designer, in 1957, and they have four children. The Hood family lives in Montreal.

Hugh Hood has published four novels, three collections of stories, and a sports documentary on the career of Montreal Canadiens' hockey star Jean Beliveau. He has also published some sixty short stories in various Canadian, American, and European magazines. Mr. Hood teaches English at the University of Montreal.

Bibliography

Flying a Red Kite. Ryerson Press, Toronto, 1962. (Stories)

White Figure, White Ground. Ryerson Press, Toronto, 1964. (Novel)

Around the Mountain: Scenes from Montreal Life. Peter Martin Associates Limited, Toronto, 1967. (Stories)

The Camera Always Lies. Longmans Canada Ltd., Toronto, 1967. (Novel)

Strength Down Centre. Prentice-Hall, Canada Ltd., Toronto, 1970 (Sports Documentary)

A Game of Touch. Longmans Canada Ltd., Toronto, 1970. (Novel)

The Fruit Man, The Meat Man, and The Manager. Oberon Press, Ottawa, 1971. (Stories)

You Can't Get There From Here. Oberon Press, Ottawa, 1972 (Novel)

Socks And Boots

". . . a natural pair . . ." Noreen Hood.

I: SOCKS

Domenico Lercaro got here by himself—from Calabria—and it wasn't easy. The effort left him bewildered and almost broke, unable to speak the same dialect as the rest of the Italians in town, and terribly cold in winter. Where he came from there were no jobs. All the young men from his birthplace on the Gulf of Taranto had moved north, some of them very far north, but none had come as far as he had.

He had not counted on our climate.

At the same time he could not wish himself back home. It had been too much of nothing, an unchanging metallic sky, crazily turbulent weather, an everlasting feeling of being at the extreme edge of the world neither in winter nor summer, a place where it was always March, where the wind never stopped, seeming to blow the people away from around you. His village was a widening in a wobbly hillside track inhabited by twenty-three men and women, an indeterminate number of children, and eight goats. He walked away and walked away north . . . north . . . took him two years to come where his work was paid for in money. Always before he had been paid in mere existence.

In Torino there were posters about Canada showing tulips, grass, lakes, boats, cities lit up at night and girls in bathing suits. He formed a mental picture of this country which was uncritical because he had nothing to compare it with except what he had left. Canada was "America" and there were millions of Italians over there. Twice he saw movies of America at a workers' club in the automotive assembly plant where he worked, and what impressed him was the speed with which everybody talked and the way in which all the space in the pictures was filled with straight lines. This made him aware of the disorganization in his own history, the blankness of what had happened to him so far, which frightened him more each time he thought of it.

Domenico Lercaro was not stupid, not unhealthy, not naturally inarticulate though he almost never spoke. He was not brutal, mean, inhumane. It was hard to say what he was. A range of possibilities, an unopened box, raw consciousness, what? He was a spot in civilization where nothing happened to be going on, just like his village, somewhere inconsidered, not worth seizing and taking trouble over, unexploitable because off to one side of ordinary wealth.

He hummed much of the time, making an unusual music without rhythm or clear intervals or words to accompany it. If anybody had listened to this loud humming, which you couldn't hear in the assembly plant, it would have sounded like unmixed life. He enjoyed the vibration of his vocal cords and the resonance in his nose and mouth and the way he could modify the sounds he made. He kept his mouth closed. Over three or four years he composed about a dozen hums—some of them surprisingly long. After he had made up enough of them to respond to most of what happened to him, he stopped inventing new ones.

He would go for peculiar walks, first hup-hup-hupping up and down on his heels like a walker in Olympic competition, then swinging his legs smooth and straight like a runner in slow motion, then trying to see how long he could walk without taking breath. Humming and walking became the book of his experience. You could hum in many ways (how many, twelve, fifteen?) and you could walk in five ways. This knowledge gave him a basis for various comparisons, and on simple comparisons more complicated ones could be built. He now saw that he did not have to work in the assembly plant because he had some money. Some. There was America and straight lines.

We were admitting Italians to Canada in large numbers so he came here. The streets were rectilinear once you got away from the dockside, which was irregular and distressful to him. Off the ship and through immigration, he walked uptown as fast as he could, using the most important of the five ways to walk, the way that gets you somewhere fast. He had not been able to walk far enough on the ship to feel in full control of himself. His first day in Montréal he walked seventeen miles and after a while began to see signs in Italian. He knew some Piedmontese now and even some Tuscan and could figure out the signs—they were in more or less standard Italian and he could read very well when he wanted to. He got a room in northeastern Montréal and made comparisons: this is a big room, three times as big as my room in Torino; there are some Fiats on the roads but more Volkswagens and many more American cars; not all Italians live on pasta. I never did. This is America, Montréal, Canada, America, it is very warm.

He began to see that an organized life might be a falsified life—construction work or gardening seemed to be open work-options. This seemed over-simple as he had never done either. He had hated heights since infancy, associating vertigo with his native village and the pressure of wind in his ears. Growing things in the soil was something he knew nothing about. He had never known anybody who did such a thing. He

86

had swept floors and pushed heavy metal carts with cylinder blocks in them. What he could do was stay on his feet for a long time and push something. His tools were his feet, which he cared for meticulously, his socks and his boots.

So he walked, walked looking, having trouble explaining himself to foremen in metropolitan Italian. He knew no French. Got a job as helper on a grocery truck, lasted ten weeks. He dropped boxes and broke eggs. He learned to smile often. Got a job as a garbageman; this was closer. For this you had to run and lift, which was like walking and pushing, so he could hold it. Was a garbageman for a long time. Winter came: sheer horror. The metal handles of the garbage cans froze to his hands and pulled the skin off. The crew was paid so much per street, according to their contract with the city, so they ran and ran and did the allotted streets in three-quarters the contracted time, so they'd have free time not to run. On the garbage crew Domenico always suspected that it would be better to walk for eight hours than run for six, but he was incapable of expressing the idea or defending it. He ran the whole winter with frozen hands and knew that there was something better he could do. This was his first reflective, considered choice, and it changed him. He had had no previous conception of a winter so long and so cold.

In the spring he married a Piedmontese girl named Vanna DiConti who immediately gave his life a structure so multiform that he felt yanked all at once out of insignificance into determined manhood. She taught him some English, a little French, put his socks away to mend them and lined up his workboots in a row—four boots. She bought him some nylon socks which never got holes in them; they felt cold and slippery on his feet, and when he wore them on the job all day they burned his skin. There was no give to them. Talk about socks became a constant element in his relations with his wife. She did not seem to understand how important his feet were. She wanted to discuss her own feet, which were always cold in bed. This was a surprise because the rest of her was always intensely warm. When he got into bed beside her she radiated heat which he found so pleasing that he would sometimes say something about it.

"But my feet are cold," Vanna would answer, grumbling like a child.

That summer the garbage stank, fermenting and liquefying in cans and cartons: scrapings of plates, clotted grease and hair, disposable diapers. Domenico shone with sweat. How could it be so cold, then so warm? In July he was afflicted by a hateful minor ailment, a rankly acid sweat which burned and itched between his toes, thickening and glistening on the flat surface on the big toe and the second, on either foot, searing the skin and blistering it an unhealthy white and red. He could hardly stand, much less walk, and was afraid of the smell from his feet and the greasy oily feel of the strange sweat.

Vanna advised bathing four times a day, constant changes of socks, then boracic acid powder. In the end the infection went away, but its effects left distrust between man and wife.

"How they stink," Vanna said, holding a pair of his socks at arm's length. She grimaced. He thought she was very pretty and felt attacked. He quit the garbage crew and spent two terrifying months looking for another job, something clean, nothing involving dirt and sweat, in the cold. He got a new job in November, good for four months. Laborer on a snow-removal gang.

These gangs are like armoured divisions, with many motorized vehicles operating according to a rigorous system. First comes the little truck which puts out the NO PARKING signs, then the tiny one-man tractor which scrapes the sidewalk, then the heavy equipment, the large plow which piles the snow and ice in enormous hillocks on one side of the road, the gigantic rotary sweeper with its blower shaft hanging up over a dump-truck which rides slowly along under the blower till it is full—then it moves ahead, away down the street, to be replaced by an empty truck. Behind the heavy equipment another small tractor turns and darts, trimming the curbs and sidewalks. The heaviest fall of snow can be disposed of like this in around forty-eight hours, even including obscure side streets.

When Domenico joined the gang he saw these mighty engines lined up in a yard, as if marshalled for parade, drivers at the ready, laborers and foremen in attendance. He felt awe. But that first awe was nothing to what he felt during blizzards. Weather predictions were closely monitored by city authorities: first flakes, tentative and idle in early afternoon, could be recognized immediately as the gestures of an infant snowstorm. Orders went out. Sanding trucks and light sweeping and salting gangs started work. As night fell and the snow came thicker, first plowing began, then more determined plowing. For twenty-four hours the gangs fought a holding operation. Then the snow would stop—eight inches, ten inches, twelve, not often more—the sun would appear. Cold might grow intense. Now came the great crews, the concentrated effort to clear off the streets before more snow came. We can live with twelve inches: twenty-four is something else. At that point traffic patterns break down, commerce is disrupted, criminality doubles. Round the clock shifts, overtime, action.

Frozen feet.

Domenico was inexperienced and lucky to have the job at all. They made him lantern man. His work consisted in backing up slowly in front of the great rotary sweeper, not too far in front of it, especially at night, along the top of the snow hills with a red lantern, to give the operator of the sweeper a line to follow in the middle of the storm of flying ice chips and sprayed slush.

Two years before in Winnipeg a child playing on such a snow hill had been gobbled up by a sweeper and cut to pieces by the powerful blades inside the mechanism which ground the iced snow into powder. Domenico didn't know this. What he knew was that he was now the servant of an immensely strong and active machine whose piercing cry was the sound of a divine beast. As he backed unevenly along the snow hills he sometimes felt a crazy wish to throw himself into the mouth of the sucking sweeper which snouted towards him. When his feet sank too deeply into heavy wet snow he was in extreme danger of which he was completely unaware. He heard the roar and grind and crunch and surrendered himself to something unspeakable.

Twelve hours of this taxed his strength viciously. He went home and took off his boots and emptied them. They were caked with dirty ice which took a while to melt. His socks were soaking, matted into hurtful lumps of coarse knitted yarn, sometimes wool, more often some artificial fabric. When the roaring and crashing of the rotary sweeper had died out of his ears, he would get up from his chair, find a towel and chafe his ankles and feet, which hurt badly. He would think of thick dry warm woollen socks without holes. It made him frantic to think how long it was that Vanna took to darn his socks. She never darned his socks. She said they stank. He wanted them dry and new.

He saw that darning his socks was servitude for her. His dirt and wet and smell repelled her. Two o'clock in the morning. He dried himself and prepared for bed, went into the bedroom and lit a shaded lamp. Vanna was sound asleep under heavy blankets. Domenico went to the window and peered out; a new fall was beginning, early flakes swirling, more overtime on the way. He turned to the bed and twitched back the blankets, then straightened up amazed. His wife's feet protruded from under the bedclothes, and on them were thick warm dry woollen socks without holes. His.

He shook all over his body and raised his arms above his head, his mouth opened in a strained circle, a silent howl. He took a quick involuntary step towards the sleeping woman. His heart burned with resentment.

II: BOOTS

My wife pays no attention to fashion, which is something to be thankful
for, so when she complained again and again about her cold wet feet
I knew she wasn't joking.

"Nobody makes good snowboots for women," she kept saying.

"They must."

"No they don't. I've looked and looked this past two winters and I
can't find anything. It's a conspiracy."

I said, "Conspiracy theories are the paranoia of intellectuals."

"I'm no intellectual," she said truthfully.

I never knew her to take this line before, attributing the cause of a
personal problem to some invisible group of evil planners. She brooded
about it. She said, "It's the international conspiracy of the snowboot
manufacturers, possibly a cartel with connections on both sides of the
iron curtain."

"Tell me all about it."

"About twenty years ago," she began, "a girl used to be able to buy
galoshes. You remember, they were usually black, made of some kind
of waterproof fabric with a rubber sole and heel, and those funny little
clip fasteners. You could get them low-cut or you could get them so
they came halfway up your calf. They had a beige lining, felt or velour.
I had one pair after another when I was growing up, and now I have
this problem about my feet, I can see that my infantile galoshes formed
a primordial image for me. Warm, fuzzy, soft. My mother would snap
them on, give me a kiss, and send me out to play in the snow. You
don't know what it was like around our house in the old days. I was
the only girl my age in the neighbourhood, and the only playmate I had
was two years older, Paddy Ann Devlin. She used to pinch me. She
used to refuse to play with me."

I could see that these reminiscences were about to pass into a familiar
track. "You've told me all about Paddy Ann," I said. "I've even met
her. I don't see what she has to do with snowboots."

"I associate warm snowboots with Paddy Ann," my wife said. "She
often had colored ones but mine were always black."

"Never mind that."

"I won't. I'll put that aside."

"You're very wise."

"Do you know, I've been all over town looking for something I could
wear over my shoes. All they make these days are little slip-on things
that won't go over a shoe, no matter what size you buy; they just aren't

90

designed to. You're supposed to carry a pair of shoes or slippers with you—an awful nuisance—and when you get where you're going, you take your boots off, get out your shoes, put them on, leave the boots to dry. When you're leaving you take your shoes off—and your feet always get dirty standing on the mat or the floor—the bottoms of your stockings get black—put the boots on, put the shoes in the bag . . . not only that, they won't keep your feet dry, the way they're cut. I haven't had a pair of winter boots in years that would keep water out. I don't say they leak, but the tops are cut wrong. They sacrifice comfort to looks."

"Who do?"

"The snowboot cartel."

"There is no snowboot cartel," I said. "Why can't you simply buy a pair of whatever's available, only a size larger so you can wear shoes under?"

"Impossible. The way the last is shaped a shoe won't go inside unless you get them three sizes too big, and then you get snow down inside because they flop around."

"Really?"

"Certainly, really! Do you think I'm making this up?"

"No. I don't think that. I tell you what I do think though. If there's a demand for an article, somebody must be supplying it. What you appear to want is a simple, well-cut boot, with a last wide enough to take your shoes inside, and an upper designed so that snow won't come in over top. Right?"

"Exactly."

"Somebody must be selling them."

"Uh-uh."

"Come on now, somebody must. You've just missed them; you can't have looked. In this affluent society. . . ."

She looked dangerous, so I stopped.

"There is no such boot," she said.

"Must be."

"No."

"I never heard of such a thing," I said. "Here, get me the Eaton's fall sale catalogue. No, not the toy catalogue. No, not the big catalogue. That's it, the sale catalogue. Let's see."

I thumbed through the book for a while, then finally consulted the index.

"Here we are. 'Women's winter footwear.' Now we'll see."

I picked out something in a brown suede effect that looked very attractive. Women's boots mean nothing to me ordinarily.

"They look very nice. How much do we want to spend?"

"Not over twelve dollars. You can't get a shoe in those."

I looked at the description of the article and she was right. Not only that, there wasn't a pair of boots on the page that would take a shoe. "That's extremely interesting," I said. It opened up a world of speculation. "I wonder why that is."

"I can't tell you that," she said, "but it's discriminatory. All I want is a comfortable snowboot, and I can't get it."

"Why don't you buy a pair of men's workboots, shearling-lined, like those ones I bought in Hartford? They're ten years old and as good as new. I'll never wear them out. Every winter you go over the soles and welts with one of those silicone waterproofings. Keep you dry as a bone."

But she has the idea that her feet are on the big side. I don't think they are. I think they're cute little feet but I can't convince her. Her attitude to her feet is more projective than descriptive.

"Don't be a fool," she said curtly.

"I'm quite serious. If you don't want to wear workboots for cosmetic reasons. . . ."

"It isn't that."

"You're a sensible woman. If the heavy workboots with the shearling piled lining, warm felt insole, water-resistant Neoprene sole and heel, don't meet your specifications. . . ."

"Stop that," she said, her mouth watering.

". . . look around and pick out another kind of man's boot. What does it matter how they look? You're wearing them for comfort and warmth, not to impress anybody. Who looks at your overshoes anyway?"

"Could we go as high as fifteen dollars?"

"Why not? Go around to some of the smaller stores; maybe they've got something in stock from years back." I thought that would be the end of it.

Well sir, she did it, something hardly anybody does anymore. Patronized the neighbourhood merchants, went the length of the shopping district along Sherbrooke from Girouard to Hampton. Our neighbourhood. Also the stores around Cavendish and Somerled: picture framers, music stores, pet shops, paint and wallpaper, those specialized little places that you look in sometimes as you pass, wondering how they stay in business. The neighbourhood. We should be more loyal to our neighbourhoods. I'm going to start buying my clothes in the district if I can find what I want.

My wife couldn't find what she wanted. She had a whole sequence of upsetting meetings with local merchants. They wouldn't, literally *wouldn't,* sell her what she wanted.

"I was in the Fit-Rite Shoestore, corner Kensington, this afternoon," she told me.

"Any good boots?"

"Do you know what that man said? He said, 'Madam, your problem is simply you've been buying a cheaper article. I've got just the thing for you.' Then he went in the back of the store and was gone fifteen minutes. I figured he was digging out some item he'd had in inventory for years, that he was going to try to stick me with. Maybe I would unearth some rare pair of overshoes, like an archaeologist on a dig."

"What happened?"

"He came back with a pair of sealskin boots. Everybody knows about sealskin boots for Heaven's sake. I could get them anywhere. I'm perfectly familiar with them."

"Look how smart," he said. "Neat. Small-looking, thong ties. You could wear them anywhere, don't need a shoe underneath. Soft and clinging."

"How much?"

"To you, thirty-nine ninety-five."

"It was the 'to you' that annoyed me," she said. "I gave it to him good. I said, 'What am I, rich or something? Do I look rich to you? I want a pair of galoshes, man, not a pair of hand-tailored gloves for my feet. What kind of a lunatic pays forty dollars for that? Do you mean to stand there and tell me you can't meet the demand?' I was a bit rude, I think."

"I'm sorry, Madam," he said. "We get no call for the kind of thing you're talking about. Mind you, mind you, I'm not saying we shouldn't; we used to sell a flock of them. Not for ten years. I blame the Beatles."

"What does your own wife wear?"

"She takes from stock. Forty dollar boots."

My wife said, "I felt sorry for the man, and went out of the store thinking, 'Do unto others as you would have them do unto you.'"

I said, "That's a great line but you can't make it stick. It seems wrong, somehow, that you have to pay forty dollars to get something good-looking and comfortable. I mean, lots of people can't pay forty dollars. We can't. At least, I mean, go ahead if you want to, but it's un-economical."

"That's just it. It isn't right that nobody's making them. Not *right.* Somebody ought to."

I said, "I don't think fashion has anything to do with morals."

"Oh, but you're so wrong. Fashion makes morals."

"I thought it was the other way around."

"No, no, no, a human being who is fool enough to wear a girdle and bra can only behave in certain ways—submissive, dependent, silly, and it's the same with snowboots. Soft and clinging! I don't know why we put up with it. I don't know why I wear these canvas and net bags on my tits. For one thing, they never fit right."

"It's none of my business but you can leave them off anytime as far as I'm concerned."

"Maybe I will," she said, looking fierce.

I expected her to strike a blow for the new feminism at almost any time, probably in the form of refusal to wear an irrationally-designed and otiose garment, nylon stockings or absurdly narrow shoes. But instead she continued to campaign on the snowboot issue, going into stores and making scenes when they refused to allow her to buy men's galoshes. "You haven't any idea . . . the prejudice, the taboos," she told me, "these men actually refuse to sell me something I want to buy. Refuse!"

"Should I go with you sometime? Between the two of us we could overpower the clerk and escape with the goods."

"Don't tease, sweetie, there's a principle involved."

When a clever woman uses the word 'principle' there's trouble in store for somebody. I hoped it wasn't me. Instead it was the owner of the Fit-Rite Shoestore, a special object of her anger. One early winter afternoon she walked into his place and ordered him to sell her the men's overshoes in the window. Calf-length, brown rubber, cut narrow with a good thick ring of synthetic fur around the inside of the uppers, and big enough to get a shoe inside.

The poor man cringed and pleaded. "I can't let you wear those out of the store, Madam, I just can't. I refuse to. Don't do it, please!" He tried to restrain her but she overcame him, seized the footwear, flung seven ninety-five plus tax on a showcase and departed.

Those boots are on their third winter now, and she's never had a pair she liked better. Goes around with a happy smile and dry feet. Now, two years later, we're beginning to see similar boots on many other girls, perhaps a sign of a new, moral fashion. I ask myself, will girls abandon unreasonable adornment? The idea upsets me.

SOBER COLORING: THE ONTOLOGY OF SUPER-REALISM

Super-realism, yes, because that is how I think of my fiction, quite deliberately and consciously, very likely unconsciously too. When I started to write novels and stories about the year 1956, I had no clear idea of what I was doing. I had had a literary education, and knew something about critical theory and method as applied to the work of other writers, the classics especially, and some moderns. I got a Ph.D. in English in late 1955. After that I did more or less what I wanted. I began to write independently, feeling liberated from the need to defer to what other people might think. I was glad to get out of the graduate school.

I had no theory of my own writing, and belonged to no school, so I wrote most of a novel which was never published, and a dozen stories, in 1956 and 1957, instinctively, making all the important artistic decisions as I went along, with no theoretical bias for one kind of writing as against all the others. Instinctively, then, I turned out to be a moral realist, not a naturalist nor a surrealist nor a magic realist nor in any way an experimental or advance guard writer. That was in effect where I began.

All my early writing dealt with the affairs of credible characters in more or less credible situations. As I look back, I see that this instinctive moral realism was tempered by an inclination to show these credible characters, in perfectly ordinary situations, nevertheless doing violent and unpredictable, and even melodramatic, things. A brother and sister go to visit their mother's grave and are unable to find it in a cemetery of nightmarish proportions; a man kills his newly-baptized girlfriend thinking that she will go straight to Heaven; a young priest molests a child sexually; a young boy goes mad under great strain. A yachtsman runs his boat on a rock and sinks it, drowning his wife and her lover, who are trapped below deck. I would never choose actions like these nowadays, not because of their violence but because of their improbability. I still write about intense feelings which lead to impulsive and sometimes violent acts, but I am better able to locate these feelings in credible occasions.

In those days, and for several years afterwards, I tried to control these melodramatic tendencies—murder, suicide, hanging about in cemeteries, drowning in burst boats—by a strong sense of the physical form of stories. I arranged my pieces according to complex numerologies.

A novel might have seven main sections, one for each of a specific week in a given year, so that the reader could tell exactly what time it was when something happened. Or the book might be divided in three main parts, each with a specific number of subdivisions. I once wrote the rough draft of a book in two main sections and when I had finished each half of the manuscript was precisely a hundred and forty-four pages long: twelve twelves doubled. This play with numbers is a recurrent feature of my work. *Around the Mountain* follows the calendar very precisely, with one story for each month from one Christmas to the next. I have always had a fondness for the cycle of the Christian liturgical year. My first, unpublished, novel was called *God Rest You Merry,* and covered the seven days from Christmas Night to New Year's Eve, in a most elaborate arrangement.

I still do this. My new novel, which will appear in the fall of 1972, *You Can't Get There From Here,* is in three parts. The first and third sections have ten chapters each; the middle part has twenty, which gives us: 10/20/10. The Christian numerological symbolism implied is very extensive. It makes a kind of scaffolding for the imagination.

I had then, and still have, an acute sense of the possibilities of close formal organization of the sentence, syntactically and grammatically, and in its phonemic sequences. I paid much attention to the difficulties of writing long sentences because I knew that simple-minded naturalists wrote short sentences, using lots of 'ands.' I did not want to be a simple-minded naturalist. I hoped to write syntactically various and graceful prose. I took care to vary the number of sentences in succeeding paragraphs. I rarely used the one-sentence paragraph; when I did so I felt mighty daring. I kept a careful eye upon the clause-structure of each sentence. I wouldn't use the ellipsis mark (. . .) because Arthur Mizener wrote to me that he considered it a weak, cop-out sort of punctuation.

I sometimes use the ellipsis now . . . and feel guilty.

My interest in the sound of sentences, in the use of color words and of the names of places, in practical stylistics, showed me that prose fiction might have an abstract element, a purely formal element, even though it continued to be strictly, morally, realistic. It might be possible to think of prose fiction the way one thinks of abstract elements in representational painting, or of highly formal music. I now began to see affinities between the art I was willy-nilly practising and the other arts, first poetry, then painting and music. I have always been passionately attached to music and painting—I have gone so far as to marry a painter on mixed grounds—and have written many stories about the arts: film-making, painting, music less often because it is on the surface such a non-narrative art. I find that it is hard to speak about music.

I have also written some stories about a kind of experience close to that of the artist: metaphysical thought. My stories "A Season of Calm Weather" (with its consciously Wordsworthian title) and "The Hole" are about metaphysicians. The second of the two tries to show a philosopher's intelligence actually at work, a hard thing to do. Like musical thought, metaphysical thought seems to take place in a non-verbal region of consciousness, if there is such a thing, and it is therefore hard to write about, but to me an irresistible challenge.

My novels *White Figure, White Ground* and *The Camera Always Lies* dealt respectively with the problems of a painter and a group of film-makers. It is the seeing-into-things, the capacity for meditative abstraction, that interests me about philosophy, the arts and religious practice. I love most in painting an art which exhibits the transcendental element dwelling in living things. I think of this as true *super-realism*. And I think of Vermeer, or among American artists of Edward Hopper, whose painting of ordinary places, seaside cottages, a roadside snack bar and gasoline station, have touched some level of my own imagination which I can only express in fictional images. In my story "Getting to Williamstown" there is a description of a roadside refreshment stand beside an abandoned gas pump, which is pretty directly imitated from a painting of Hopper's. I see this now, though I didn't when I wrote the story. That is what I mean by the unconscious elements in my work which co-operate with my deliberate intentions.

I have to admit at this point that my Ph.D. thesis discussed the theory of the imagination of the Romantic poets and its background. The argument of the thesis was that Romantic imagination-theory was fundamentally a revision of the theory of abstraction as it was taught by Aristotle and the mediaeval philosophers. The kind of knowing which Wordsworth called "reason in its most exalted mood" and which Coleridge exalted as creative artistic imagination, *does the same thing* as that power which Saint Thomas Aquinas thought of as the active intellect. I do not think of the imagination and the active intellect as separate and opposed to one another. No more are emotion and thought *lived* distinct and apart. The power of abstraction, in the terms of traditional psychology, is not a murderous dissection of living beings; on the contrary it is an intimate penetration into their physical reality. "No ideas but in things" said William Carlos Williams. I believe that Aquinas would concur in that—the idea lives in the singular real being. The intellect is not set over against emotion, feelings, instincts, memory

97

and the imagination, but intimately united to them. The artist and the metaphysician are equally contemplatives; so are the saints.

Like Vermeer or Hopper or that great creator of musical form, Joseph Haydn, I am trying to concentrate on knowable form as it lives in the physical world. These forms are abstract, not in the sense of being inhumanly non-physical, but in the sense of communicating the perfection of the essences of things—the formal realities which create things as they are in themselves. A transcendentalist must first study the things of this world, and get as far inside them as possible. My story "The Hole" tries to show a philosopher working out this idea in his own experience. Here, as everywhere in my writing, I have studied as closely and intensely as I can the *insides* of things which are not me. The great metaphor in human experience for truly apprehending another being is sexual practice. Here, perhaps only here, do we get inside another being. Alas, the entrance is only metaphorical. In plain fact no true penetration happens in love-making. It is not possible for one physical being to merge into another, as D. H. Lawrence finally realized. Bodies occupy different places; there is nothing to be done about this. Sex is a metaphor for union, not itself achieved union.

What we are united to in this world is not the physical insides of persons or things, but the knowable principle in them. Inside everything that exists is essence, not in physical space and time, but as forming space and time and the perceptions possible within them. What I know, love, and desire in another person isn't inside him like a nut in its shell, but it is everywhere that he is, forming him. My identity isn't inside me—it is *how I am*. It is hard to express the way we know the forms of things, but this is the knowing that art exercises.

Art after all, like every other human act, implies a philosophical stance: either you think that there is nothing to things that is not delivered in their appearances, or you think that immaterial forms exist in these things, conferring identity on them. These are not the only ontological alternatives, but they are extreme ones, and they state a classical ontological opposition. The bias of most contemporary thought has been towards the first alternative, until the very recent past. But perhaps we are again beginning to be able to think about the noumenal element in things, their essential and intelligible principles, what Newman called the "illative" aspect of being. The danger of this sort of noumenalism is that you may dissolve the hard, substantial shapes of things, as they can be seen to be, into an idealistic mish-mash—something I'm not inclined to do. I'm not a Platonist or a dualist of any kind. I think with Aristotle that the body and the soul are one; the form of a thing is totally united to its matter. The soul is the body. No ideas but in things.

That is where I come out: the spirit is totally *in* the flesh. If you pay close enough attention to things, stare at them, concentrate on them as hard as you can, not just with your intelligence, but with your feelings and instincts—with your prick too—you will begin to apprehend the forms in them. Knowing is not a matter of sitting in an armchair while engaged in some abstruse conceptual calculus of weights and measures and geometrical spaces. Knowing includes making love, and making pieces of art, and wanting and worshipping *and* calculating (because calculation is also part of knowing) and in fact knowing is what Wordsworth called it, a "spousal union" of the knower and the known, a marriage full of flesh.

I want to propose the Wordsworthian account of the marriage of the mind and the thing as a model of artistic activity. I don't think that the Romantic movement failed. I think we are still in the middle of it. Of the Romantic masters, Wordsworth seems to me to have understood best how things move in themselves, how they exist as they are when they are possessing themselves, having their identities, living. Wordsworth has an extraordinary grasp of the movement, the running motion, of the physical, the roll of water or sweep of wind, changing textures of fog or mist, all that is impalpable and yet material. In this fleeting, running movement of physical existence, for Wordsworth there is always the threat of an illumination, "splendor in the grass, glory in the flower." Things are full of the visionary gleam.

The illuminations in things are there, really and truly *there,* in those things. They are not run over them by projective intelligence, and yet there is a sense in which the mind, in uniting itself to things, creates illumination in them.

> *"The clouds that gather round the setting sun*
> *Do take a sober coloring from an eye*
> *That hath kept watch o'er man's mortality;"*

This is a triple eye, that of the setting sun which colors the clouds, and that of the sober human moral imagination, and finally that of God as brooding, creative Father of all. The coloring of the clouds is given to them by the Deity in the original act of creation. Every evening the sun re-enacts the illumination. The moral imagination operates in the same way, though it is not originally creative; it projects coloring into things, true, but the coloring has already been put there by the divine creation. The act of the human knower is an act of reciprocity. It half creates, and half perceives "the mighty world of eye and ear."

"I have at all times endeavoured to look steadily at my subject," said Wordsworth, very justly. His regard to things is concentrated and accurate; he insists everywhere on the utter necessity of the sensory process, of seeing and hearing, of taking in the sensible world and transforming it. He proposed "to throw a certain coloring of the imagination over incidents and situations taken from common life." This is the same metaphor as that of the final stanza of the "Intimations Ode." The eye in seeing gives color to things; but the color is there.

The poetry of Wordsworth supplies us again and again with examples of this coloring of imagination spread over incidents and situations from common life. The figure of the old Leech-Gatherer in "Resolution and Independence" is perhaps the most overwhelming example of this capacity of very ordinary persons and scenes to yield, on close inspection, an almost intolerable significance.

> *"In my mind's eye I seemed to see him pace*
> *About the weary moors continually,*
> *Wandering about alone and silently."*

The concentrating eye, interior/exterior, giving to things their sober hues, is constant in Wordsworth. I have imitated it from him in my work. In the deliberately paired stories "Socks" and "Boots" I have chosen incidents from ordinary life and characters such as may be met with everywhere, and I have attempted to look steadily at these persons in the hope that something of the noumenal will emerge.

These stories are, to begin with, political; they are about the ways in which living in society modifies our personal desires, a very Wordsworthian theme. Domenico Lercaro in "Socks" does not want to work so hard. Nobody wants to work that hard. He doesn't want to work on a garbage truck or do snow removal, but he is driven to it by the need to survive. The fictional "my wife" in the story "Boots" wants to buy a certain specific kind of winter footwear, but the stores simply don't stock the boots she wants. We can buy only what we are offered, and our range of choice is surprisingly limited.

I have tried to move beyond the fiction of social circumstance by taking a very attentive look at my two main characters. In "Socks" poor Domenico sees the enormous, noisy, snow-removal machine turn before his eyes into a divine beast or Leviathan. Everyone who has seen these machines at work recognizes their intimations of violence, in their noise

100

and in the sharpness of their rotary blades. They have actually killed and eaten people. Modern life is full of these mechanical beasts.

"My wife" in "Boots" feels trivialized by fashion; most women in middle-class circumstances do, I think. To wear high heels and a girdle is to enslave yourself—to adopt the badges of a humiliating subservience. This story tries to make its readers sense the galling limits on their activities felt by intelligent women in the face of the clothes which fashion and *chic* propose for them: the necessary sexual exhibitionism, the silly posturing, the faked little-girlishness.

The two stories insinuate larger issues than their subjects would suggest; they are following Wordsworth's prescription. I have at all times endeavoured to look steadily at my subjects. I hope that my gaze has helped to light them up.

HUGH HOOD

Margaret Laurence

Margaret Laurence was born in 1926 in Neepawa, Manitoba.
She attended the University of Manitoba and married in 1947.
She went with her husband to Somaliland and Ghana where he
was employed as an engineer. She has a son and daughter.
For the last few years she has been living in Buckinghamshire
in England but plans to return to Canada. She spent the
academic year 1969-70 as Writer-in-Residence at the
University of Toronto.

Her books are published in Canada, America and England.
A Jest of God appeared as the successful film *Rachel, Rachel.*
She is currently working on a new novel.

Bibliography

This Side Jordan. McClelland and Stewart, Toronto, 1960. (Novel)

The Prophet's Camel Bell. McClelland and Stewart, Toronto, 1963. (Travel)

The Tomorrow-Tamer. McClelland and Stewart, Toronto, 1963. (Novel)

The Stone Angel. McClelland and Stewart, Toronto, 1964. (Novel)

A Jest of God. McClelland and Stewart, Toronto, 1966. (Novel)

Long Drums and Cannons. McClelland and Stewart, Toronto, 1968. (Essays on Nigerian literature)

A Bird in the House. McClelland and Stewart, Toronto, 1970. (Stories)

Jason's Quest. McClelland and Stewart, Toronto, 1970. (Children's Book)

The Loons

Just below Manawaka, where the Wachakwa River ran brown and noisy over the pebbles, the scrub oak and grey-green willow and chokecherry bushes grew in a dense thicket. In a clearing at the centre of the thicket stood the Tonnerre family's shack. The basis of this dwelling was a small square cabin made of poplar poles and chinked with mud, which had been built by Jules Tonnerre some fifty years before, when he came back from Batoche with a bullet in his thigh, the year that Riel was hung and the voices of the Metis entered their long silence. Jules had only intended to stay the winter in the Wachakwa Valley, but the family was still there in the thirties, when I was a child. As the Tonnerres had increased, their settlement had been added to, until the clearing at the foot of the town hill was a chaos of lean-tos, wooden packing cases, warped lumber, discarded car tyres, ramshackle chicken coops, tangled strands of barbed wire and rusty tin cans.

The Tonnerres were French halfbreeds, and among themselves they spoke a *patois* that was neither Cree nor French. Their English was broken and full of obscenities. They did not belong among the Cree of the Galloping Mountain reservation, further north, and they did not belong among the Scots-Irish and Ukrainians of Manawaka, either. They were, as my Grandmother MacLeod would have put it, neither flesh, fowl, nor good salt herring. When their men were not working at odd jobs or as section hands on the C.P.R., they lived on relief. In the summers, one of the Tonnerre youngsters, with a face that seemed totally unfamiliar with laughter, would knock at the doors of the town's brick houses and offer for sale a lard-pail full of bruised wild strawberries, and if he got as much as a quarter he would grab the coin and run before the customer had time to change her mind. Sometimes old Jules, or his son Lazarus, would get mixed up in a Saturday-night brawl, and would hit out at whoever was nearest, or howl drunkenly among the offended shoppers on Main Street, and then the Mountie would put them for the night in the barred cell underneath the Court House, and the next morning they would be quiet again.

Piquette Tonnerre, the daughter of Lazarus, was in my class at school. She was older than I, but she had failed several grades, perhaps because her attendance had always been sporadic and her interest in schoolwork negligible. Part of the reason she had missed a lot of school was that she had had tuberculosis of the bone, and had once spent many months in hospital. I knew this because my father was the doctor who had

104

looked after her. Her sickness was almost the only thing I knew about her, however. Otherwise, she existed for me only as a vaguely embarrassing presence, with her hoarse voice and her clumsy limping walk and her grimy cotton dresses that were always miles too long. I was neither friendly nor unfriendly towards her. She dwelt and moved somewhere within my scope of vision, but I did not actually notice her very much until that peculiar summer when I was eleven.

"I don't know what to do about that kid," my father said at dinner one evening. "Piquette Tonnerre, I mean. The damn bone's flared up again. I've had her in hospital for quite a while now, and it's under control all right, but I hate like the dickens to send her home again."

"Couldn't you explain to her mother that she has to rest a lot?" my mother said.

"The mother's not there," my father replied. "She took off a few years back. Can't say I blame her. Piquette cooks for them, and she says Lazarus would never do anything for himself as long as she's there. Anyway, I don't think she'd take much care of herself, once she got back. She's only thirteen, after all. Beth, I was thinking—what about taking her up to Diamond Lake with us this summer? A couple of months rest would give that bone a much better chance."

My mother looked stunned.

"But Ewen—what about Roddie and Vanessa?"

"She's not contagious," my father said. "And it would be company for Vanessa."

"Oh dear," my mother said in distress, "I'll bet anything she has nits in her hair."

"For Pete's sake," my father said crossly, "do you think Matron would let her stay in the hospital for all this time like that? Don't be silly, Beth."

Grandmother MacLeod, her delicately featured face as rigid as a cameo, now brought her mauve-veined hands together as though she were about to begin a prayer.

"Ewen, if that half-breed youngster comes along to Diamond Lake, I'm not going," she announced. "I'll go to Morag's for the summer."

I had trouble in stifling my urge to laugh, for my mother brightened visibly and quickly tried to hide it. If it came to a choice between Grandmother MacLeod and Piquette, Piquette would win hands down, nits or not.

"It might be quite nice for you, at that," she mused. "You haven't seen Morag for over a year, and you might enjoy being in the city for a while. Well, Ewen dear, you do what you think best. If you think it would do Piquette some good, then we'll be glad to have her, as long as she behaves herself."

So it happened that several weeks later, when we all piled into my father's old Nash, surrounded by suitcases and boxes of provisions and toys for my ten-month-old brother, Piquette was with us and Grandmother MacLeod, miraculously, was not. My father would only be staying at the cottage for a couple of weeks, for he had to get back to his practice, but the rest of us would stay at Diamond Lake until the end of August.

Our cottage was not named, as many were, "Dew Drop Inn" or "Bide-a-Wee," or "Bonnie Doon." The sign on the roadway bore in austere letters only our name, MacLeod. It was not a large cottage, but it was on the lakefront. You could look out the windows and see, through the filigree of the spruce trees, the water glistening greenly as the sun caught it. All around the cottage were ferns, and sharp-branched raspberry bushes, and moss that had grown over fallen tree trunks. If you looked carefully among the weeds and grass, you could find wild strawberry plants which were in white flower now and in another month would bear fruit, the fragrant globes hanging like miniature scarlet lanterns on the thin hairy stems. The two grey squirrels were still there, gossiping at us from the tall spruce beside the cottage, and by the end of the summer they would again be tame enough to take pieces of crust from my hands. The broad moose antlers that hung above the back door were a little more bleached and fissured after the winter, but otherwise everything was the same. I raced joyfully around my kingdom, greeting all the places I had not seen for a year. My brother, Roderick, who had not been born when we were here last summer, sat on the car rug in the sunshine and examined a brown spruce cone, meticulously turning it round and round in his small and curious hands. My mother and father toted the luggage from car to cottage, exclaiming over how well the place had wintered, no broken windows, thank goodness, no apparent damage from storm-felled branches or snow.

Only after I had finished looking around did I notice Piquette. She was sitting on the swing, her lame leg held stiffy out, and her other foot scuffing the ground as she swung slowly back and forth. Her long hair hung black and straight around her shoulders, and her broad coarse-featured face bore no expression—it was blank, as though she no longer dwelt within her own skull, as though she had gone elsewhere. I approached her very hesitantly.

"Want to come and play?"

106

Piquette looked at me with a sudden flash of scorn.

"I ain't a kid," she said.

Wounded, I stamped angrily away, swearing I would not speak to her for the rest of the summer. In the days that followed, however, Piquette began to interest me, and I began to want to interest her. My reasons did not appear bizarre to me. Unlikely as it may seem, I had only just realised that the Tonnerre family, whom I had always heard called half-breeds, were actually Indians, or as near as made no difference. My acquaintance with Indians was not extensive. I did not remember ever having seen a real Indian, and my new awareness that Piquette sprang from the people of Big Bear and Poundmaker, of Tecumseh, of the Iroquois who had eaten Father Brebeuf's heart—all this gave her an instant attraction in my eyes. I was a devoted reader of Pauline Johnson at this age, and sometimes would orate aloud and in an exalted voice, *West Wind, blow from your prairie nest; Blow from the mountains, blow from the west*—and so on. It seemed to me that Piquette must be in some way a daughter of the forest, a kind of junior prophetess of the wilds, who might impart to me, if I took the right approach, some of the secrets which she undoubtedly knew—where the whippoorwill made her nest, how the coyote reared her young, or whatever it was that it said in Hiawatha.

I set about gaining Piquette's trust. She was not allowed to go swimming, with her bad leg, but I managed to lure her down to the beach—or rather, she came because there was nothing else to do. The water was always icy, for the lake was fed by springs, but I swam like a dog, thrashing my arms and legs around at such speed and with such an output of energy that I never grew cold. Finally, when I had had enough, I came out and sat beside Piquette on the sand. When she saw me approaching, her hand squashed flat the sand castle she had been building, and she looked at me sullenly, without speaking.

"Do you like this place?" I asked, after a while, intending to lead on from there into the question of forest lore.

Piquette shrugged. "It's okay. Good as anywhere."

"I love it," I said. "We come here every summer."

"So what?" Her voice was distant, and I glanced at her uncertainly, wondering what I could have said wrong.

"Do you want to come for a walk?" I asked her. "We wouldn't need to go far. If you walk just around the point there, you come to a bay where great big reeds grow in the water, and all kinds of fish hang around there. Want to? Come on."

She shook her head.

"Your dad said I ain't supposed to do no more walking than I got to."
I tried another line.

"I bet you know a lot about the woods and all that, eh?" I began respectfully.

Piquette looked at me from her large dark unsmiling eyes.

"I don't know what in hell you're talkin' about," she replied. "You nuts or somethin'? If you mean where my old man, and me, and all them live, you better shut up, by Jesus, you hear?"

I was startled and my feelings were hurt, but I had a kind of dogged perseverance. I ignored her rebuff.

"You know something, Piquette? There's loons here, on this lake. You can see their nests just up the shore there, behind those logs. At night, you can hear them even from the cottage, but it's better to listen from the beach. My dad says we should listen and try to remember how they sound, because in a few years when more cottages are built at Diamond Lake and more people come in, the loons will go away."

Piquette was picking up stones and snail shells and then dropping them again.

"Who gives a good goddamn?" she said.

It became increasingly obvious that, as an Indian, Piquette was a dead loss. That evening I went out by myself, scrambling through the bushes that overhung the steep path, my feet slipping on the fallen spruce needles that covered the ground. When I reached the shore, I walked along the firm damp sand to the small pier that my father had built, and sat down there. I heard someone else crashing through the undergrowth and the bracken, and for a moment I thought Piquette had changed her mind, but it turned out to be my father. He sat beside me on the pier and we waited, without speaking.

At night the lake was like black glass with a streak of amber which was the path of the moon. All around, the spruce trees grew tall and close-set, branches blackly sharp against the sky, which was lightened by a cold flickering of stars. Then the loons began their calling. They rose like phantom birds from the nests on the shore, and flew out onto the dark still surface of the water.

No one can ever describe that ululating sound, the crying of the loons, and no one who has heard it can ever forget it. Plaintive, and yet with a quality of chilling mockery, those voices belonged to a world separated by aeons from our neat world of summer cottages and the lighted lamps of home.

"They must have sounded just like that," my father remarked, "before any person ever set foot here."

108

Then he laughed. "You could say the same, of course, about sparrows, or chipmunks, but somehow it only strikes you that way with the loons."

"I know," I said.

Neither of us suspected that this would be the last time we would ever sit here together on the shore, listening. We stayed for perhaps half an hour, and then we went back to the cottage. My mother was reading beside the fireplace. Piquette was looking at the burning birch log, and not doing anything.

"You should have come along," I said, although in fact I was glad she had not.

"Not me," Piquette said. "You wouldn' catch me walkin' way down there jus' for a bunch of squawkin' birds."

Piquette and I remained ill at ease with one another. I felt I had somehow failed my father, but I did not know what was the matter, nor why she would not or could not respond when I suggested exploring the woods or playing house. I thought it was probably her slow and difficult walking that held her back. She stayed most of the time in the cottage with my mother, helping her with the dishes or with Roddie, but hardly ever talking. Then the Duncans arrived at their cottage, and I spent my days with Mavis, who was my best friend. I could not reach Piquette at all, and I soon lost interest in trying. But all that summer she remained as both a reproach and a mystery to me.

That winter my father died of pneumonia, after less than a week's illness. For some time I saw nothing around me, being completely immersed in my own pain and my mother's. When I looked outward once more, I scarcely noticed that Piquette Tonnerre was no longer at school. I do not remember seeing her at all until four years later, one Saturday night when Mavis and I were having Cokes in the Regal Café. The jukebox was booming like tuneful thunder, and beside it, leaning lightly on its chrome and its rainbow glass, was a girl.

Piquette must have been seventeen then, although she looked about twenty. I stared at her, astounded that anyone could have changed so much. Her face, so stolid and expressionless before, was animated now with a gaiety that was almost violent. She laughed and talked very loudly with the boys around her. Her lipstick was bright carmine, and her hair was cut short and frizzily permed. She had not been pretty as a child, and she was not pretty now, for her features were still heavy and blunt. But her dark and slightly slanted eyes were beautiful, and her skin-tight skirt and orange sweater displayed to enviable advantage a soft and slender body.

109

She saw me, and walked over. She teetered a little, but it was not due to her once-tubercular leg, for her limp was almost gone.

"Hi, Vanessa." Her voice still had the same hoarseness. "Long time no see, eh?"

"Hi," I said. "Where've you been keeping yourself, Piquette?"

"Oh, I been around," she said. "I been away almost two years now. Been all over the place—Winnipeg, Regina, Saskatoon. Jesus, what I could tell you! I come back this summer, but I ain't stayin'. You kids goin' to the dance?"

"No," I said abruptly, for this was a sore point with me. I was fifteen, and thought I was old enough to go to the Saturday-night dances at the Flamingo. My mother, however, thought otherwise.

"Y'oughta come," Piquette said. "I never miss one. It's just about the on'y thing in this jerkwater town that's any fun. Boy, you couldn' catch me stayin' here. I don' give a shit about this place. It stinks."

She sat down beside me, and I caught the harsh over-sweetness of her perfume.

"Listen, you wanna know something, Vanessa?" she confided, her voice only slightly blurred. "Your dad was the only person in Manawaka that ever done anything good to me."

I nodded speechlessly. I was certain she was speaking the truth. I knew a little more than I had that summer at Diamond Lake, but I could not reach her now any more than I had then. I was ashamed, ashamed of my own timidity, the frightened tendency to look the other way. Yet I felt no real warmth towards her—I only felt that I ought to, because of that distant summer and because my father had hoped she would be company for me, or perhaps that I would be for her, but it had not happened that way. At this moment, meeting her again, I had to admit that she repelled and embarrassed me, and I could not help despising the self-pity in her voice. I wished she would go away. I did not want to see her. I did not know what to say to her. It seemed that we had nothing to say to one another.

"I'll tell you something else," Piquette went on. "All the old bitches an' biddies in this town will sure be surprised. I'm gettin' married this fall—my boyfriend, he's an English fella, works in the stockyards in the city there, a very tall guy, got blond wavy hair. Gee, is he ever handsome. Got this real classy name. Alvin Gerald Cummings—some handle, eh? They call him Al."

For the merest instant, then, I saw her. I really did see her, for the first and only time in all the years we had both lived in the same town.

110

Her defiant face, momentarily, became unguarded and unmasked, and in her eyes there was a terrifying hope.

"Gee, Piquette—" I burst out awkwardly, "that's swell. That's really wonderful. Congratulations—good luck—I hope you'll be happy—"

As I mouthed the conventional phrases, I could only guess how great her need must have been, that she had been forced to seek the very things she so bitterly rejected.

When I was eighteen, I left Manawaka and went away to college. At the end of my first year, I came back home for the summer. I spent the first few days in talking non-stop with my mother, as we exchanged all the news that somehow had not found its way into letters—what had happened in my life and what had happened here in Manawaka while I was away. My mother searched her memory for events that concerned people I knew.

"Did I ever write you about Piquette Tonnerre, Vanessa?" she asked one morning.

"No, I don't think so," I replied. "Last I heard of her, she was going to marry some guy in the city. Is she still there?"

My mother looked perturbed, and it was a moment before she spoke, as though she did not know how to express what she had to tell and wished she did not need to try.

"She's dead," she said at last. Then, as I stared at her, "Oh, Vanessa, when it happened, I couldn't help thinking of her as she was that summer —so sullen and gauche and badly dressed. I couldn't help wondering if we could have done something more at that time—but what could we do? She used to be around in the cottage there with me all day, and honestly it was all I could do to get a word out of her. She didn't even talk to your father very much, although I think she liked him in her way."

"What happened?" I asked.

"Either her husband left her, or she left him," my mother said. "I don't know which. Anyway, she came back here with two youngsters, both only babies—they must have been born very close together. She kept house, I guess, for Lazarus and her brothers, down in the valley there, in the old Tonnerre place. I used to see her on the street some-times, but she never spoke to me. She'd put on an awful lot of weight, and she looked a mess, to tell you the truth, a real slattern, dressed any old how. She was up in court a couple of times—drunk and disorderly, of course. One Saturday night last winter, during the coldest weather, Piquette was alone in the shack with the children. The Tonnerres made home brew all the time, so I've heard, and Lazarus said later she'd been drinking most of the day when he and the boys went out that evening.

They had an old woodstove there—you know the kind, with exposed pipes. The shack caught fire. Piquette didn't get out, and neither did the children."

I did not say anything. As so often with Piquette, there did not seem to be anything to say. There was a kind of silence around the image in my mind of the fire and the snow, and I wished I could put from my memory the look that I had seen once in Piquette's eyes.

I went up to Diamond Lake for a few days that summer, with Mavis and her family. The MacLeod cottage had been sold after my father's death, and I did not even go to look at it, not wanting to witness my long-ago kingdom possessed now by strangers. But one evening I went down to the shore by myself.

The small pier which my father had built was gone, and in its place there was a large and solid pier built by the government, for Galloping Mountain was now a national park, and Diamond Lake had been re-named Lake Wapakata, for it was felt that an Indian name would have a greater appeal to tourists. The one store had become several dozen, and the settlement had all the attributes of a flourishing resort—hotels, a dance-hall, cafés with neon signs, the penetrating odours of potato chips and hot dogs.

I sat on the government pier and looked out across the water. At night the lake at least was the same as it had always been, darkly shining and bearing within its black glass the streak of amber that was the path of the moon. There was no wind that evening, and everything was quiet all around me. It seemed too quiet, and then I realized that the loons were no longer here. I listened for some time, to make sure, but never once did I hear that long-drawn call, half mocking and half plaintive, spearing through the stillness across the lake.

I did not know what had happened to the birds. Perhaps they had gone away to some far place of belonging. Perhaps they had been unable to find such a place, and had simply died out, having ceased to care any longer whether they lived or not.

I remembered how Piquette had scorned to come along, when my father and I sat there and listened to the lake birds. It seemed to me now that in some unconscious and totally unrecognised way, Piquette might have been the only one, after all, who had heard the crying of the loons.

To Set Our House in Order

When the baby was almost ready to be born, something went wrong and my mother had to go into hospital two weeks before the expected time. I was wakened by her crying in the night, and then I heard my father's footsteps as he went downstairs to phone. I stood in the doorway of my room, shivering and listening, wanting to go to my mother but afraid to go lest there be some sight there more terrifying than I could bear.

"Hello—Paul?" my father said, and I knew he was talking to Dr. Cates. "It's Beth. The waters have broken, and the fetal position doesn't seem quite—well, I'm only thinking of what happened the last time, and another like that would be—I wish she were a little huskier, damn it—she's so—no, don't worry, I'm quite all right. Yes, I think that would be the best thing. Okay, make it as soon as you can, will you?"

He came back upstairs, looking bony and dishevelled in his pyjamas, and running his fingers through his sand-coloured hair. At the top of the stairs, he came face to face with Grandmother MacLeod, who was standing there in her quilted black satin dressing gown, her slight figure held straight and poised, as though she were unaware that her hair was bound grotesquely like white-feathered wings in the snare of her coarse night-time hairnet.

"What is it, Ewen?"

"It's all right, Mother. Beth's having—a little trouble. I'm going to take her into the hospital. You go back to bed."

"I told you," Grandmother MacLeod said in her clear voice, never loud, but distinct and ringing like the tap of a sterling teaspoon on a crystal goblet, "I did tell you, Ewen, did I not, that you should have got a girl in to help her with the housework? She would have rested more."

"I couldn't afford to get anyone in," my father said. "If you thought she should've rested more, why didn't you ever—oh God, I'm out of my mind tonight—just go back to bed, Mother, please. I must get back to Beth."

When my father went down to the front door to let Dr. Cates in, my need overcame my fear and I slipped into my parents' room. My mother's black hair, so neatly pinned up during the day, was startingly spread across the white pillowcase. I stared at her, not speaking, and then she smiled and I rushed from the doorway and buried my head upon her.

113

"It's all right, honey," she said. "Listen, Vanessa, the baby's just going to come a little early, that's all. You'll be all right. Grandmother MacLeod will be here."

"How can she get the meals?" I wailed, fixing on the first thing that came to mind. "She never cooks. She doesn't know how."

"Yes, she does," my mother said. "She can cook as well as anyone when she has to. She's never had to very much, that's all. Don't worry —she'll keep everything in order, and then some."

My father and Dr. Cates came in, and I had to go, without ever saying anything I had wanted to say. I went back to my own room and lay with the shadows all around me. I listened to the night murmurings that always went on in that house, sounds which never had a source, rafters and beams contracting in the dry air, perhaps, or mice in the walls, or a sparrow that had flown into the attic through the broken skylight there. After a while, although I would not have believed it possible, I slept.

The next morning I questioned my father. I believed him to be not only the best doctor in Manawaka, but also the best doctor in the whole of Manitoba, if not in the entire world, and the fact that he was not the one who was looking after my mother seemed to have something sinister about it.

"But it's always done that way, Vanessa," he explained. "Doctors never attend members of their own family. It's because they care so much about them, you see, and—"

"And what?" I insisted, alarmed at the way he had broken off. But my father did not reply. He stood there, and then he put on that difficult smile with which adults seek to conceal pain from children. I felt terrified, and ran to him, and he held me tightly.

"She's going to be fine," he said. "Honestly she is. Nessa, don't cry—"

Grandmother MacLeod appeared beside us, steel-spined despite her apparent fragility. She was wearing a purple silk dress and her ivory pendant. She looked as though she were all ready to go out for afternoon tea.

"Ewen, you're only encouraging the child to give way," she said. "Vanessa, big girls of ten don't make such a fuss about things. Come and get your breakfast. Now, Ewen, you're not to worry. I'll see to everything."

Summer holidays were not quite over, but I did not feel like going out to play with any of the kids. I was very superstitious, and I had the feeling that if I left the house, even for a few hours, some disaster would overtake my mother. I did not, of course, mention this feeling to Grandmother MacLeod, for she did not believe in the existence of fear, or if

114

she did, she never let on. I spent the morning morbidly, in seeking hidden places in the house. There were many of these—odd-shaped nooks under the stairs, small and loosely nailed-up doors at the back of clothes closets, leading to dusty tunnels and forgotten recesses in the heart of the house where the only things actually to be seen were drab oil paintings stacked upon the rafters, and trunks full of outmoded clothing and old photograph albums. But the unseen presences in these secret places I knew to be those of every person, young or old, who had ever belonged to the house and had died, including Uncle Roderick who got killed on the Somme, and the baby who would have been my sister if only she had managed to come to life. Grandfather MacLeod, who had died a year after I was born, was present in the house in more tangible form. At the top of the main stairs hung the mammoth picture of a darkly uniformed man riding upon a horse whose prancing stance and dilated nostrils suggested that the battle was not yet over, that it might indeed continue until Judgment Day. The stern man was actually the Duke of Wellington, but at the time I believed him to be my grandfather MacLeod, still keeping an eye on things.

We had moved in with Grandmother MacLeod when the Depression got bad and she could no longer afford a housekeeper, but the MacLeod house never seemed like home to me. Its dark red brick was grown over at the front with Virginia creeper that turned crimson in the fall, until you could hardly tell brick from leaves. It boasted a small tower in which Grandmother MacLeod kept a weedy collection of anaemic ferns. The verandah was embellished with a profusion of wrought-iron scrolls, and the circular rose-window upstairs contained glass of many colours which permitted an outlooking eye to see the world as a place of absolute sapphire or emerald, or if one wished to look with a jaundiced eye, a hateful yellow. In Grandmother MacLeod's opinion, their features gave the house style.

Inside, a multitude of doors led to rooms where my presence, if not actually forbidden, was not encouraged. One was Grandmother MacLeod's bedroom, with its stale and old-smelling air, the dim reek of medicines and lavender sachets. Here resided her monogrammed dresser silver, brush and mirror, nail-buffer and button hook and scissors, none of which must even be fingered by me now, for she meant to leave them to me in her will and intended to hand them over in the same flawless and unused condition in which they had always been kept. Here, too, were the silver-framed photographs of Uncle Roderick—as a child, as a boy, as a man in his Army uniform. The massive walnut spool bed had obviously been designed for queens or giants, and my tiny grandmother used to lie within it all day when she had migraine, contriving somehow to look like a giant queen.

The living room was another alien territory where I had to tread warily, for many valuable objects sat just-so on tables and mantelpiece, and dirt must not be tracked in upon the blue Chinese carpet with its birds in eternal motionless flight and its water-lily buds caught forever just before the point of opening. My mother was always nervous when I was in this room.

"Vanessa, honey," she would say, half apologetically, "why don't you go and play in the den, or upstairs?"

"Can't you leave her, Beth?" my father would say. "She's not doing any harm."

"I'm only thinking of the rug," my mother would say, glancing at Grandmother MacLeod, "and yesterday she nearly knocked the Dresden shepherdess off the mantel. I mean, she can't help it, Ewen, she has to run around—"

"Goddamn it, I know she can't help it," my father would growl, glaring at the smirking face of the Dresden shepherdess.

"I see no need to blaspheme, Ewen," Grandmother MacLeod would say quietly, and then my father would say he was sorry, and I would leave.

The day my mother went to the hospital, Grandmother MacLeod called me at lunch-time, and when I appeared, smudged with dust from the attic, she looked at me distastefully as though I had been a cockroach that had just crawled impertinently out of the woodwork.

"For mercy's sake, Vanessa, what have you been doing with yourself? Run and get washed this minute. Here, not that way—you use the back stairs, young lady. Get along now. Oh—your father phoned."

I swung around. "What did he say? How is she? Is the baby born?"

"Curiosity killed a cat," Grandmother MacLeod said, frowning. "I cannot understand Beth and Ewen telling you all these things, at your age. What sort of vulgar person you'll grow up to be, I dare not think. No, it's not born yet. Your mother's just the same. No change."

I looked at my grandmother, not wanting to appeal to her, but unable to stop myself. "Will she—will she be all right?"

Grandmother MacLeod straightened her already-straight back. "If I said definitely yes, Vanessa, that would be a lie, and the MacLeods do not tell lies, as I have tried to impress upon you before. What happens is God's will. The Lord giveth, and the Lord taketh away."

Appalled, I turned away so she would not see my face and my eyes.

116

Surprisingly, I heard her sigh and felt her papery white and perfectly manicured hand upon my shoulder.

"When your Uncle Roderick got killed," she said, "I thought I would die. But I didn't die, Vanessa."

At lunch, she chatted animatedly, and I realised she was trying to cheer me in the only way she knew.

"When I married your Grandfather MacLeod," she related, "he said to me, 'Eleanor, don't think because we're going to the prairies that I expect you to live roughly. You're used to a proper house, and you shall have one.' He was as good as his word. Before we'd been in Manawaka three years, he'd had this place built. He earned a good deal of money in his time, your grandfather. He soon had more patients than either of the other doctors. We ordered our dinner service and all our silver from Birks' in Toronto. We had resident help in those days, of course, and never had less than twelve guests for dinner parties. When I had a tea, it would always be twenty or thirty. Never any less than half a dozen different kinds of cake were ever served in this house. Well, no one seems to bother much these days. Too lazy, I suppose."

"Too broke," I suggested. "That's what Dad says."

"I can't bear slang," Grandmother MacLeod said. "If you mean hard up, why don't you say so? It's mainly a question of management, anyway. My accounts were always in good order, and so was my house. No unexpected expenses that couldn't be met, no fruit cellar running out of preserves before the winter was over. Do you know what my father used to say to me when I was a girl?"

"No," I said. "What?"

"God loves Order," Grandmother MacLeod replied with emphasis. "You remember that, Vanessa. God loves Order—he wants each one of us to set our house in order. I've never forgotten those words of my father's. I was a MacInnes before I got married. The MacInnes is a very ancient clan, the lairds of Morven and the constables of the Castle of Kinlochaline. Did you finish that book I gave you?"

"Yes," I said. Then, feeling some additional comment to be called for, "It was a swell book, Grandmother."

This was somewhat short of the truth. I had been hoping for her cairngorm brooch on my tenth birthday, and had received instead the plaid-bound volume entitled *The Clans and Tartans of Scotland*. Most of it was too boring to read, but I had looked up the motto of my own family and those of some of my friends' families. *Be then a wall of brass. Learn to suffer. Consider the end. Go carefully.* I had not found any of these slogans reassuring. What with Mavis Duncan learning to

117

suffer, and Laura Kennedy considering the end, and Patsy Drummond going carefully, and I spending my time in being a wall of brass, it did not seem to me that any of us were going to lead very interesting lives. I did not say this to Grandmother MacLeod.

"The MacInnes motto is *Pleasure Arises from Work*," I said.

"Yes," she agreed proudly. "And an excellent motto it is, too. One to bear in mind."

She rose from the table, rearranging on her bosom the looped ivory beads that held the pendant on which a fullblown ivory rose was stiffly carved.

"I hope Ewen will be pleased," she said.

"What at?"

"Didn't I tell you?" Grandmother MacLeod said. "I hired a girl this morning, for the housework. She's to start tomorrow."

When my father got home that evening, Grandmother MacLeod told him her good news. He ran one hand distractedly across his forehead.

"I'm sorry, Mother, but you'll just have to unhire her. I can't possibly pay anyone."

"It seems distinctly odd," Grandmother MacLeod snapped, "that you can afford to eat chicken four times a week."

"Those chickens," my father said in an exasperated voice, "are how people are paying their bills. The same with the eggs and the milk. That scrawny turkey that arrived yesterday was for Logan MacCardney's appendix, if you must know. We probably eat better than any family in Manawaka, except Niall Cameron's. People can't entirely dispense with doctors or undertakers. That doesn't mean to say I've got any cash. Look, Mother, I don't know what's happening with Beth. Paul thinks he may have to do a Caesarean. Can't we leave all this? Just leave the house alone. Don't touch it. What does it matter?"

"I have never lived in a messy house, Ewen," Grandmother MacLeod said, "and I don't intend to begin now."

"Oh Lord," my father said. "Well, I'll phone Edna, I guess, and see if she can give us a hand, although God knows she's got enough, with the Connor house and her parents to look after."

"I don't fancy having Edna Connor in to help," Grandmother MacLeod objected.

"Why not?" my father shouted. "She's Beth's sister, isn't she?"

"She speaks in such a slangy way," Grandmother MacLeod said. "I have never believed she was a good influence on Vanessa. And there is no need for you to raise your voice to me, Ewen, if you please."

118

I could hardly control my rage. I thought my father would surely rise to Aunt Edna's defence. But he did not.

"It'll be all right," he soothed her. "She'd only be here for part of the day, Mother. You could stay in your room."

Aunt Edna strode in the next morning. The sight of her bobbed black hair and her grin made me feel better at once. She hauled out the carpet sweeper and the weighted polisher and got to work. I dusted while she polished and swept, and we got through the living room and front hall in next to no time.

"Where's her royal highness, kiddo?" she enquired.

"In her room," I said. "She's reading the catalogue from Robinson & Cleaver."

"Good Glory, not again?" Aunt Edna cried. "The last time she ordered three linen tea-cloths and two dozen serviettes. It came to fourteen dollars. Your mother was absolutely frantic. I guess I shouldn't be saying this."

"I knew anyway," I assured her. "She was at the lace handkerchiefs section when I took up her coffee."

"Let's hope she stays there. Heaven forbid she should get onto the banqueting cloths. Well, at least she believes the Irish are good for two things—manual labour and linen-making. She's never forgotten Father used to be a blacksmith, before he got the hardware store. Can you beat it? I wish it didn't bother Beth."

"Does it?" I asked, and immediately realised this was a wrong move, for Aunt Edna was suddenly scrutinising me.

"We're making you grow up before your time," she said. "Don't pay any attention to me, Nessa. I must've got up on the wrong side of the bed this morning."

But I was unable to leave the subject.

"All the same," I said thoughtfully, "Grandmother MacLeod's family were the lairds of Morven and the constables of the Castle of Kinlochaline. I bet you didn't know that."

Aunt Edna snorted. "Castle, my foot. She was born in Ontario, just like your Grandfather Connor, and her father was a horse doctor. Come on, kiddo, we'd better shut up and get down to business here."

We worked in silence for a while.

"Aunt Edna—" I said at last, "what about Mother? Why won't they let me go and see her?"

"Kids aren't allowed to visit maternity patients. It's tough for you, I know that. Look, Nessa, don't worry. If it doesn't start tonight, they're going to do the operation. She's getting the best of care."

I stood there, holding the feather duster like a dead bird in my hands. I was not aware that I was going to speak until the words came out.

"I'm scared," I said.

Aunt Edna put her arms around me, and her face looked all at once stricken and empty of defences.

"Oh, honey, I'm scared, too," she said.

It was this way that Grandmother MacLeod found us when she came stepping lightly down into the front hall with the order in her hand for two dozen lace-bordered handkerchiefs of pure Irish linen.

I could not sleep that night, and when I went downstairs, I found my father in the den. I sat down on the hassock beside his chair, and he told me about the operation my mother was to have the next morning. He kept on saying it was not serious nowadays.

"But you're worried," I put in, as though seeking to explain why I was.

"I should at least have been able to keep from burdening you with it," he said in a distant voice, as though to himself. "If only the baby hadn't got itself twisted around—"

"Will it be born dead, like the little girl?"

"I don't know," my father said. "I hope not."

"She'd be disappointed, wouldn't she, if it was?" I said bleakly, wondering why I was not enough for her.

"Yes, she would," my father replied. "She won't be able to have any more, after this. It's partly on your account that she wants this one, Nessa. She doesn't want you to grow up without a brother or sister."

"As far as I'm concerned, she didn't need to bother," I retorted angrily.

My father laughed. "Well, let's talk about something else, and then maybe you'll be able to sleep. How did you and Grandmother make out today?"

"Oh, fine, I guess. What was Grandfather MacLeod like, Dad?"

"What did she tell you about him?"

"She said he made a lot of money in his time."

"Well, he wasn't any millionaire," my father said, "but I suppose he did quite well. That's not what I associate with him, though."

He reached across to the bookshelf, took out a small leather-bound volume and opened it. On the pages were mysterious marks, like doodling, only much neater and more patterned.

"What is it?" I asked.

"Greek," my father explained. "This is a play called *Antigone*. See,

120

here's the title in English. There's a whole stack of them on the shelves there. *Oedipus Rex. Electra. Medea.* They belonged to your Grandfather MacLeod. He used to read them often."

"Why?" I enquired, unable to understand why anyone would pore over those undecipherable signs.

"He was interested in them," my father said. "He must have been a lonely man, although it never struck me that way at the time. Sometimes a thing only hits you a long time afterwards."

"Why would he be lonely?" I wanted to know.

"He was the only person in Manawaka who could read these plays in the original Greek," my father said. "I don't suppose many people, if anyone, had even read them in English translations. Maybe he would have liked to be a classical scholar—I don't know. But his father was a doctor, so that's what he was. Maybe he would have liked to talk to somebody about these plays. They must have meant a lot to him."

It seemed to me that my father was talking oddly. There was a sadness in his voice that I had never heard before, and I longed to say something that would make him feel better, but I could not, because I did not know what was the matter.

"Can you read this kind of writing?" I asked hesitantly.

My father shook his head. "Nope. I was never very intellectual, I guess. Rod was always brighter than I, in school, but even he wasn't interested in learning Greek. Perhaps he would've been later, if he'd lived. As a kid, all I ever wanted to do was go into the merchant marine."

"Why didn't you, then?"

"Oh well," my father said offhandedly, "a kid who'd never seen the sea wouldn't have made much of a sailor. I might have turned out to be the seasick type."

I had lost interest now that he was speaking once more like himself.

"Grandmother MacLeod was pretty cross today about the girl," I remarked.

"I know," my father nodded. "Well, we must be as nice as we can to her, Nessa, and after a while she'll be all right."

Suddenly I did not care what I said.

"Why can't she be nice to us for a change?" I burst out. "We're always the ones who have to be nice to her."

My father put his hand down and slowly tilted my head until I was forced to look at him.

"Vanessa," he said, "she's had troubles in her life which you really don't know much about. That's why she gets migraine sometimes and has to go to bed. It's not easy for her these days, either—the house is still the

121

same, so she thinks other things should be, too. It hurts her when she finds they aren't."

"I don't see—" I began.

"Listen," my father said, "you know we were talking about what people are interested in, like Grandfather MacLeod being interested in Greek plays? Well, your grandmother was interested in being a lady, Nessa, and for a long time it seemed to her that she was one."

I thought of the Castle of Kinlochaline, and of horse doctors in Ontario.

"I didn't know—" I stammered.

"That's usually the trouble with most of us," my father said. "You go on up to bed now. I'll phone tomorrow from the hospital as soon as the operation's over."

I did sleep at last, and in my dreams I could hear the caught sparrow fluttering in the attic, and the sound of my mother crying, and the voices of the dead children.

My father did not phone until afternoon. Grandmother McLeod said I was being silly, for you could hear the phone ringing all over the house, but nevertheless I refused to move out of the den. I had never before examined my father's books, but now, at a loss for something to do, I took them out one by one and read snatches here and there. After I had been doing this for several hours, it dawned on me that most of the books were of the same kind. I looked again at the titles.

Seven-League Boots. Arabia Deserta. The Seven Pillars of Wisdom. Travels in Tibet. Count Lucknor the Sea Devil. And a hundred more. On a shelf by themselves were copies of the *National Geographic* magazine, which I looked at often enough, but never before with the puzzling compulsion which I felt now, as though I were on the verge of some discovery, something which I had to find out and yet did not want to know. I riffled through the picture-filled pages. Hibiscus and wild orchids grew in a soft-petalled confusion. The Himalayas stood lofty as gods, with the morning sun on their peaks of snow. Leopards snarled from the vined depths of a thousand jungles. Schooners buffetted their white sails like the wings of giant angels against the great sea winds.

"What on earth are you doing?" Grandmother MacLeod enquired waspishly, from the doorway. "You've got everything scattered all over the place. Pick it all up this minute, Vanessa, do you hear?"

So I picked up the books and magazines, and put them all neatly away, as I had been told to do.

When the telephone finally rang, I was afraid to answer it. At last I picked it up. My father sounded faraway, and the relief in his voice made it unsteady.

"It's okay, honey. Everything's fine. The boy was born alive and kicking after all. Your mother's pretty weak, but she's going to be all right."

I could hardly believe it. I did not want to talk to anyone. I wanted to be by myself, to assimilate the presence of my brother, towards whom, without ever having seen him yet, I felt such tenderness and such resentment.

That evening, Grandmother MacLeod approached my father, who, still dazed with the unexpected gift of neither life now being threatened, at first did not take her seriously when she asked what they planned to call the child.

"Oh, I don't know. Hank, maybe, or Joe. Fauntleroy, perhaps."

She ignored his levity.

"Ewen," she said, "I wish you would call him Roderick."

My father's face changed. "I'd rather not."

"I think you should," Grandmother MacLeod insisted, very quietly, but in a voice as pointed and precise as her silver nail-scissors.

"Don't you think Beth ought to decide?" my father asked.

"Beth will agree if you do."

My father did not bother to deny something that even I knew to be true. He did not say anything. Then Grandmother MacLeod's voice, astonishingly, faltered a little.

"It would mean a great deal to me," she said.

I remembered what she had told me—*When your Uncle Roderick got killed, I thought I would die. But I didn't die.* All at once, her feeling for that unknown dead man became a reality for me. And yet I held it against her, as well, for I could see that it had enabled her to win now.

"All right," my father said tiredly. "We'll call him Roderick."

Then, alarmingly, he threw back his head and laughed.

"Roderick Dhu!" he cried. "That's what you'll call him, isn't it? Black Roderick. Like before. Don't you remember? As though he were a character out of Sir Walter Scott, instead of an ordinary kid who—"

He broke off, and looked at her with a kind of desolation in his face.

"God, I'm sorry, Mother," he said. "I had no right to say that."

Grandmother MacLeod did not flinch, or tremble, or indicate that she felt anything at all.

"I accept your apology, Ewen," she said.

My mother had to stay in bed for several weeks after she arrived home. The baby's cot was kept in my parents' room, and I could go in and look at the small creature who lay there with his tightly closed fists and his feathery black hair. Aunt Edna came in to help each morning, and when she had finished the housework, she would have coffee with my mother. They kept the door closed, but this did not prevent me from eavesdropping, for there was an air register in the floor of the spare room, which was linked somehow with the register in my parents' room. If you put your ear to the iron grille, it was almost like a radio.

"Did you mind very much, Beth?" Aunt Edna was saying.

"Oh, it's not the name I mind," my mother replied. "It's just the fact that Ewen felt he had to. You know that Rod had only the sight of one eye, didn't you?"

"Sure, I knew. So what?"

"There was only a year and a half between Ewen and Rod," my mother said, "so they often went around together when they were youngsters. It was Ewen's air-rifle that did it."

"Oh Lord," Aunt Edna said heavily. "I suppose she always blamed him?"

"No, I don't think it was so much that, really. It was how he felt himself. I think he even used to wonder sometimes if—but people shouldn't let themselves think like that, or they'd go crazy. Accidents do happen, after all. When the war came, Ewen joined up first. Rod should never have been in the Army at all, but he couldn't wait to get in. He must have lied about his eyesight. It wasn't so very noticeable unless you looked at him closely, and I don't suppose the medicals were very thorough in those days. He got in as a gunner, and Ewen applied to have him in the same company. He thought he might be able to watch out for him, I guess, Rod being—at a disadvantage. They were both only kids. Ewen was nineteen and Rod was eighteen when they went to France. And then the Somme. I don't know, Edna, I think Ewen felt that if Rod had had proper sight, or if he hadn't been in the same outfit and had been sent somewhere else—you know how people always think these things afterwards, not that it's ever a bit of use. Ewen wasn't there when Rod got hit. They'd lost each other somehow, and Ewen was looking for him, not bothering about anything else, you know, just frantically looking. Then he stumbled across him quite by chance. Rod was still alive, but—"

"Stop it, Beth," Aunt Edna said. "You're only upsetting yourself."

"Ewen never spoke of it to me," my mother went on, "until once his mother showed me the letter he'd written to her at the time. It was a peculiar letter, almost formal, saying how gallantly Rod had died, and all that. I guess I shouldn't have, but I told him she'd shown it to me. He was very angry that she had. And then, as though for some reason he

124

were terribly ashamed, he said—*I had to write something to her, but men don't really die like that, Beth. It wasn't that way at all.* It was only after the war that he decided to came back and study medicine and go into practice with his father."

"Had Rod meant to? Aunt Edna asked.

"I don't know," my mother said slowly. "I never felt I should ask Ewen that."

Aunt Edna was gathering up the coffee things, for I could hear the clash of cups and saucers being stacked on the tray.

"You know what I heard her say to Vanessa once, Beth? *The Mac-Leods never tell lies.* Those were her exact words. Even then, I didn't know whether to laugh or cry."

"Please, Edna—" my mother sounded worn out now. "Don't."

"Oh Glory," Aunt Edna said remorsefully, "I've got all the delicacy of a two-ton truck. I didn't mean Ewen, for heaven's sake. That wasn't what I meant at all. Here, let me plump up your pillows for you."

Then the baby began to cry, so I could not hear anything more of interest. I took my bike and went out beyond Manawaka, riding aimlessly along the gravel highway. It was late summer, and the wheat had changed colour, but instead of being high and bronzed in the fields, it was stunted and desiccated, for there had been no rain again this year. But in the bluff where I stopped and crawled under the barbed wire fence and lay stretched out on the grass, the plentiful poplar leaves were turning to a luminous yellow and shone like church windows in the sun. I put my head down very close to the earth and looked at what was going on there. Grasshoppers with enormous eyes ticked and twitched around me, as though the dry air were perfect for their purposes. A ladybird laboured mightily to climb a blade of grass, fell off, and started all over again, seeming to be unaware that she possessed wings and could have flown up.

I thought of the accidents that might easily happen to a person—or, of course, might not happen, might happen to somebody else. I thought of the dead baby, my sister, who might as easily have been I. Would she, then, have been lying here in my place, the sharp grass making its small toothmarks on her brown arms, the sun warming her to the heart? I thought of the leather-bound volumes of Greek, and the six different kinds of iced cakes that used to be offered always in the MacLeod house, and the pictures of leopards and green seas. I thought of my brother, who had been born alive after all, and now had been given his life's name.

I could not really comprehend these things, but I sensed their strangeness, their disarray. I felt that whatever God might love in this world, it was certainly not order.

TIME AND THE NARRATIVE VOICE

The treatment of time and the handling of the narrative voice—these two things are of paramount importance to me in the writing of fiction. Oddly enough, although they might seem to be two quite separate aspects of technique, in fact they are inextricably bound together. When I say "time," I don't mean clock-time, in this context, nor do I mean any kind of absolute time—which I don't believe to exist, in any event. I mean historical time, variable and fluctuating.

In any work of fiction, the span of time present in the story is not only as long as the time-span of every character's life and memory; it also represents everything acquired and passed on in a kind of memory-heritage from one generation to another. The time which is present in any story, therefore, must—by implication at least—include not only the totality of the characters' lives but also the inherited time of perhaps two or even three past generations, in terms of parents' and grandparents' recollections, and the much much longer past which has become legend, the past of a collective cultural memory. Obviously, not all of this can be conveyed in a single piece of prose. Some of it can only be hinted at; some of it may not be touched on at all. Nevertheless, it is *there* because it exists in the minds of the characters. How can one even begin to convey this sense of time? What parts of the time-span should be conveyed? These are questions which I always find enormously troubling, and before beginning any piece of writing, I tend to brood for quite a long time (clockwise) on these things. Not that the brooding does very much good, usually, or perhaps it bears fruit at some unrecognized subconscious level, because when the writing begins, a process of selection takes place in a way not consciously chosen, and this is where the long-time-span implicit in every story or novel is directly and intimately related to the narrative voice.

Most of the fiction I have written in recent years has been written in the first person, with the main character assuming the narrative voice. Even when I have written in the third person, as I did in part of my novel *The Fire-Dwellers*, it is really a first-person narrative which happens to be written in the third person, for the narrative voice even here is essentially that of the main character, and the writer does not enter in as commentator. Some people hold the erroneous belief that this kind of fiction is an evasion—the writer is hiding behind a mask, namely one of the characters. Untrue. The writer is every bit as vulnerable here as in directly autobiographical fiction. The character is not a mask but an individual, separate from the writer. At the same time, the character is one of the writer's voices and selves, and fiction writers tend to have a mental trunk full of these—in writers, this quality is known as richness of imagination; in certain inmates of mental hospitals it has other names, the only significant difference being that writers are creating their private worlds with the ultimate hope of throwing open the doors to other humans. This means of writing fiction, oriented almost totally towards an individual character, is obviously not the only way, but it appears to be the only way I can write.

Once the narrative voice is truly established—that is, once the writer has listened, really listened, to the speech and idiom and outlook of the character—it is then not the writer but the character who, by some process of transferal, bears the responsibility for the treatment of time within the work. It is the character who chooses which parts of the personal past, the family past and the ancestral past have to be revealed in order for the present to be realized and the future to happen. This is not a morbid dwelling on the past on the part of the writer or the character. It is, rather, an expression of the feeling which I strongly hold about time—that the past and the future are both always present, *present* in both senses of the word, always now and always here with us. It is only through the individual presence of the characters that the writer can hope to convey even a fragment of this sense of time, and this is one reason, among others, why it is so desperately important to discover the true narrative voice—which really means knowing the characters so well that one can take on their past, their thoughts, their responses, can in effect for awhile *become* them. It has sometimes occurred to me that I must be a kind of Method writer, in the same way that some actors become the characters they play for the moments when they are portraying these characters. I didn't plan it this way, and possibly it sounds like gibberish, but this is how it appears to take place.

Theorizing, by itself, is meaningless in connection with fiction, just as any concept of form is meaningless in isolation from the flesh and blood of content and personality, just as a skelton is only dry bone by itself but when it exists inside a living being it provides the support for the whole creature. I'll try to show something of what I mean about time and voice by reference to the two stories of mine which appear in this book.

These stories are part of a collection called *A Bird in the House*, eight in all, published separately before they were collected in a single volume, but conceived from the beginning as a related group. Each story is self-contained in the sense that it is definitely a short story and not a chapter from a novel, but the net effect is not unlike that of a novel. Structurally, however, these stories as a group are totally unlike a novel. I think the outlines of a novel (mine, anyway) and those of a group of stories such as these interrelated ones may be approximately represented in visual terms. In a novel, one might perhaps imagine the various themes and experiences and the interaction of characters with one another and with themselves as a series of wavy lines, converging, separating, touching, drawing apart, but moving in a *horizontal* direction. The short stories have flow-lines which are different. They move very close together but parallel and in a *vertical* direction. Each story takes the girl Vanessa along some specific course of her life and each follows that particular thread closely, but the threads are presented separately and not simultaneously. To this extent, the structure of these stories is a good deal simpler than that of a novel. Nevertheless, the relationship of time and the narrative voice can be seen just as plainly in the stories as in a novel.

"To Set Our House in Order" takes place when Vanessa is ten years old. Her age remains constant throughout the story. The actual time-span of the story itself is short, a few days in her life, immediately before, during and after the birth of her brother. The things which happen on the surface are simple, but the things that happen inside Vanessa's head are more complex.

The narrative voice is, of course, that of Vanessa herself, but an older Vanessa, herself grown up, remembering how it was when she was ten. When I was trying to write this story, I felt as I did with all the stories in *A Bird in the House*, that this particular narrative device was a tricky one, and I cannot even now personally judge how well it succeeds. What I tried to do was definitely *not* to tell the story as though it were being narrated by a child. This would have been impossible for me and also would have meant denying the story one of its dimensions, a time-dimension, the viewing from a distance of events which had happened in childhood. The narrative voice had to be that of an older Vanessa, but at the same time the narration had to be done in such a way that the ten-year-old would be conveyed. The narrative voice, therefore, had to speak as though from two points in time, simultaneously.

Given this double sense of time-present, Vanessa herself had to recollect those things which were most meaningful to her, and in doing so, she reveals (at least I hope she does to the reader as she does to me) what the story is really about. It is actually a story about the generations, about the pain and bewilderment of one's knowledge of other people, about the reality of other people which is one way of realizing one's own reality, about the fluctuating and accidental quality of life (God really doesn't love Order), and perhaps more than anything, about the strangeness and mystery of the very concepts of *past, present* and *future*. Who is Vanessa's father? The doctor who is struggling to support his family during the depression and who seems a pillar of strength to the little girl? Or the man who has collected dozens of travel books because once he passionately wanted to go far beyond Manawaka and now knows he won't? Or the boy who long ago half-blinded his brother accidentally with an air-rifle? Or the nineteen-year-old soldier who watched his brother die in the First World War? Ewen is all of these, and many many more, and in the story Vanessa has the sudden painful knowledge of his reality and his intricacy as a person, bearing with him the mental baggage of a lifetime, as all people do, and as she will have to do. The events of the story will become (and have become, to the older Vanessa) part of her mental baggage, part of her own spiritual fabric. Similarly, her father passes on to her some actual sense of her grandparents, his parents—the adamant Grandmother MacLeod, whose need it has been to appear a lady in her own image of herself; the dead Grandfather MacLeod, who momentarily lives for his granddaughter when she sees for the first time the loneliness of a man who could read the Greek tragedies in their original language and who never knew anyone in the small prairie town with whom he could communicate.

In "The Loons," the narrative voice is also that of the older Vanessa, but in her portrayal of herself in past years, she ranges in age from eleven to eighteen. This meant, of course, that the tone of the narration had to change as Vanessa recalled herself at different ages, and this meant, for me, trying to feel my way into her mind at each age. Here again, the narrative voice chooses what will be recalled, and here again, the element of time is of great importance in the story. The eleven-year-old Vanessa sees the Métis girl, Piquette Tonnerre, in terms of romanticized notions of Indians, and is hurt when Piquette does not respond in the expected way. That summer lies submerged in Vanessa's mind until she encounters Piquette at a later time, but even then her reaction is one mainly of embarrassment and pity, not any real touching, and Piquette's long experience of hurt precludes anything except self-protectiveness on her part. It is only when Vanessa hears of Piquette's death that she realizes that she, too, like the entire town, is in part responsible. But the harm and alienation started a long way back, longer even than the semi-mythical figure of Piquette's grandfather, Jules Tonnerre, who fought with Riel at Batoche. The loons, recurring in the story both in their presence and in their absence, are connected to an ancestral past which belongs to Piquette, and the older Vanessa can see the irony of the only way in which Piquette's people are recognized by the community, in the changing of the name Diamond Lake to the more tourist-appealing Lake Wapakata.

What I said earlier may perhaps be more clearly seen now to show a little of the relationship between the narrative voice and the treatment of time—it is the character who chooses which parts of the personal past, the family past and the ancestral past have to be revealed in order for the present to be realized and the future to happen.

MARGARET LAURENCE

John Metcalf

John Metcalf was born in Carlisle, England, in 1938. He attended Bristol University and came to Canada a year after graduating. He has worked as a teacher of English in and around Montreal. In 1965 he married Gale Courey: they have a daughter, Elizabeth.

Metcalf's work has been published in such magazines as *West Coast Review, Prism, Tamarack,* and *Fiddlehead* and broadcast on the CBC. Stories have been included in recent Canadian, American and English anthologies.

Bibliography

New Canadian Writing 1969. Clarke, Irwin and Co. Ltd., Toronto, 1969. (Stories) This book contains five stories by Metcalf, four by D. O. Spettigue, and three by C. J. Newman.

The Lady Who Sold Furniture. Clarke, Irwin and Co. Ltd., Toronto, 1970. (Stories)

Going Down Slow. McClelland and Stewart, Toronto, 1972. (Novel)

The Children Green and Golden

David waited outside the gate while Pete went up the steps to the front door. They didn't like going to Rory's house because his mother was funny. She always said things like, "So you are Rory's little friends," and she never seemed to get dressed. She was always wearing a nightdress and her toe-nails were bright red. Rory's father had gone away. Rory used to steal money from her purse and one day he had watched her through the keyhole when she was having a bath.

"Good morning, Mrs. Callaghan. Can Rory come out, please?"

"Rory! Rory, darling! Your friends are here for you."

They walked slowly along the hot pavement, towels under their arms and hands in pockets, towards the path that led down to the Promenade. The sun was already melting the tar between the paving-stones and forcing it up into shining bubbles. In the gardens, the sweet-chestnut trees with their mounds of cool leaves were quite still in the morning heat. Pete was rattling a careless stick along the slats of the fences. Turning to the others he said, "Who's got any money on them?"

"I've got a couple of bob," said Rory.

"Let's get ten *Weights.*"

"No. *Park Drive*. They're stronger."

David stopped stamping on the tar bubbles and said, "And three banana ices at Rossi's."

"Whose money *is* it?" said Rory.

"All right. All right," said David. "She give it to you?"

"No, I nicked it. So what? *You* got any money?"

"Yes. It just so happens that I have."

"Show us then."

David slipped back behind Rory and Pete, pretending to grope in his pocket, and flicked his towel at the back of Rory's head. As David ran out into the road Rory shouted, "You wait, sodguts," and they chased each other back and forth across the road fighting with their towels. Suddenly Pete shouted, "Squirrel!" and the three of them searched the gutter for stones and pebbles.

When they neared the cliff-path Pete said, "Let's go along the top and through the park."

"What about going across the golf-course? See if we can find some balls."

"Yes, but if we go through the park we can have a deck at the ponds, can't we?"

They strolled along the cliff-top path leading to the park, stopping every now and then to throw stones at the grey squirrels or to hurl their pen-knives into the tree trunks. The morning was heavy with the smell of pine trees and the sun came in brilliant yellow patches through their shade. David stabbed at the top of a fence post but the blade of his knife closed and cut his little finger.

They stopped at the wooden kiosk by the park gates and Rory said to the old man, "Can I have ten *Park Drive*, please?"

"I can't sell cigarettes to minors, son. You can see the notice for yourself."

"Oh, they're not for me. They're for my Dad. He's waiting down on the beach."

"Well if you're sure they're not for you. . . ."

Rory called to David, "Did he say he wanted matches?"

"No. He's got his lighter, hasn't he?"

"Yes. That's all, thank you."

And they strolled on into the park. The park-benches were grouped around two oblong fish-ponds which were covered with water-lilies. The ponds were teeming with orange and silver goldfish, huge lazy fish lying near the surface under the lily-pads. The park-keeper in his brown suit walked round and round.

"You could get them with a spear," said Pete. "One of those with three prongs like they use for dabfish."

"Or nightlines," said David.

"Bombs would be best," said Rory. "You could climb in at night and dynamite them."

They stood staring at the fish. Suddenly Rory said, "Come on. Let's get going. The parkie's coming and we don't want to be recognized."

They left the park and wandered down the path towards the dunes.

"Shall we go to the cliff?" said Pete.

"Hey, yes. Perhaps those swifts are nesting again."

"They're not swifts," said Pete. "They're swallows."

"Swifts. You can tell by the shape of the tail."

"Swallows. They're swallows, I tell you. Didn't you see the blue on their backs?"

"It'd be difficult to get up there," said Rory. "You'd need ropes and climbing irons. Or you could lower someone on a rope from the top."

They were still arguing as the path petered out into the loose sand of the dunes. The coarse silver-green dune grass cut against their bare legs. Suddenly Rory checked them with an outstretched hand. He pointed over to the right where, half-hidden behind a rise, a man and woman lay in the sun. He gestured Pete to the right and David to the left and they crouched low and worked their way towards the dune. When they were getting close, all three sank flat into the sand and wormed their way nearer.

They peered over the edge into the hollow. The man was lying beside the woman, one arm around her. The straps of her bathing costume were undone and the man was rubbing sun-tan oil on her back. They stared at the white bulge of her breasts which the loosened costume revealed. When she rolled over completely onto her stomach Rory gestured them back. They slid carefully down the bank. He raised his eyebrows in question and Pete and David nodded. Pete was biting on his fingers to keep from laughing. Rory nodded and they sprang up in sight of the couple and he shouted, "Give her a big belly!"

And then they were running. Running with their mouths open and their hearts pounding; running and stumbling for dear life through the heavy sand of the dunes. They did not look back, but ran and ran until the blood pounded in their temples and their throats were dry and aching and they could run no more. Eventually, with shaking legs, they collapsed into the dunes near their favourite cliff.

David was fighting for breath and crying tears of laughter at the same time. Pete shouted, in a voice trembling with laughter, "Give her a big belly!" and hurled himself upon Rory. They wrestled backwards and forwards until Pete threw Rory and sat on his chest, pinning his arms to the ground. He said, "Did you see them coming after us, Dave?"

"I didn't look. I was going too fast."

"Hey, get off, Pete, you silly bugger. You're hurting."

"Did you see him, Rory?"

Rory sprang to his feet, and shook the sand out of his hair. "No. I didn't happen to be watching."

"He was coming fast. I think we just made it. Hey, what if he'd caught us?"

"There's three of us. We could have got him down."

"We'd have beat him up."

"We'd have given him a rabbit punch."

"Hit him right in the neck with a rabbit punch."

They settled back, using their towels as pillows, and stared up into the blue of the sky. Gulls dipped and floated lazily over the edge of the cliff towards the sea. David took off his shoes and socks and dug his feet into the sand, letting it trickle between his toes. He unbuttoned his shirt to let the heat sink into his chest and stomach and wriggled his shoulders in the loose sand until he was comfortable. It was so quiet they could hear the whisper of the dune grass. High up against the sandstone cliff the black shapes of the swallows flickered like the blink of an eyelash. The heat seemed to roll in waves.

Pete said, "Are you going in today, Dave?" David only grunted.

"Are you?"

"Dunno."

"Got your cozzie?"

"Mmmm. Got it on."

Rory was lying on his stomach looking over the edge of the low cliff. Below, there was a level stretch of beach, an arc contained in the curve of the cliffs.

"Hey! Come and look at this," called Rory.

"What?"

"Come and look."

Near the tide-line a few small children were playing with buckets and spades, but nearer to the foot of the cliff a man and woman were putting up a sort of flag or banner which drooped between two poles. The boys could not read what it said because it faced out towards the beach. Near the banner were two boxes, like huge suitcases.

"What do you think they're doing?" said Rory.

"Dunno. Can't see from here."

"Let's go down and look."

"Shall we?"

"Yes, come on. We can look at the swallow nests later."

With their towels round their necks, they scrambled down the fault where the cliff had crumbled into large boulders and heaps of rubble, and ran the final few yards onto the beach.

Uncle Michael held up his handkerchief. "On your marks!" The boys and girls forced their toes into the sand. "Get set!" A boy with ginger hair called Brian made a false start.

"Get set!"

"Go!"

They sprinted towards the woman called Auntie Mary who was standing holding another handkerchief to mark the finishing line. Pete finished first and Uncle Michael shouted, "Oh, well done! Well done. Peter, isn't it? A beautiful race!"

He trotted up to the group of boys and girls who were standing around Auntie Mary. "Who came second and third?" he asked.

"These two were tied for second place," said Auntie Mary. "John and. . . ."

135

"David."

"Oh, yes. David."

"Well I think an effort like that deserves a prize," said Uncle Michael. "So I'm going to give Peter here two cards and John and David one each. That'll make a grand start for your album."

He gave the cards to the winners and Rory said to Pete, "What did you get?" They looked at the coloured pictures and read the titles. One was *Christ Cleanses the Temple of the Money-Changers,* and the other was *Christ Baptized of John the Baptist.*

Uncle Michael, clapping his hands for attention, said, "Now then, everybody. You're not too tired, are you? Let's play a quick game of Leap-Frog. Yes, *and* you smaller ones. It's great fun. Come along, now. Let's make a long line."

Rory said to Pete, "Bloody hot, isn't it?"

Bending down, hands braced on knees, Uncle Michael shouted, "I'll be Frog."

They played energetically for a few minutes until one of the bigger boys banged his knee against a small boy's head. The game quickly collapsed. While Auntie Mary held the boy and stroked his hair, the others drifted away into small groups. A few chased each other throwing sand until Uncle Michael called, "I say, steady on there. We don't want anyone to get sand in their eyes, do we?" Four of the boys were holding a competition to see who could do the most push-ups. A girl called Mary kept slapping her young sister and saying, "Just wait till I get you home." A small boy in a blue bathing-costume was quietly burying a small girl.

David said to Brian, the boy with ginger hair, "What school do you go to?"

"Brentwood Junior."

"Pete and Rory and me go to Parkview Junior."

"You in the scholarship class?"

"Yes, you?"

Uncle Michael came and interrupted their conversation. "Would you chaps like to gather everyone together for me," he said. "We're going to have a story next."

Auntie Mary said to the little boy, "Big boys don't cry, do they?"

"No," said the little boy.

"And you don't want to be a cry-baby, do you?"

"No," snuffed the little boy.

"And if you're brave, perhaps we'll give you a present. Would you like that?"

"Yes."

"A nice present for your book?"

The boy smiled watery through the big tears.

"There you are," she said. "Shall we go and join the others now?"

Holding his hand she walked towards the semi-circle sitting around Uncle Michael. He was wearing grey flannels and a white shirt, open at the neck, with a paisley choker. Behind him hung the drooping banner which read SUFFER THE CHILDREN CAMPAIGN.

Rory whispered to Pete, "See that kid. She gave him a card."

"That's not fair, is it?"

"Well, I mean he didn't win it, did he?"

"Come along, now!" said Uncle Michael. "We can't have everyone talking at once, can we?" He smiled at Pete and Rory. "Now. If we're all listening. I'm going to tell you a story.

"Once there was a little boy, just like some of you, and his name was Jack. But he wasn't *quite* like you because, you see, nobody loved him. His father used to drink and when he was drunk he would sometimes beat Jack for no reason at all. You see, he wasn't *in control of himself*. And that's what drinking can do for you. . . ." Uncle Michael stopped, and looked seriously and slowly around the group.

"And what about Jack's mother? Well, Jack's mother had nine other children to look after and she was too tired to pay a lot of attention to poor Jack. So what do you think poor Jack decided to do? He felt *so* unhappy that one night, after his father and mother had gone to bed, he packed up the few clothes he had and put them in his suitcase and he. . . . Well, what do you think he was going to do?"

One of the small boys put up his hand and said, "My name is Andrew and I think he was going to run away."

"Yes. That's right. Jack was *so* unhappy he was going to run away! He was going to run away to LONDON. But poor Jack hadn't any money so he had to try and get a lift in a car or on a lorry. So he stood by the side of the road for hours and hours but nobody stopped and he was getting colder and colder. And then a very strange thing happened! A car stopped and who do you think was driving it?"

Andrew said, "His father."

"No. No, you'll never guess. It was the minister of the church that Jack attended! And so the minister said, 'Hello, Jack, my lad. Where are you off to at this time of night?' And Jack told him his story."

"Silly bastard," whispered Rory.

" 'Cheer up, Jack,' said the minister, when he'd finished. 'Someone loves you very much.' Jack stared at the minister but he couldn't think

137

who it might be. . . . Can any of you think who it was who loved Jack so much?"

Uncle Michael smiled at the silent group in front of him, the sunlight glinting on his spectacles.

"No? Can't anybody guess? Well Jack couldn't either. So the minister said, 'There's someone who loves each and every one of us, Jack, and that someone is God. Why, He must have sent me to you tonight when you were so unhappy.' And the minister told Jack how God really does love us all, and especially boys and girls. And the minister took Jack home with him and gave him a cup of hot chocolate before he phoned his father."

"Told you," whispered Rory.

"And after that, whenever Jack felt unhappy he always prayed to God as the minister had taught him and he always felt at peace.

"And now I want everyone to close their eyes and we're going to say the prayer that Jack said."

Led by Uncle Michael they recited the Lord's Prayer. As soon as the prayer was finished he nodded to Auntie Mary who sat down at the harmonium and started to play.

"No, it isn't a piano. It's a sort of organ," he explained as they all gathered round. "And how would you like to sing a few songs? I think we could persuade Auntie Mary to play for us." He smiled across at her, his eyes twinkling. "And I've even got some papers here with the words on."

Pete looked across at Rory and said, "I'm afraid we'll have to be going now. We have to be back for tea."

"That's fine, boys," smiled Uncle Michael. "But you'll come again tomorrow, won't you? Remember the badges are for attending three days in a row."

"Oh, yes," said David. "We'll see you tomorrow. Bye."

"See you," said Brian.

As they walked away and started to climb the cliff the singing started. At first it was thin and ragged but it soon gathered strength drowning the shush of the sea and the cries of the gulls.

A sunbeam, a sunbeam,
Jesus wants me for a sunbeam,
A sunbeam, a sunbeam,
I'll be a sunbeam for Him.

David, Pete and Rory received the badges on their third day. The badges were blue with the letters S.C.C. in gilt. Each badge was in a tiny box and wrapped in tissue-paper.

For each day they received a picture-card. Each album had fifty spaces and after attending for five days the empty slots seemed endless. "It'd take us years," said Pete. "Yes, but you can win 'em," David said.

Rory had ten cards but he'd given one of the small boys two piggy-backs in return for an *Agony in the Garden* and a *Do This in Remembrance of Me.*

The morning was already hot as they turned into the park on the cliff-top. They did not linger by the fishponds as they used to do, but followed the path that led out onto the dunes. Near the park-gates Pete stopped and bent over a poplar-sapling, turning the silver underside of the leaves.

"What are you doing?"

"Looking for hawkmoth caterpillars. Poplar hawks. Jim said he'd got some near here last Saturday."

"Oh, come on, Pete. We haven't got time now."

"All right, all right. What's so important?"

"You know he likes us there early," said David.

"Oh, piss," said Pete. "You go on and I'll catch you up."

When they neared the sandstone cliff they could hear the sounds of the children playing and the voice of Auntie Mary. She was playing tag with four little girls and the small boy called Andrew. The little girls ran after her squealing with delight and Auntie Mary kept shouting, "You can't catch *me*! You can't catch *me*!"

Uncle Michael was striding along the beach with his head bent. As they scrambled down the last few yards and approached him he was saying ". . . nineteen, twenty, twenty-one, twenty-two. . . ." They followed him. He stopped at "twenty-five" and ground his heel into the sand.

"Good morning, boys. Isn't Peter with you today?"

"Yes, he's just coming. What are you doing?"

"Marking out a pitch. Would you like to help me before the others get here?"

"O.K. What do you want us to do?"

"Get a stick and draw lines from the four marks I've made. It's for a game of touch football."

As they edged the first line they saw Pete climbing down the cliff. A voice behind them said, "It's no use whining. You're here and you're going to stay here." Mary and her little sister. Rory called to her, "Hey! You've got a big spot on your back!" She turned and blushed. "I'm not going to speak to you so you needn't think that I am," she said. "So there."

Pete sauntered up to them holding a *Craven A* packet in his hand.

"Where you been?"

"Up the top."

"You'd better put those fags away," said David.

Peter grinned. "I haven't got any fags."

"What is it?"

"What you got, Pete?"

They dropped the sticks and looked at the packet as Pete eased it open. Inside was a Poplar-hawk caterpillar. It was about two inches long and beautifully coloured. The back was a soft dove-grey and the underside a pale lime-green. Along its sides were rows of scarlet dots like eyes.

"Isn't it a beauty?" said Pete.

"Are there any more?"

"Hey, come on. Let's go."

"I didn't *see* any more."

"Come on, you chaps," a voice shouted. "Let's get that marking finished."

"Oh, shut-up!" said Rory quietly.

"I'm going to keep it until it turns into a moth," said Pete.

"Isn't it *big*!" said David.

They watched the caterpillar in fascination as it reared its head and lifted the front part of its body off the ground, weaving from side to side as though seeing dimly with the scarlet eyes of its markings.

"Come on, you three!" shouted Uncle Michael.

"*All right!*" shouted Rory.

While they had been talking most of the others had arrived. Uncle Michael shepherded the crowd over towards the pitch and explained the rules of the game. Auntie Mary had taken the small children and was playing "Black Pudding" with them.

"Now remember!" shouted Uncle Michael. "All passes must be *forward* passes. Brian! Let's have you over here as captain of Red Team." He put his hand round Brian's shoulder and looked at the group in front of him. "And . . . Rory . . . you're Blue Team, here." He took a sixpence from his pocket and spun it into the air. "Call! Heads it is. Brian, you have first pick."

The teams were quickly sorted out. Rory, as he chose last, was left with the thin boy with thick glasses who ran with his arms held at a funny angle. Punctuated by silver blasts on Uncle Michael's whistle, the game got under way. There were seven players on each side and the ball was fumbled and hassled from end to end of the pitch. Every few minutes Uncle Michael would shout, "Oh, well done! A beautiful pass! Play *up*, Blue Team!"

Red Team was four goals ahead and most of the players were crowded down around Rory's goal when Peter suddenly caught the ball which Rory had flicked out from the centre of the struggling mob. Rory and he started to run up the nearly empty pitch towards Brian's goal. Three players sprinted towards Peter to intercept him. "Pete!" yelled Rory. "Over here! Pass over here. *Pass*, you silly bastard!"

The silver whistle cut the game short. Uncle Michael trotted out into the centre of the pitch. "Rory?" he called. "That isn't the sort of language we use, is it? Is it, Rory?"

"No."

"Now, I must insist that you apologize to Peter and be a good sports-man about it."

Rory stared at him incredulously. Then turning towards Peter, he said, "I'm sorry I called you a. . . ."

"Rory!"

"I'm sorry I was rude to you."

"Now, I don't want to cut your game short," said Uncle Michael, "but Auntie Mary and I have prepared a surprise for you, so if we all sit down for a few minutes to catch our breath I can tell you about it after the story."

The group of boys and girls trailed over towards the harmonium where Auntie Mary already had the small children sitting quietly. David and Pete sat at one end of the semi-circle so that they were partially hidden by the harmonium. Uncle Michael and Auntie Mary came along the line handing out the picture-cards. Pete already had the cigarette-packet open on the sand by his side. He put his card into his shirt-pocket and uncovered the cigarette-packet again. David's card was *The Soldiers Dice For Jesus's Robe.*

"Hey Pete."

"What?"

"Do you want to swap me?"

"Swap what?"

"My card for the caterpillar."

"You've got a hope!" laughed Peter.

Uncle Michael clapped his hands sharply to silence the chatter and said, smiling, "Now, when we're all ready, I'm going to tell you a story. It's not a new story. Actually, it's a very old one, one that Jesus himself told. It's called the *Parable of the Sower.* Who knows what a parable is? Anybody? Yes? Charles, isn't it?"

The thin boy with thick glasses said, "Well it's sort of a story . . . and it isn't really . . . well, I mean. . . ." He picked nervously at the cluster of white spots near his lip. ". . . well it isn't about what it's about."

"Good!" said Uncle Michael. "That's right. It's a story that has two meanings. And now here's the story just as Our Lord told it.

"Once upon a time, a man was sowing wheat in his field and as he threw each handful some of the seeds fell in different places.

"Some of the seeds fell onto the path that ran along the side of his field and it was crushed underfoot as the people walked along or it was eaten by the crows and sparrows.

"And some of the seeds fell onto places where there were lots of stones and rocks and. . . ."

—"Why do you think it's got that little horn on top of its head?" whispered David.

"It's to make it look fierce," said Pete, "so birds won't peck at it."

"Does it just eat poplar leaves?"

"Yes, but it should be nearly ready to turn into a cocoon now."

"And some of the seeds fell into good ground and grew up into strong plants that gave a hundred seeds from the *one* they had grown from."

He paused, and there was silence. "Now what is the story *really* about?" There was no reply. Suddenly in the silence Rory said, "*I* don't know."

Uncle Michael's face tightened slightly and then he smiled again as he said, "Is there anybody who *does* know?"

Rory flicked sand at Mary's back, hoping that she would turn around, but she took no notice. The voice went on and on. Rory watched the slow swoop of a gull as it dipped down over the cliff. At the edge of the shore where the waves ran up and frothed upon the sand, he could just see the white, scurrying shapes of sand-pipers.

"And the rocky ground stands for the sort of people who are very enthusiastic at first but give way as soon as temptation comes along. I expect that all of you. . . ."

The caterpillar humped its body and started to flow over the edge of the cigarette-packet. Its body creased into a row of folds like a tiny concertina. Pete headed it off with a matchstick.

". . . close our eyes and pray to our Lord Jesus that we may be like the *good* ground.

"Oh God, Our Holy Father, look down on these thy little ones, and grant that they, in thy infinite Mercy, may find Salvation and that eternal peace which Thou hast promised. Lead them, guide them, shelter them under thy wings of Love; take away from them the burden of their Sin,

142

that they may, at the last, enter Thy Kingdom, perfect in Thy Holy Love. . . . Amen."

After a slight pause, Uncle Michael raised his head and said in a bright voice, "And now boys and girls, Auntie Mary is going to tell us about the surprise she has for us."

Auntie Mary moved across to stand by Uncle Michael's side. She clasped her hands in front of her and stirred the sand with the toe of her gym-shoe.

"Well, children," she started.

"Children!" whispered Pete.

"We're going to have a treasure hunt!"

The smaller children started to squirm about in the sand and even Mary unbent to say to her little sister, "A treasure hunt! *Isn't* that nice?"

"And," continued Auntie Mary, "we're going to give you all the first clue on a slip of paper, then you must find the others. When you find the first hiding-place you come to me for the second clue. And so on."

The first clue said, "Under a red **** near the cliff. (What Jesus called Peter)."

Everyone split up into small groups and wandered aimlessly about the beach.

"What's it *mean*?" said Pete.

"I dunno. Where's Rory?"

"He's walking around with that girl."

"Do you reckon there's any more?"

"What?"

"Caterpillars."

"Yes, I should think there *probably* are."

Uncle Michael was standing near the fallen rubble at the base of the cliff. When people came near him he would cry, "That's the spirit. Warm. Warmer. Oh, *very* warm! No. No. Cold, I'm afraid. Completely cold."

Most of the smaller children were playing at their own concerns, building castles, digging holes or just sitting and patting the smooth sand happily.

David and Peter, tiring of the search, sat down to play with the caterpillar. Uncle Michael called to them, "That's not a warm place at all. Come on, fellows, you'd be very warm *indeed* over here!"

They were just getting to their feet when Rory passed them and beckoned with a turn of his head. As they caught up with him they said, "What's up?"

"Come on. We're going."

"Why? What's wrong?"

"Nothing. Let's get going."

Rory's face was set with a contained and infectious delight.

"What is it, Rory?"

Rory hurried on, the current of his excitement drawing them after him. They started to scramble their way up the cliff-path, Rory setting the pace.

"Hey, you three!" shouted Uncle Michael. "You're *very* cold up there."

They paused for a moment and looked down on him, then struggled on towards the lip of the cliff and the dunes beyond.

They hurried to the hidden hollow in the dunes, almost running, caught by Rory's excitement.

"What did you do?"

"What is it, Rory?"

Rory unbuttoned his shirt and groped inside. He brought out a fountain pen. It was blue with a gold arrow for a clip.

"Nicked it out of his jacket," explained Rory.

They examined it carefully. "Hey, it's one of those good ones," said Pete.

"It's a Parker 51," said David. "They're worth a lot of money."

"Let's sell it," said Pete.

"Yeah, we could sell it at school," said David.

"No," said Rory. His tone of voice made them look at him. "I nicked it; so I'm deciding what to do with it."

"What *are* you going to do then?"

Rory stood considering. Then he stuck the pen into the sand. "I'm going to throw rocks at it," he said. Pete and David hung back while Rory threw a stone. He missed and, almost frantically, started to hunt for stones and pebbles.

Pete and David watched him. Their silence seemed to drive him on. He tore and grubbed for stones at the roots of the tough dune-grass as though he were possessed. Standing twenty paces off, he threw the stones from his pile as fast as he could bend to pick them up, and as he threw he began to laugh.

He became more and more incapable as his laughter consumed him and Pete and David started to pick up the wild-thrown stones. Soon the stones were raining down around the pen and the echoes of their laughter filled the air.

"Got it!" shouted Pete.

David ran to set it up again.

"And again!" shouted Rory. "Bombs away!"

With a lucky shot David smashed the top part of the pen away.

144

"It's mine!" shouted Rory. "Leave it alone!" And picking up a heavy rock, he held it directly above the stump of the pen and let it go. The rock hit the pen at an angle and smashed the casing. Ink spurted out onto the sand and Rory stamped on the broken pieces driving them out of sight. His eyes were shining with excitement. He stamped on the fragments until his foot had worn a small crater in the sand. Then suddenly, without warning, he rushed at Pete and grabbed him in a wrestling hold.

"Give in?"

Pete grunted and squirmed and bucked, trying to throw him off.

"You wait, bloody Callaghan."

Rory worked his knees into Pete's arms.

"Give in?"

"Come on, Rory. Get off. You're hurting."

Rory rolled off into the warm sand and pillowed his head on his hands. David propped himself up and lighted a cigarette. The heat seemed to roll in waves. High up against the sandstone cliff the black shapes of the swallows flickered like the blink of an eyelash. With a sigh of contentment, David unbuttoned his shirt and settled down to let the warmth soak through him. Swimming in the darkness behind his closed eyes were gentle globes of light, red and glowing.

Pete said, "We could try for those swallow-nests this afternoon."

"Swifts," murmured David.

"Swallows."

"Mmmm," sighed David happily.

Robert, standing

The hot-water bottle bulgy in his lap, Robert pushed himself down the passage and into the bathroom. The wheels of his chair rippled over the uneven woodblock floor and squawked as he made the turn. A strong push with his right hand brought the chair round to face the washbasin. Gripping the edge of the basin with his right hand, he pulled the chair closer.

Tipping the chair forward, he reached up and over the basin to open the bathroom cabinet. He took down the bottle of *Dettol* and stood it between the taps. Holding the hot-water bottle pressed against his chest with his left arm, he unscrewed the stopper and then poured the urine down the sink.

He ran the water for a few moments and then flopped the mouth of the hot-water bottle under the tap. When it was half full he held it pressed against the edge of the basin with his left hand while he poured in some *Dettol* so that it wouldn't smell.

He pushed against the basin and moved himself over to the bath. Leaning out from the chair, he turned on both taps. The bath was an old fashioned one his brother had bought from a demolition company, legs and claw feet, its enamel chipped away in spots leaving blue-black roughnesses. The original bath had been too low for him to get into without help.

He took off his pyjama jacket and draped it over the back of his chair. He lifted himself with his good arm and worked the pyjama bottoms from under him, pushing them down his legs to wrinkle round his ankles. He sat naked in the canvas chair as the bathroom filled with steam.

From his broad shoulders hung the single, paunchy mound of his chest and stomach. His left arm was stick thin, the wrist and hand twisted, fingers splayed. Below, both legs were thin and useless, the kneecaps rising like huge swellings. At the end of the wasted legs his feet sat like big boots on a rag puppet.

He freed his feet from the folds of the pyjamas and then, jamming the wheelchair against the tub, worked himself forward to the edge of the blue canvas seat. Holding the pressure against the bath to try and stop the chair from being pushed away, he heaved up his bulk on the strength of his right arm. The chair tipping, sliding, he lurched sideways, straining upwards to lodge one buttock on the white enamel. The breath soughing in and out of him, he rested there for a moment, and then worked himself higher until he was sitting on the edge of the tub.

Using both arms, he lifted up his right leg, hoisted it over the rim, and dumped it into the water. Then the left leg. He sat resting again, facing the wall.

The skin of his back and buttocks was pitted with the scars of boils and sores, wounds which erupted again and again from the same chafed sites leaving scar tissue like soft scale.

He shuffled himself along the edge of the bath to the curved end. His legs dragged out behind him. Then, getting a good grip with his hand, he allowed his buttocks to slide down. His quivering arm held for a moment and then his bulk fell, water slopping out onto the floor. The shock of the hot water stopped his breath. He lay motionless as the water surged up and down. When his breathing returned, he levered himself into a sitting position and hauled at his legs to straighten them out.

Sweat was standing out on his forehead. A vein, a muscle, something in his neck was jerking. He lay back in the rising steam, his eyes closed, waiting for the pounding of his heart to slow. He could feel the water still lapping at the island of his stomach. He opened his eyes and stared up at the tiled wall. It was furred with gathering beads of moisture.

Grey cement lines between the white spaces climbing, zigzags, verticals, building block lines, near the top edge a band of blue tiles, a single drop hung. Already impossibly heavy. Still on his desk. The weekly folder of playscripts from the CBC still lay on his desk. They'd have to be mailed off today or he'd have to pay for special delivery. But if he could finish reading the last play and write the four reports by eleven and then get the last three chapters of the novel read for the *Gazette* review—say twelve, twelve-thirty—he could get the carriage out and go to the drive-in on Decarie for lunch. The drop of water pulled others tributary and hung swelling. It broke suddenly into a meandering run. It was three days now since he'd been out. But if he went a bit later she wouldn't be so busy. One-thirty. One-thirty might be better, when the cars had thinned out.

As it checked, and paused, and changed direction to run again, it was leaving a clear trail shining down the tiles. One-thirty might be better. The soap slipped from his hand and he groped for it under his wasted thighs.

Bringing his tray, the edge of the peasant blouse decorated with blue and pink stitched flowers. Leaning into the carriage, the blouse falling away, a tiny gold crucifix on a gold chain deep between her breasts. The drop of water gathered again and then streaked down below the edge of the tub and out of sight.

"Are you going to be long, Bob?" yelled his brother.

"Nearly finished," he called back.

He could hear Jim in the kitchen now; the tap running, a pan on the gas-stove. He pushed himself higher and twisted round to reach the two towels on the chair behind him. He spread the first on the seat of his wheelchair so that he wouldn't have to sit on wet canvas for hours. He draped the other down the inside curve of the bath and splashed water on it. He heaved himself up again on his right arm and grunted his way up the towel's roughness until he was lodged on the rim of the bath.

Jim rapped on the bathroom door and rushed in. He was wearing a dark suit and carrying a briefcase. "Sorry, Bob," he said. "It's half-past eight." He wrenched on the cold tap and splashed water on his face.

"Didn't you sleep again?" he said.

"Fair. I just woke up early."

Jim squeezed toothpaste onto his brush and leaned over the basin.

147

When he had wiped his mouth, Robert said, "You've still got toothpaste on your moustache."

"O.K. See you tonight then. There's some coffee for you in the kitchen." He peered into the mirror again. "Nothing you want?"

"No, I don't think so, thanks." Then he called after him, "Jim! Are you going to be late tonight?"

"No. Usual."

"Shall I make supper?"

"O.K. Bye."

The front door slammed shut. Robert sat on the edge of the bath.

He struggled back into his chair and started to dry himself. When he touched his legs the flesh dented into white fingerprints which slowly faded up again to red.

He wheeled himself over to the basin and waited for the water to run hot. He propped the small hand-mirror between the taps and reached down his razor and the can of foam. As he peered into the mirror his fingertips explored a nest of spots under the angle of his jaw.

He put his hand into the water to test the heat and sat staring down into the basin. No scrubbing ever cleaned his calloused palm and fingers which were grimy with an ingrained dirt from the rubber wheels. He sat in the silence, staring. His hand looked disembodied, yellowish, like some strange creature in an aquarium.

Before going back to his room, he dusted his buttocks and groin with *Johnson's Baby Powder*.

Sitting tailor fashion on his bed, he worked the socks onto his feet. Then pulling his legs apart, he stuffed his feet into his underpants. He got the pants up round his knees and then rolled onto his back to pull them up. He repeated the manoeuvre to get his trousers on. As he had decided on going out, he put on his new turtle-neck sweater. Then he rolled back into his chair again and wheeled himself over to face his desk.

The empty apartment was shifting, settling into silence. He moved the folder of plays to one side and taking a large manilla envelope from the middle drawer wrote:

    The Script Department,
        CBC,
            P.O. Box 500,
            Toronto.

He found his mind drifting into the clock's rhythm, speeding up and slowing down, emphasizing now this beat, now that. He could hear the faint twinge of cooling metal from the gas-stove in the kitchen. Outside on the street he could hear the rattle of tricycles, the faint shouts of children. If he looked up he would see the side wall of the next duplex and in the top left corner of the window part of a branch. The desk top was a sheen of light.

The room behind him was familiar country, his own unchanging landscape. On top of the chest of drawers stood the photographs of his mother and father, ebony and silver frames. Beside them stood the small silver cup won long ago in his school days. On the end wall were the two rows of Hogarth prints—a complete set of *The Rake's Progress* and three odd prints from *Marriage á la Mode*. By the fake fireplace and the green armchair were his record-player, tape-recorder, and the FM radio. And the rank and order of his books memorized, the colours of their bindings.

Facing him on the desk were three shoeboxes. They were packed with file cards—the bones of his abandoned thesis for the University of Montreal. He was always intending to move the boxes and put them away but he never seemed to get round to it.

The wild yapping of the upstairs dog aroused him. His eyes focused and he found that his pen had covered the envelope with doodling lines and squiggles. He quickly wheeled himself out to the front door. The mailman was just walking up the concrete ramp.

"Hello!" said Robert. "How are you?"

"Oh, fine. Just fine."

He handed Robert two letters.

"Did you go away anywhere?" Robert asked.

"No, I took it easy, you know. Did a few jobs round the house."

He smiled and started to walk away down the slope.

"The man replacing you got everybody's mail mixed up all the time," called Robert.

"Oh, these temporaries, *they* don't care," he said.

"It must be hard getting back to it after a holiday," Robert called. The mailman paused on the pavement and shrugged. "Oh, it gets kind of boring round the house," he said. He hitched up his bag and walked on up the road. Robert sat in the open doorway and looked at the letters. One was a bill from *Hydro-Quebec* and the other contained a three cent voucher for *New Luxol* detergent.

He backed his chair and closed the door. He knew it must be at least nine-thirty. Perhaps more coffee would help. He was just about to wheel himself into the kitchen when the dog started its frantic barking again. He sat in the hall waiting. It had to be somebody for upstairs. But then the bell rang. He waited for a few moments and then moved up to open the door. Two young women stood looking at him.

"Good morning," said one.

"We're messengers of the Lord," said the other.

"Well you'd better come in, then," said Robert.

He ushered them into his room. "Do sit down," he said, pointing to the armchair by the record-player. "I'll just. . . ." He started to drag over a wooden kitchen chair.

"Can I help you with that?" asked the younger one.

"No, no. I can manage, thank you."

He placed the chair and the two of them sat down. The older one smoothed her skirt carefully, pulling it down taut over her knees. Robert guessed she was in her late twenties. She had straight hair, cut short, and a pale, almost pasty face. She bent to take something from her briefcase.

The younger one was prettier except that her hair was rigidly permed. She was wearing white ankle socks, a tartan skirt and a blue blazer with brass buttons.

"Well," said the older one, "we'd like to talk with you for a few minutes if you can spare us the time?"

"Sure," said Robert. "Certainly."

"We'd like to talk about the Lord Jesus?"

"Can I get you anything?" asked Robert. "Tea, coffee?"

"No, thank you."

He moved his wheelchair so that he could look at both of them at once.

"We're members of the Church of Jesus Christ of Latterday Saints?" said the younger one.

"Commonly called 'Mormons'," said the other, pointing to a blue, paperback book she had taken from her briefcase. On the bookcover, a man in gold robes was blowing a trumpet. "After this book, *The Book of Mormon*."

"Yes," said Robert. "Would you like some lemonade, perhaps?"

"We should have introduced ourselves," said the older one. "This is Miss Adetti and I'm Miss Stevens."

"Hardwick," said Robert. "Robert Hardwick."

"Tell me, Mr. Hardwick, are you a member of a church?"

"No, I don't go to church," said Robert.

"Do you believe in the Lord Jesus Christ?" asked Miss Stevens.

"Not in any active way," said Robert.

"We'd like to present the Lord Jesus to you this morning, if you'll let us?" said Miss Stevens.

"By all means. . . ." said Robert.

She fixed him with her eyes. "Mr. Hardwick. Why did the Lord Jesus come into the world?"

"Allegedly to save it," said Robert.

"And he cometh into the world that he may save all men if they harken unto his voice; for behold, he suffereth the pains of all men, yea, the pains of every living creature. . . ." said Miss Stevens.

"Second Book of Nephi. Chapter Nine. Verse twenty-one," said Miss Adetti.

"There are many misconceptions about the Mormon faith, Mr. Hardwick," said Miss Stevens.

"You mean wives and so on?" said Robert.

"Some people say we aren't even Christians and that the *Book of Mormon* is our Bible," said Miss Stevens.

"Which just isn't true," said Miss Adetti.

"*The Book of Mormon*," said Miss Stevens, "*reinforces* the Bible. It *doesn't* replace it. It adds its witness to Christ's word."

" 'Wherefore murmur ye,' " said Miss Adetti, " 'because that ye shall receive more of my word?' "

"And again from Second Nephi," said Miss Stevens. " 'And because my words shall hiss forth—many of the Gentiles shall say: A Bible! A Bible! We have got a Bible and there cannot be any more Bible.' "

She paused and then said, "And what was the Lord God's answer, Mr. Hardwick?"

" 'O fools!' " said Miss Adetti.

"Well that certainly seems a reasonable point," said Robert.

Miss Stevens bent into her briefcase again and came out with a long cylinder. She took the cap off and pulled out an assortment of metal rods. Robert hauled his feet further in on the footplate and shifted his buttocks on the hard canvas. Miss Stevens did not shave her legs and he stared at the matted hair under her nylons.

"*The Book of Mormon*," she said—her fingers were building the rods into a sort of frame or easel—"was first given to the world in 1830. We'd like to tell you a little of the miraculous history of that book. I have here a visual aid. . . ." She stretched over and stood the easel thing on top of the record-player. Robert saw with sudden interest that her baggy blouse concealed absolutely enormous breasts.

"But you see," said Robert, "it's not history that concerns me. Before we bother about history we ought to answer other questions. How do we know that the Lord God even exists?"

" 'And by the power of the Holy Ghost ye may know the truth of all things,' " said Miss Adetti. "Moroni 10:4-5," she added.

"But I don't know that the Holy Ghost exists," said Robert.

"I have known the Lord Jesus in my life, Mr. Hardwick," said Miss Stevens.

"But I haven't," said Robert.

"You must have faith," said Miss Adetti, " 'for the natural man is an enemy to God and has been from the fall of Adam, and will be, forever and ever, unless he yields to the enticings of the Holy Spirit.' Mosiah 3: 19-20."

" 'He who wishes to become a saint must become as a child,' " said Miss Stevens. " ' Submissive, meek, humble, patient, full of love, willing to submit to all things which the Lord seeth fit to inflict upon him, even. . . .' "

"But how," interrupted Robert, "can you have faith in something you don't believe in?"

"There's such a beautiful story in the *Book of Alma*," said Miss Adetti, "that answers that very question. May I tell it to you?" Miss Stevens nodded.

" 'Korihor said to Alma: If thou wilt show me a sign that I may be convinced that there is a God'—you see— the very question you asked us—'But Alma said unto him: Thou hast had signs enough; will ye tempt your God? Will ye say, Show unto me a sign, when ye have the testimony of all these thy brethren, and also all the holy prophets? The scriptures are laid before thee, yea, and all things denote there is a God; yea, even the earth, and all things that are upon the face of it, yea, and its motion, yea, and also all the planets which move in their regular form do witness that there is a Supreme Creator.' "

She finished and there was a silence. Her face was flushed. The silence deepened. Robert nodded slowly. He bent and pushed his left foot forward on the footplate. He straightened up and looked at them.

"Oh, Mr. Hardwick!" burst out Miss Stevens. "Let the Lord Jesus enter into your life!"

"Let us say a prayer!" said Miss Adetti.

He leaned back in his chair and watched them. They screwed up their eyes tight like children and lifted up their faces. They intoned their words antiphonally and his eyes followed from face to face.

"And let us," said Miss Stevens, "remind ourselves of that promise thou hast made to us in the *Book of Moroni*: 'If ye by the grace of God are perfect in Christ, and deny not his power, then are ye sanctified in Christ by the grace of God. . . .' "

152

Miss Adetti's voice took up, " 'through the shedding of the blood of Christ, which is in the covenant of the Father. . . .' "

Both voices rose in unison, " ' unto the remission of your sins, that ye become holy, without spot.' "

They lowered their heads and sat for a few moments in silence.

"Thank you," said Robert quietly.

Miss Stevens glanced at Miss Adetti and then said, "Mr. Hardwick, we'd like to leave this book with you for a few days. We'd like to have you read it?" She stood up and picked up her briefcase. Miss Adetti got up and took the wooden chair back to the other side of the room. "And perhaps we could call back on you in a few days' time?"

"I shall look forward to it," said Robert. He wheeled himself ahead of them and opened the door. As they stood by the front door, Miss Adetti said, "Well it's been just fine meeting you, Mr. Hardwick." She smiled warmly at him.

He backed his chair away and started to close the door. They were just turning out onto the pavement. Miss Stevens hitched her briefcase higher under her arm. Suddenly he pulled the door open again and rammed his chair forward, bucking the wheels over the fibre mat.

"Hey! You!"

Two startled faces turned to stare at him. His body bent forward from the chair.

"If I was standing up," he bellowed, "I'd be six foot three."

SOAPING A MEDITATIVE FOOT
(Notes for a Young Writer)

1) If you write as balm for a broken heart, if you find writing therapeutic, read no further.

2) If you find offensive the assertion that writing has little or nothing to do with 'sincerity' and spontaneity, read no further.

3) Do not confuse your politics with your writing. Party political positions are necessary in the larger world; the literary world is necessarily aristocratic.

   Do not hope to write for the masses—it is a fate worse than death.

   Don't write propaganda—be warned by the example of those who did. (Read the poetry which came out of the Spanish War. Or worse, the bad poetry by some excellent poets which is coming out of the Viet Nam War.)

   Do not feel ashamed that you are not carrying a gun or digging a ditch. Let the cobbler stick to his last.

   Remember that all writing is political, all great writing subversive.

4) Stories, novels, and poems are neither idea nor opinion. They are the distillation of experience.

   ("Particular life is still the best map to truth. When we search our hearts and strip our pretenses, we all know this. Particular life—we know only what we *know*." Herbert Gold.)

   If you have an idea, don't start writing until you feel better.

5) "To sustain, nourish and enrich the climate for creative growth and progress, Titanic is embarked on the most comprehensive quest for new ideas in the company's history.

   "The formal vehicle for this quest is an imaginative and long-range planning programme that was launched last year and is being executed with skill and vigour. The programme is a continuing, in-depth effort that is adding and will add new directions and novel dimensions to the on-going and imaginative activities of the company's strategic planning department."

   (Extract from *Annual Report* of Titanic Oil Company.)

   This is not *merely* effluent; it is your *active* enemy, the tide against which you must swim.

6) Take joy in the Placing of words.

   "How had he made his bad impression? The most likely thing, he always thought, was his having inflicted a superficial wound on the Professor of English in his first week. This man, a youngish ex-Fellow of a Cambridge college, had been standing on the front steps when Dixon, coming round the corner from the library, had kicked violently at a small round stone lying on the macadam. Before reaching the top of its trajectory it had struck the other just below the left kneecap at a distance of fifteen yards or more. Averting his head, Dixon had watched in terrified amazement; it had been useless to run, as the nearest cover was far beyond reach. At the moment of impact he'd turned and begun to walk down the drive, but knew well enough that he was the only visible entity capable of stone-propulsion. He looked back once and saw the Professor of English huddled up on one leg and looking at him." (*Lucky Jim*. Kingsley Amis. Gollancz, London, 1957.)

Consider the word 'looking' and its setting.

7) It is understandable but futile to take the 20th Century as a personal affront.

8) Know the weight, colour, and texture of *things*.

"For what seemed an immensely long time, I gazed without knowing, even without wishing to know, what it was that confronted me. At any other time I would have seen a chair barred with alternate light and shade. Today the percept had swallowed up the concept. I was so completely absorbed in looking, so thunderstruck by what I actually saw, that I could not be aware of anything else. Where the shadows fell on the canvas upholstery, stripes of a deep but glowing indigo alternated with stripes of an incandescence so intensely bright that it was hard to believe that they could be made of anything but blue fire. Garden furniture, laths, sunlight, shadow—these were no more than names and notions, mere verbalizations, for utilitarian purposes, after the event. The event was this succession of azure furnace doors separated by gulfs of unfathomable gentian. It was inexpressibly wonderful, wonderful to the point, almost, of being terrifying. And suddenly I had an inkling of what it must feel like to be mad."

(*The Doors of Perception*. Aldous Huxley. Harper and Brothers, New York, 1954.)

9) The real poetry—the names of materials and tools in the trades. Visit hardware stores.

10) Avoid, so far as possible, articles made of plastic.

155

11) Certain foods should be avoided on aesthetic and spiritual grounds. (eg. all forms of styrofoam 'bread'.)

12) Do not watch television. It is debilitating and leads to the belief that one or two programmes are not really all that bad.

13) The consumption of vast amounts of alcohol or dope or both is not necessarily the outward and visible sign of genius.

14) Fill your mind with useless information. *Brewer's Dictionary of Phrase and Fable* is invaluable.

15) Buy the *SOED* and *Webster's*.

16) Consult Fowler's *Modern English Usage*.

17) Read Jane Austen.

18) Avoid literary criticism which moves away from the word on the printed page and ascends to theories of God, Archetypes, Myth, Psyche, The Garden of Eden, The New Jerusalem, and Orgone Boxes. Stick to the study of the placement of commas.

19) If your main interest is prose, study poets.

20) Good films are cross-fertilizing.

21) "... a good talker can talk away the substance of twenty books in as many evenings. He will describe the central idea of the book he means to write until it revolts him."
    (From *Enemies of Promise*. Cyril Connolly. Routledge and Kegan Paul, London, Revised Edition, 1949.)

22) Read *Enemies of Promise*.

23) Study Arthur Waley's translations of Chinese poetry—the modern short story in capsule form.

24) Don't be pious about Literature. Take what you need and don't feel too guilty about what you leave. (With the exception of Jane Austen.)

25) Approach Dylan Thomas with extreme caution; he is insidious and, on prose writers, a Bad Influence.
    Avoid *richness*. A love of Keats and a love of sweet sherry are not unrelated.
    Tio Pepe for preference.

156

26) Study the Grand Masters. For years. After you have decided who they are.

Shakespeare has been widely praised for the audacity of his quintuple 'Never' and for the poignant simplicity of 'I pray you undo this button' but who has praised P. G. Wodehouse for daring to write:

Tum tiddle umpty-pum
Tum tiddle umpty-pum
Tum tiddle umpty-pum?

These masterly lines are enshrined in the following context.

"I don't know if you happen to be familiar with a poem called 'The Charge of the Light Brigade' by the bird Tennyson whom Jeeves had mentioned when speaking of the fellow whose strength was as the strength of ten. It is, I believe, fairly well known, and I used to have to recite it at the age of seven or thereabouts when summoned to the drawing-room to give visitors a glimpse of the young Wooster. 'Bertie recites so nicely,' my mother used to say— getting her facts twisted, I may mention, because I practically always fluffed my lines—and after trying to duck for safety and being hauled back I would snap into it. And very unpleasant the whole thing was, so people have told me.

"Well, what I was about to say, when I rambled off a bit on the subject of the dear old days, was that though in the course of the years most of the poem of which I speak has slid from the memory, I still recall its punch line. The thing goes, as you probably know,

Tum tiddle umpty-pum
Tum tiddle umpty-pum
Tum tiddle umpty-pum

and this brought you to the snapperoo or pay-off, which was

Someone had blundered.

"I always remember that bit, and the reason I bring it up now is that, as I stood blinking at this pink-boudoir-capped girl, I was feeling just as those Light Brigade fellows must have felt. Obviously someone had blundered here, and that someone was Aunt Dahlia."

(From *Jeeves and the Feudal Spirit*. P. G. Wodehouse. Herbert Jenkins, London, 1954.)

"Grand Master?"

"Well, in one way, yes."

The tragedy of Wodehouse is that he is not a comic writer but, rather, a comedian. If only C. P. Snow, Doris Lessing, or Joseph Heller had shared his grace.

(Examine a few paragraphs of Heller's lumbering humour in *Catch 22*; soggy as old bread pudding.)

"But Grand Master!"

"Don't be pious!"

Here is Wodehouse doing Nature. It is a performance, a comedian's routine, but it can teach you more of the art of writing than all the Writers' Conferences and Schools advertised in the summer issues of *Saturday Review*.

"A thing I never know when I'm telling a story is how much scenery to bung in. I've asked one or two scriveners of my acquaintance, and their views differ. A fellow I met at a cocktail party in Bloomsbury said that he was all for describing kitchen sinks and frowsty bedrooms and squalor generally, but the beauties of Nature no. Whereas, Freddie Oaker, of the Drones, who does tales of pure love for the weeklies under the pen-name of Alicia Seymour, once told me that he reckoned that flowery meadows in springtime alone were worth at least a hundred quid a year to him.

"Personally, I've always rather barred long descriptions of the terrain, so I will be on the brief side. As I stood there that morning, what the eye rested on was the following. There was a nice little splash of garden, containing a bush, a tree, a couple of flower beds, a lily pond with a statue of a nude child with a bit of tummy on him, and to the right a hedge. Across this hedge, Brinkley, my new man, was chatting with our neighbour, Police Sergeant Voules, who seemed to have looked in with a view to selling eggs.

"There was another hedge straight ahead, with the garden gate in it, and over this one espied the placid waters of the harbour, which was much about the same as any other harbour, except that sometime during the night a whacking great yacht had rolled up and cast anchor in it. And of all the objects under my immediate advisement I noted this yacht with the most pleasure and approval. White in colour, in size resembling a young liner, it lent a decided tone to the Chuffnell Regis foreshore.

"Well, such was the spreading prospect. Add a cat sniffing at a snail on the path and me at the door smoking a gaspar, and you have the complete picture."

(From *Thank you Jeeves*. P. G. Wodehouse. Herbert Jenkins, London, 1934.)

27) Do not expect much recognition financial or critical for the years of hard work ahead of you.

In 1968, Alice Munro gave us *Dance of the Happy Shades*— the finest collection of short stories yet published in Canada. You can *still* buy (and should) copies of the first printing. Allen Ginsburg once said that most critics couldn't recognize good poetry if it came up and buggered them in broad daylight. Canadian critics seem equally insensitive to quality in the short story.

28) A reply to those who ask you what your stories *mean*.

"There is easy reading. And there is literature. There are easy writers, and there are writers. There are people whose ears have never grown, or have fallen off, or have merely lost the power to listen. And there are people with ears. . . .

" 'I write. Let the reader learn to read.' I must be as skillful as I can. I am obliged to be the best craftsman I can be. I must be free to choose my subject and my language, and I am at liberty to experiment, to grow, to express, if need be, the complexity of my experience with whatever resources are at hand. I will talk baby talk to babies and dog talk to dogs, but I cannot tell you in baby talk or dog talk of the excitement of being an adult human being in a world so wondrous with hope and sorrow and loyalty and defeat and anguish and delight.

"All of us who *write* once made the decision to write out the best that is in us. It had nothing to do with integrity, only with taste and preference. Loath to tape our ears to our skulls, we said, instead, We shall let our ears grow up and away and see what happens.

"We want to tell the jokes we want to tell, and we can tell them only to people with ears to listen, people who will bring to the evening talents to challenge our own, who will work as goddam hard to read as we work who write."

(From *Easy Does It Not*. Mark Harris, from *The Living Novel*. ed. Granville Hicks. Macmillan, New York, 1957.)

29) Rewrite.

30) Rewrite.

JOHN METCALF

Alice Munro

Alice Munro was born in 1931 in Wingham, a small town in western Ontario. She later attended the University of Western Ontario in London. She married in 1951 and moved to British Columbia. She now lives in Victoria with her husband and three daughters. Her work has been widely anthologized in Canada, England and America. In 1968 she won the Governor-General's Award for Literature. She is currently working on a second novel.

Bibliography

Dance of the Happy Shades. Ryerson Press, Toronto, 1968. (Stories)
Lives of Girls and Women. McGraw-Hill Ryerson Limited, Toronto, 1971
    (Novel)

Images

Now that Mary McQuade had come, I pretended not to remember her. It seemed the wisest thing to do. She herself said, "If you don't remember me you don't remember much," but let the matter drop, just once adding, "I bet you never went to your Grandma's house last summer. I bet you don't remember that either."

It was called, even that summer, my grandma's house, though my grandfather was then still alive. He had withdrawn into one room, the largest front bedroom. It had wooden shutters on the inside of the windows, like the living room and dining room; the other bedrooms had only blinds. Also, the verandah kept out the light so that my grandfather lay in near-darkness all day, with his white hair, now washed and tended and soft as a baby's, and his white nightshirt and pillows, making an island in the room which people approached with diffidence, but resolutely. Mary McQuade in her uniform was the other island in the room, and she sat mostly not moving where the fan, as if it was tired, stirred the air like soup. It must have been too dark to read or knit, supposing she wanted to do those things, and so she merely waited and breathed, making a sound like the fan made, full of old indefinable complaint.

I was so young then I was put to sleep in a crib—not at home but this was what was kept for me at my grandma's house—in a room across the hall. There was no fan there and the dazzle of outdoors—all the flat fields round the house turned, in the sun, to the brilliance of water—made lightning cracks in the drawn-down blinds. Who could sleep? My mother's my grandmother's my aunts' voices wove their ordinary repetitions, on the verandah in the kitchen in the dining room (where with a little brass-handled brush my mother cleaned the white cloth, and the lighting-fixture over the round table hung down unlit flowers of thick, butterscotch glass). All the meals in that house, the cooking, the visiting, the conversation, even someone playing on the piano (it was my youngest aunt, Edith, not married, singing and playing with one hand, *Nita, Juanita, softly falls the southern moon*); all this life going on. Yet the ceilings of the rooms were very high and under them was a great deal of dim wasted space, and when I lay in my crib too hot to sleep I could look up and see that emptiness, the stained corners, and feel, without knowing what it was, just what everybody else in the house must have felt—under the sweating heat the fact of death-contained, that little lump of magic ice. And Mary McQuade waiting in her starched white dress, big and gloomy as an iceberg herself, implacable, waiting and breathing. I held her responsible.

So I pretended not to remember her. She had not put on her white uniform, which did not really make her less dangerous but might mean, at least, that the time of her power had not yet come. Out in the daylight, and not dressed in white, she turned out to be freckled all over, everywhere you could see, as if she was sprinkled with oatmeal, and she had a crown of frizzy, glinting, naturally brass-coloured hair. Her voice was loud and hoarse and complaint was her everyday language. "Am I going to have to hang up this wash all by myself?" she shouted at me, in the yard, and I followed her to the clothesline platform where with a groan she let down the basket of wet clothes. "Hand me them clothespins. One at a time. Hand me them right side up. I shouldn't be out in this wind at all, I've got a bronchial condition." Head hung, like an animal chained to her side, I fed her clothespins. Outdoors, in the cold March air, she lost some of her bulk and her smell. In the house I could always smell her, even in the rooms she seldom entered. What was her smell like? It was like metal and like some dark spice (cloves—she did suffer from toothache) and like the preparation rubbed on my chest when I had a cold. I mentioned it once to my mother, who said, "Don't be silly, *I* don't smell anything." So I never told about the taste, and there was a taste too. It was in all the food Mary McQuade prepared and perhaps in all food eaten in her presence—in my porridge at breakfast and my fried potatoes at noon and the slice of bread and butter and brown sugar she gave me to eat in the yard—something foreign, gritty, depressing. How could my parents not know about it? But for reasons of their own they would pretend. This was something I had not known a year ago.

After she had hung out the wash she had to soak her feet. Her legs came straight up, round as drainpipes, from the steaming basin. One hand on each knee, she bent into the steam and gave grunts of pain and satisfaction.

"Are you a nurse?" I said, greatly daring, though my mother had said she was.

"Yes I am and I wish I wasn't."

"Are you my aunt too?"

"If I was your Aunt you would call me Aunt Mary, wouldn't you? Well you don't, do you? I'm your cousin, I'm your father's cousin. That's why they get me instead of getting an ordinary nurse. I'm a practical nurse. And there is always somebody sick in this family and I got to go to them. I never get a rest."

I doubted this. I doubted that she was asked to come. She came, and cooked what she liked and rearranged things to suit herself, complaining about draughts, and let her power loose in the house. If she had never come my mother would never have taken to her bed.

My mother's bed was set up in the dining room, to spare Mary McQuade climbing the stairs. My mother's hair was done in two little thin dark braids, her cheeks were sallow, her neck warm and smelling of raisins as it always did, but the rest of her under the covers had changed into some large, fragile and mysterious object, difficult to move. She spoke of herself gloomily in the third person, saying, "Be careful, don't hurt Mother, don't sit on Mother's legs." Every time she said Mother I felt chilled, and a kind of wretchedness and shame spread through me as it did at the name of Jesus. This *Mother* that my own real, warm-necked, irascible and comforting human mother set up between us was an everlastingly wounded phantom, sorrowing like Him over all the wickedness I did not yet know I would commit.

My mother crocheted squares for an afghan, in all shades of purple. They fell among the bedclothes and she did not care. Once they were finished she forgot about them. She had forgotten all her stories which were about Princes in the Tower and a queen getting her head chopped off while a little dog was hiding under her dress and another queen sucking poison out of her husband's wound; and also about her own childhood, a time as legendary to me as any other. Given over to Mary's care she whimpered childishly, "Mary, I'm dying for you to rub my back." "Mary, could you make me a cup of tea? I feel if I drink any more tea I'm going to bob up to the ceiling, just like a big balloon, but you know it's all I want." Mary laughed shortly. "You," she said, "you're not going to bob up anywhere. Take a derrick to move *you*. Come on now, raise up, you'll be worse before you're better!" She shooed me off the bed and began to pull the sheets about with not very gentle jerks. "You been tiring your Momma out? What do you want to bother your Momma for on this nice a day?" "I think she's lonesome," my mother said, a weak and insincere defence. "She can be lonesome in the yard just as well as here," said Mary, with her grand, vague, menacing air. "You put your things on, out you go!"

My father, too, had altered since her coming. When he came in for his meals she was always waiting for him, some joke swelling her up like a bullfrog, making her ferocious-looking and red in the face. She put uncooked white beans in his soup, hard as pebbles, and waited to see if good manners would make him eat them. She stuck something to the bottom of his water glass to look like a fly. She gave him a fork with a prong missing, pretending it was by accident. He threw it at her, and missed, but startled me considerably. My mother and father, eating supper, talked quietly and seriously. But in my father's family even grownups played tricks with rubber worms and beetles, fat aunts were always invited to sit on little rickety chairs and uncles broke wind in public and said, "Whoa, hold on there!" proud of themselves as if they had whistled a complicated tune. Nobody could ask your age without a rigmarole of teasing. So with Mary McQuade my father returned to family ways, just as he went back to eating heaps of fried potatoes and side meat and thick, floury pies, and drinking tea black and strong as medicine out of a tin pot, saying gratefully, "Mary, you know what it is a man ought to eat!" He followed that up with, "Don't you think it's time you got a man of your own to feed?" which earned him, not a fork thrown, but the dishrag.

His teasing of Mary was always about husbands. "I thought up one for you this morning!" he would say. "Now Mary I'm not fooling you, you give this some consideration." Her laughter would come out first in little angry puffs and explosions through her shut lips, while her face grew redder than you would have thought possible and her body twitched and rumbled threateningly in its chair. There was no doubt she enjoyed all this, all these preposterous imagined matings, though my mother would certainly have said it was cruel, cruel and indecent, to tease an old maid about men. In my father's family of course it was what she was always teased about, what else was there? And the heavier and coarser and more impossible she became, the more she would be teased. A bad thing in that family was to have them say you were *sensitive,* as they did of my mother. All the aunts and cousins and uncles had grown tremendously hardened to any sort of personal cruelty, reckless, even proud, it seemed, of a failure or deformity that could make for general laughter.

At supper-time it was dark in the house, in spite of the lengthening days. We did not yet have electricity. It came in soon afterwards, maybe the next summer. But at present there was a lamp on the table. In its light my father and Mary McQuade threw gigantic shadows, whose heads wagged clumsily with their talk and laughing. I watched the shadows instead of the people. They said, "What are you dreaming about?" but I was not dreaming, I was trying to understand the danger, to read the signs of invasion.

My father said, "Do you want to come with me and look at the trap?" He had a trapline of muskrats along the river. When he was younger he used to spend days, nights, weeks in the bush, following creeks all up and down Wawanash County, and he trapped not only muskrat then but red fox, wild mink, marten, all animals whose coats are prime in the fall. Muskrat is the only thing you can trap in the spring. Now that he was married and settled down to farming he just kept the one line, and that for only a few years. This may have been the last year he had it.

We went across a field that had been plowed the previous fall. There was a little snow lying in the furrows but it was not real snow, it was a thin crust like frosted glass that I could shatter with my heels. The field went downhill slowly, down to the river flats. The fence was down in some places from the weight of the snow, we could step over it.

My father's boots went ahead. His boots were to me as unique and familiar, as much an index to himself as his face was. When he had taken them off they stood in a corner of the kitchen, giving off a complicated smell of manure, machine oil, caked black mud, and the ripe and disintegrating material that lined their soles. They were a part of himself, temporarily discarded, waiting. They had an expression that was dogged and uncompromising, even brutal, and I thought of that as part of my father's look, the counterpart of his face, with its readiness for jokes and courtesies. Nor did that brutality surprise me; my father came back to us always, to my mother and me, from places where our judgment could not follow.

For instance, there was a muskrat in the trap. At first I saw it waving at the edge of the water, like something tropical, a dark fern. My father drew it up and the hairs ceased waving, clung together, the fern became a tail with the body of the rat attached to it, sleek and dripping. Its teeth were bared, its eyes wet on top, dead and dull beneath, glinted like washed pebbles. My father shook it and whirled it around, making a little rain of icy river water. "This is a good old rat," he said. "This is a big old king rat. Look at his tail!" Then perhaps thinking that I was worried, or perhaps only wanting to show me the charm of simple, perfect mechanical devices, he lifted the trap out of the water and explained to me how it worked, dragging the rat's head under at once and mercifully drowning him. I did not understand or care. I only wanted, but did not dare, to touch the stiff, soaked body, a fact of death.

My father baited the trap again using some pieces of yellow, winter-wrinkled apple. He put the rat's body in a dark sack which he carried slung over his shoulder, like a pedlar in a picture. When he cut the apple I had seen the skinning knife, its slim bright blade.

Then we went along the river, the Wawanash River, which was high, running full, silver in the middle where the sun hit it and where it arrowed in to its swiftest motion. That is the current, I thought, and I pictured the current as something separate from the water, just as the wind was separate from the air and had its own invading shape. The banks were steep and slippery and lined with willow bushes, still bare and bent over and looking weak as grass. The noise the river made was not loud but deep, and seemed to come from away down in the middle of it, some hidden place where the water issued with a roar from underground.

The river curved, I lost my sense of direction. In the traps we found more rats, released them, shook them and hid them in the sack, replaced the bait. My face, my hands, my feet grew cold, but I did not mention it. I could not, to my father. And he never told me to be careful, to stay away from the edge of the water, he took it for granted that I would have sense enough not to fall in. I never asked how far we were going, or if the trapline would ever end. After a while there was a bush behind us, the afternoon darkened. It did not occur to me, not till long afterwards, that this was the same bush you could see from our yard, a fan-shaped hill rising up in the middle of it with bare trees in wintertime that looked like bony little twigs against the sky.

Now the bank, instead of willows, grew thick bushes higher than my head. I stayed on the path, about halfway up the bank, while my father went down to the water. When he bent over the trap, I could no longer see him. I looked around slowly and saw something else. Further along, and higher up the bank, a man was making his way down. He made no noise coming through the bushes and moved easily, as if he followed a path I could not see. At first I could just see his head and the upper part of his body. He was dark, with a high bald forehead, hair long behind the ears, deep vertical creases in his cheeks. When the bushes thinned I could see the rest of him, his long clever legs, thinness, drab camouflaging clothes, and what he carried in his hand, gleaming where the sun caught it—a little axe, or hatchet.

I never moved to warn or call my father. The man crossed my path somewhere ahead, continuing down to the river. People say they have been paralyzed by fear, but I was transfixed, as if struck by lightning, and what hit me did not feel like fear so much as recognition. I was not surprised. This is the sight that does not surprise you, the thing you have always known was there that comes so naturally, moving delicately and contentedly and in no hurry, as if it was made, in the first place, from a wish of yours, a hope of something final, terrifying. All my life I had known there was a man like this and he was behind doors, around the corner at the dark end of a hall. So now I saw him and just waited, like a child in an old negative, electrified against the dark noon sky, with blazing hair and burned-out Orphan Annie eyes. The man slipped down through the bushes to my father. And I never thought, or even hoped for, anything but the worst.

My father did not know. When he straightened up, the man was not three feet away from him and hid him from me. I heard my father's voice come out, after a moment's delay, quiet and neighbourly.

"Hello, Joe. Well. Joe. I haven't seen you in a long time."

The man did not say a word, but edged around my father giving him a close look. "Joe, you know me," my father told him. "Ben Jordan. I been out looking at my traps. There's a lot of good rats in the river this year, Joe."

The man gave a quick not-trusting look at the trap my father had baited.

"You ought to set a line out yourself."

No answer. The man took his hatchet and chopped lightly at the air.

"Too late this year, though. The river is already started to go down."

"Ben Jordan," the man said with a great splurt, a costly effort, like somebody leaping over a stutter.

"I thought you'd recognize me, Joe."

"I never knew it was you, Ben. I thought it was one them Silases."

"Well I been telling you it was me."

"They's down here all the time choppin my trees and pullin down my fences. You know they burned me out, Ben. It was them done it."

"I heard about that," my father said.

"I didn't know it was you, Ben. I never knew it was you. I got this axe, I just take it along with me to give them a little scare. I wouldn't of if I'd known it was you. You come on up and see where I'm living now."

My father called me. "I got my young one out following me today."

"Well you and her both come up and get warm."

We followed this man, who still carried and carelessly swung his hatchet, up the slope and into the bush. The trees chilled the air, and underneath them was real snow, left over from winter, a foot, two feet deep. The tree trunks had rings around them, a curious dark space like the warmth you make with your breath.

We came out in a field of dead grass, and took a track across it to another, wider, field where there was something sticking out of the ground. It was a roof, slanting one way, not peaked, and out of the roof came a pipe with a cap on it, smoke blowing out. We went down the sort of steps that lead to a cellar, and that was what it was—a cellar with a roof on. My father said, "Looks like you fixed it up all right for yourself, Joe."

"It's warm. Being down in the ground the way it is, naturally it's warm. I thought what is the sense of building a house up again, they burned it down once, they'll burn it down again. What do I need a house for anyways? I got all the room I need here, I fixed it up comfortable." He opened the door at the bottom of the steps. "Mind your head here. I don't say everybody should live in a hole in the ground, Ben. Though animals do it, and what an animal does, by and large it makes sense. But if you're married, that's another story." He laughed. "Me, I don't plan on getting married."

It was not completely dark. There were the old cellar windows, letting in a little grimy light. The man lit a coal-oil lamp, though, and set it on the table.

"There, you can see where you're at."

It was all one room, an earth floor with boards not nailed together, just laid down to make broad paths for walking, a stove on a sort of platform, table, couch, chairs, even a kitchen cupboard, several thick, very dirty blankets of the type used in sleighs and to cover horses. Perhaps if it had not had such a terrible smell—of coal oil, urine, earth and stale heavy air—I would have recognized it as the sort of place I would like to live in myself, like the houses I made under snow drifts, in winter, with sticks of firewood for furniture, like another house I had made long ago under the verandah, my floor the strange powdery earth that never got sun or rain.

But I was wary, sitting on the dirty couch, pretending not to look at anything. My father said, "You're snug here, Joe, that's right." He sat by the table, and there the hatchet lay.

"You should of seen me before the snow started to melt. Wasn't nothing showing but a smokestack."

"Nor you don't get lonesome?"

"Not me. I was never one for lonesome. And I got a cat, Ben. Where is that cat? There he is, in behind the stove. He don't relish company, maybe." He pulled it out, a huge, grey tom with sullen eyes. "Show you what he can do." He took a saucer from the table and a Mason jar from the cupboard and poured something into the saucer. He set it in front of the cat.

"Joe that cat don't drink whisky, does he?"

"You wait and see."

The cat rose and stretched himself stiffly, took one baleful look around and lowered his head to drink.

168

"Straight whisky," my father said.

"I bet that's a sight you ain't seen before. And you ain't likely to see it again. That cat'd take whisky ahead of milk any day. A matter of fact he don't get no milk, he's forgot what it's like. You want a drink, Ben?"

"Not knowing where you got that. I don't have a stomach like your cat."

The cat, having finished, walked sideways from the saucer, waited a moment, gave a clawing leap and landed unsteadily, but did not fall. It swayed, pawed the air a few times, meowing despairingly, then shot forward and slid under the end of the couch.

"Joe, you keep that up, you're not going to have a cat."

"It don't hurt him, he enjoys it. Let's see, what've we got for the little girl to eat?" Nothing, I hoped, but he brought a tin of Christmas candies, which seemed to have melted then hardened then melted again, so the coloured stripes had run. They had a taste of nails.

"It's them Silases botherin me, Ben. They come by day and by night. People won't ever quit botherin me. I can hear them on the roof at night. Ben, you see them Silases you tell them what I got waitin for them." He picked up the hatchet and chopped down at the table, splitting the rotten oilcloth. "Got a shotgun too."

"Maybe they won't come and bother you no more, Joe."

The man groaned and shook his head. "They never will stop. No. They never will stop."

"Just try not paying any attention to them, they'll tire out and go away."

"They'll burn me in my bed. They tried to before."

My father said nothing, but tested the axe blade with his finger. Under the couch, the cat pawed and meowed in more and more feeble spasms of delusion. Overcome with tiredness, with warmth after cold, with bewilderment quite past bearing, I was falling asleep with my eyes open.

My father set me down. "You're woken up now. Stand up. See. I can't carry you and this sack full of rats both."

We had come to the top of a long hill and that is where I woke. It was getting dark. The whole basin of country drained by the Wawanash River lay in front of us—greenish brown smudge of bush with the leaves not out yet and evergreens, dark, shabby after winter, showing through, straw-brown fields and the others, darker from last year's plowing, with scales of snow faintly striping them (like the field we had walked across hours, hours earlier in the day) and the tiny fences and colonies of grey barns, and houses set apart, looking squat and small.

169

"Whose house is that?" my father said, pointing.

It was ours, I knew it after a minute. We had come around in a half-circle and there was the side of the house that nobody saw in winter, the front door that went unopened from November to April and was still stuffed with rags around its edges to keep out the east wind.

"That's no more'n half a mile away and downhill. You can easy walk home. Soon we'll see the light in the dining room where your Momma is."

On the way I said, "Why did he have an axe?"

"Now listen," my father said. "Are you listening to me? He don't mean any harm with that axe. It's just his habit, carrying it around. But don't say anything about it at home. Don't mention it to your Momma or Mary, either one. Because they might be scared about it. You and me aren't, but they might be. And there is no use of that."

After a while he said, "What are you not going to mention about?" and I said, "The axe."

"You weren't scared, were you?"

"No," I said hopefully. "Who is going to burn him and his bed?"

"Nobody. Less he manages it himself like he did last time."

"Who is the Silases?"

"Nobody," my father said. "Just nobody."

"We found the one for you today, Mary. Oh, I wisht we could've brought him home."

"We thought you'd fell in the Wawanash River," said Mary McQuade furiously, ungently pulling off my boots and my wet socks.

"Old Joe Phippen that lives up in no man's land beyond the bush."

"Him!" said Mary like an explosion. "He's the one burned his house down, I know him!"

"That's right, and now he gets along fine without it. Lives in a hole in the ground. You'd be as cosy as a groundhog, Mary."

"I bet he lives in his own dirt, all right." She served my father his supper and he told her the story of Joe Phippen, the roofed cellar, the boards across the dirt floor. He left out the axe but not the whisky and the cat. For Mary, that was enough.

"A man that'd do a thing like that ought to be locked up."

"Maybe so," my father said. "Just the same I hope they don't get him for a while yet. Old Joe."

"Eat your supper," Mary said, bending over me. I did not for some time realize that I was no longer afraid of her. "Look at her," she said. "Her eyes dropping out of her head, all she's been and seen. Was he feeding the whisky to her too?"

170

"Not a drop," said my father, and looked steadily down the table at me. Like the children in fairy stories who have seen their parents make pacts with terrifying strangers, who have discovered that our fears are based on nothing but the truth, but who come back fresh from marvellous escapes and take up their knives and forks, with humility and good manners, prepared to live happily ever after—like them, dazed and powerful with secrets, I never said a word.

Dance of the Happy Shades

Miss Marsalles is having another party. (Out of musical integrity, or her heart's bold yearning for festivity, she never calls it a recital.) My mother is not an inventive or convincing liar, and the excuses which occur to her are obviously second-rate. The painters are coming. Friends from Ottawa. Poor Carrie is having her tonsils out. In the end all she can say is: Oh, but won't all that be too much trouble, *now*? *Now* being weighted with several troublesome meanings; you may take your choice. Now that Miss Marsalles has moved from the brick and frame bungalow on Bank Street, where the last three parties have been rather squashed, to an even smaller place—if she has described it correctly—on Bala Street. (Bala Street, where is that?) Or: now that Miss Marsalles' older sister is in bed, following a stroke; now that Miss Marsalles herself—as my mother says, we must face these things—is simply getting *too old*.

Now? asks Miss Marsalles, stung, pretending mystification, or perhaps for that matter really feeling it. And she asks how her June party could ever be too much trouble, at any time, in any place? It is the only entertainment she ever gives any more (so far as my mother knows it is the only entertainment she ever has given, but Miss Marsalles' light old voice, undismayed, indefatigably social, supplies the ghosts of tea parties, private dances, At Homes, mammoth Family Dinners). She would suffer, she says, as much disappointment as the children, if she were to give it up. Considerably more, says my mother to herself, but of course she cannot say it aloud; she turns her face from the telephone with that look of irritation—as if she had seen something messy which she was unable to clean up—which is her private expression of pity. And she promises to come; weak schemes for getting out of it will occur to her during the next two weeks, but she knows she will be there.

She phones up Marg French who like herself is an old pupil of Miss Marsalles and who has been having lessons for her twins, and they commiserate for a while and promise to go together and buck each other up. They remember the year before last when it rained and the little hall was full of raincoats piled on top of each other because there was no place to hang them up, and the umbrellas dripped puddles on the dark floor. The little girls' dresses were crushed because of the way they all had to squeeze together, and the living room windows would not open. Last year a child had a nosebleed.

"Of course that was not Miss Marsalles' fault."

They giggle despairingly. "No. But things like that did not used to happen."

And that is true; that is the whole thing. There is a feeling that can hardly be put into words about Miss Marsalles' parties; things are getting out of hand, anything may happen. There is even a moment, driving in to such a party, when the question occurs: will anybody else be there? For one of the most disconcerting things about the last two or three parties has been the widening gap in the ranks of the regulars, the old pupils whose children seem to be the only new pupils Miss Marsalles ever has. Every June reveals some new and surely significant dropping-out. Mary Lambert's girl no longer takes; neither does Joan Crimble's. What does this mean? think my mother and Marg French, women who have moved to the suburbs and are plagued sometimes by a feeling that they have fallen behind, that their instincts for doing the right thing have become confused. Piano lessons are not so important now as they once were; everybody knows that. Dancing is believed to be more favourable to the development of the whole child—and the children, at least the girls, don't seem to mind it as much. But how are you to explain that to Miss Marsalles, who says, "All children need music. All children love music in their hearts"? It is one of Miss Marsalles' indestructible beliefs that she can see into children's hearts, and she finds there a treasury of good intentions and a natural love of all good things. The deceits which her spinster's sentimentality has practised on her original good judgment are legendary and colossal; she has this way of speaking of children's hearts as if they were something holy; it is hard for a parent to know what to say.

In the old days, when my sister Winifred took lessons, the address was in Rosedale; that was where it had always been. A narrow house, built of soot-and-raspberry-coloured brick, grim little ornamental balconies curving out from the second-floor windows, no towers anywhere but somehow a turreted effect; dark, pretentious, poetically ugly—the family home. And in Rosedale the annual party did not go off too badly. There was always an awkward little space before the sandwiches, because the

172

woman they had in the kitchen was not used to parties and rather slow, but the sandwiches when they did appear were always very good: chicken, asparagus rolls, wholesome, familiar things—dressed-up nursery food. The performances on the piano were, as usual, nervous and choppy or sullen and spiritless, with the occasional surprise and interest of a lively disaster. It will be understood that Miss Marsalles' idealistic view of children, her tender- or simple-mindedness in that regard, made her almost useless as a teacher; she was unable to criticize except in the most delicate and apologetic way and her praises were unforgivably dishonest; it took an unusually conscientious pupil to come through with anything like a creditable performance.

But on the whole the affair in those days had solidity, it had tradition, in its own serenely out-of-date way it had style. Everything was always as expected; Miss Marsalles herself, waiting in the entrance hall with the tiled floor and the dank, church-vestry smell, wearing rouge, an antique hairdo adopted only on this occasion, and a floor-length dress of plum and pinkish splotches that might have been made out of old upholstery material, startled no one but the youngest children. Even the shadow behind her of another Miss Marsalles, slightly older, larger, grimmer, whose existence was always forgotten from one June to the next, was not discomfiting—though it was surely an arresting fact that there should be not one but two faces like that in the world, both long, gravel-coloured, kindly and grotesque, with enormous noses and tiny, red, sweet-tempered and shortsighted eyes. It must finally have come to seem like a piece of luck to them to be so ugly, a protection against life to be marked in so many ways, *impossible,* for they were gay as invulnerable and childish people are; they appeared sexless, wild and gentle creatures, bizarre yet domestic, living in their house in Rosedale outside the complications of time.

In the room where the mothers sat, some on hard sofas, some on folding chairs, to hear the children play "The Gypsy Song," "The Harmonious Blacksmith" and the "Turkish March," there was a picture of Mary, Queen of Scots, in velvet, with a silk veil, in front of Holyrood Castle. There were brown misty pictures of historical battles, also the Harvard Classics, iron firedogs and a bronze Pegasus. None of the mothers smoked, nor were ashtrays provided. It was the same room, exactly the same room, in which they had performed themselves; a room whose dim impersonal style (the flossy bunch of peonies and spirea dropping petals on the piano was Miss Marsalles' own touch and not entirely happy) was at the same time uncomfortable and reassuring. Here they found themselves year after year—a group of busy, youngish

173

women who had eased their cars impatiently through the archaic streets of Rosedale, who had complained for a week previously about the time lost, the fuss over the children's dresses and, above all, the boredom, but who were drawn together by a rather implausible allegiance—not so much to Miss Marsalles as to the ceremonies of their childhood, to a more exacting pattern of life which had been breaking apart even then but which survived, and unaccountably still survived, in Miss Marsalles' living room. The little girls in dresses with skirts as stiff as bells moved with a natural awareness of ceremony against the dark walls of books, and their mothers' faces wore the dull, not unpleasant look of acquiescence, the touch of absurd and slightly artificial nostalgia which would carry them through any lengthy family ritual. They exchanged smiles which showed no lack of good manners, and yet expressed a familiar, humorous amazement at the sameness of things, even the selections played on the piano and the fillings of the sandwiches; so they acknowledged the incredible, the wholly unrealistic persistence of Miss Marsalles and her sister and their life.

After the piano-playing came a little ceremony which always caused some embarrassment. Before the children were allowed to escape to the garden—very narrow, a town garden, but still a garden, with hedges, shade, a border of yellow lilies—where a long table was covered with crepe paper in infants' colours of pink and blue, and the woman from the kitchen set out plates of sandwiches, ice cream, prettily tinted and tasteless sherbet, they were compelled to accept, one by one, a year's-end gift, all wrapped and tied with ribbon, from Miss Marsalles. Except among the most naive new pupils this gift caused no excitement of anticipation. It was apt to be a book, and the question was, where did she find such books? They were of the vintage found in old Sunday-school libraries, in attics and the basements of second-hand stores, but they were all stiff-backed, unread, brand new. *Northern Lakes and Rivers, Knowing the Birds, More Tales by Grey-Owl, Little Mission Friends.* She also gave pictures: "Cupid Awake and Cupid Asleep," "After the Bath," "The Little Vigilantes"; most of these seemed to feature that tender childish nudity which our sophisticated prudery found most ridiculous and disgusting. Even the boxed games she gave us proved to be insipid and unplayable—full of complicated rules which allowed everybody to win.

The embarrassment the mothers felt at this time was due not so much to the presents themselves as to a strong doubt whether Miss Marsalles could afford them; it did not help to remember that her fees had gone up only once in ten years (and even when that happened, two or three

174

mothers had quit). They always ended up by saying that she must have other resources. It was obvious—otherwise she would not be living in this house. And then her sister taught—or did not teach any more, she was retired but she gave private lessons, it was believed, in French and German. They must have enough, between them. If you are a Miss Marsalles your wants are simple and it does not cost a great deal to live.

But after the house in Rosedale was gone, after it had given way to the bungalow on Bank Street, these conversations about Miss Marsalles' means did not take place; this aspect of Miss Marsalles' life had passed into that region of painful subjects which it is crude and unmannerly to discuss.

"I will die if it rains," my mother says. "I will die of depression at this affair if it rains." But the day of the party it does not rain and in fact the weather is very hot. It is a hot gritty summer day as we drive down into the city and get lost, looking for Bala Street.

When we find it, it gives the impression of being better than we expected, but that is mostly because it has a row of trees, and the other streets we have been driving through, along the railway embankment, have been unshaded and slatternly. The houses here are of the sort that are divided in half, with a sloping wooden partition in the middle of the front porch; they have two wooden steps and a dirt yard. Apparently it is in one of these half-houses that Miss Marsalles lives. They are red brick, with the front door and the window trim and the porches painted cream, grey, oily-green and yellow. They are neat, kept-up. The front part of the house next to the one where Miss Marsalles lives has been turned into a little store; it has a sign that says: GROCERIES AND CONFECTIONERY.

The door is standing open. Miss Marsalles is wedged between the door, the coatrack and the stairs; there is barely room to get past her into the living room, and it would be impossible, the way things are now, for anyone to get from the living room upstairs. Miss Marsalles is wearing her rouge, her hairdo and her brocaded dress, which it is difficult not to tramp on. In this full light she looks like a character in a masquerade, like the feverish, fancied-up courtesan of an unpleasant Puritan imagination. But the fever is only her rouge; her eyes, when we get close enough to see them, are the same as ever, red-rimmed and merry and without apprehension. My mother and I are kissed—I am greeted, as always, as if I were around five years old—and we get past. It seemed to me that Miss Marsalles was looking beyond us as she kissed us; she was looking up the street for someone who has not yet arrived.

The house has a living room and a dining room, with the oak doors pushed back between them. They are small rooms. Mary Queen of Scots hangs tremendous on the wall. There is no fireplace so the iron firedogs are not there, but the piano is, and even a bouquet of peonies and spirea from goodness knows what garden. Since it is so small the living room looks crowded, but there are not a dozen people in it, including children. My mother speaks to people and smiles and sits down. She says to me, Marg French is not here yet, could she have got lost too?

The woman sitting beside us is not familiar. She is middle-aged and wears a dress of shot taffeta with rhinestone clips; it smells of the cleaners. She introduces herself as Mrs. Clegg, Miss Marsalles' neighbour in the other half of the house. Miss Marsalles has asked her if she would like to hear the children play, and she thought it would be a treat; she is fond of music in any form.

My mother, very pleasant but looking a little uncomfortable, asks about Miss Marsalles' sister; is she upstairs?

"Oh, yes, she's upstairs. She's not herself though, poor thing."

That is too bad, my mother says.

"Yes it's a shame. I give her something to put her to sleep for the afternoon. She lost her powers of speech, you know. Her powers of control generally, she lost." My mother is warned by a certain luxurious lowering of the voice that more lengthy and intimate details may follow and she says quickly again that it is too bad.

"I come in and look after her when the other one goes out on her lessons."

"That's very kind of you. I'm sure she appreciates it."

"Oh well I feel kind of sorry for a couple of old ladies like them. They're a couple of babies, the pair."

My mother murmurs something in reply but she is not looking at Mrs. Clegg, at her brick-red healthy face or the—to me—amazing gaps in her teeth. She is staring past her into the dining room with fairly well-controlled dismay.

What she sees there is the table spread, all ready for the party feast; nothing is lacking. The plates of sandwiches are set out, as they must have been for several hours now; you can see how the ones on top are beginning to curl very slightly at the edges. Flies buzz over the table, settle on the sandwiches and crawl comfortably across the plate of little iced cakes brought from the bakery. The cut-glass bowl, sitting as usual in the centre of the table, is full of purple punch, without ice apparently and going flat.

"I tried to tell her not to put it all out ahead of time," Mrs. Clegg whispers, smiling delightedly, as if she were talking about the whims and

176

errors of some headstrong child. "You know she was up at five o'clock this morning making sandwiches. I don't know what things are going to taste like. Afraid she wouldn't be ready I guess. Afraid she'd forget something. They hate to forget."

"Food shouldn't be left out in the hot weather," my mother says.

"Oh, well I guess it won't poison us for once. I was only thinking what a shame to have the sandwiches dry up. And when she put the ginger-ale in the punch at noon I had to laugh. But what a waste."

My mother shifts and rearranges her voile skirt, as if she has suddenly become aware of the impropriety, the hideousness even, of discussing a hostess's arrangements in this way in her own living room. "Marg French isn't here," she says to me in a hardening voice. "She did say she was coming."

"I am the oldest girl here," I say with disgust.

"Shh. That means you can play last. Well. It won't be a very long programme this year, will it?"

Mrs. Clegg leans across us, letting loose a cloud of warm unfresh odour from between her breasts. "I'm going to see if she's got the fridge turned up high enough for the ice cream. She'd feel awful if it was all to melt."

My mother goes across the room and speaks to a woman she knows and I can tell that she is saying, Marg French *said* she was *coming*. The women's faces in the room, made up some time before, have begun to show the effects of heat and a fairly general uneasiness. They ask each other when it will begin. Surely very soon now; nobody has arrived for at least a quarter of an hour. How mean of people not to come, they say. Yet in this heat, and the heat is particularly dreadful down here, it must be the worst place in the city—well you can almost see their point. I look around and calculate that there is no one in the room within a year of my age.

The little children begin to play. Miss Marsalles and Mrs. Clegg applaud with enthusiasm; the mothers clap two or three times each, with relief. My mother seems unable, although she makes a great effort, to take her eyes off the dining-room table and the complacent journeys of the marauding flies. Finally she achieves a dreamy, distant look, with her eyes focused somewhere above the punch-bowl, which makes it possible for her to keep her head turned in that direction and yet does not in any positive sense give her away. Miss Marsalles as well has trouble keeping her eyes on the performers; she keeps looking towards the door. Does she expect that even now some of the unexplained absentees may turn up? There are far more than half a dozen presents in the inevitable box beside the piano, wrapped in white paper and tied with silver ribbon—not real ribbon, but the cheap kind that splits and shreds.

It is while I am at the piano, playing the minuet from *Berenice*, that the final arrival, unlooked-for by anybody but Miss Marsalles, takes place. It must seem at first that there has been some mistake. Out of the corner of my eye I see a whole procession of children, eight or ten in all, with a red-haired woman in something like a uniform, mounting the front step. They look like a group of children from a private school on an excursion of some kind (there is that drabness and sameness about their clothes) but their progress is too scrambling and disorderly for that. Or this is the impression I have; I cannot really look. Is it the wrong house, are they really on their way to the doctor for shots, or to Vacation Bible Classes? No, Miss Marsalles has got up with a happy whisper of apology; she has gone to meet them. Behind my back there is a sound of people squeezing together, of folding chairs being opened, there is an inappropriate, curiously unplaceable giggle.

And above or behind all this cautious flurry of arrival there is a peculiarly concentrated silence. Something has happened, something unforseen, perhaps something disastrous; you can feel such things behind your back. I go on playing. I fill the first harsh silence with my own particularly dogged and lumpy interpretation of Handel. When I get up off the piano bench I almost fall over some of the new children who are sitting on the floor.

One of them, a boy nine or ten years old, is going to follow me. Miss Marsalles takes his hand and smiles at him and there is no twitch of his hand, no embarrassed movement of his head to disown this smile. How peculiar; and a boy, too. He turns his head towards her as he sits down; she speaks to him encouragingly. But my attention has been caught by his profile as he looks up at her—the heavy, unfinished features, the abnormally small and slanting eyes. I look at the children seated on the floor and I see the same profile repeated two or three times; I see another boy with a very large head and fair shaved hair, fine as a baby's; there are other children whose features are regular and unexceptional, marked only by an infantile openness and calm. The boys are dressed in white shirts and short grey pants and the girls wear dresses of grey-green cotton with red buttons and sashes.

"Sometimes that kind is quite musical," says Mrs. Clegg.

"Who are they?" my mother whispers, surely not aware of how upset she sounds.

"They're from that class she has out at the Greenhill School. They're nice little things and some of them quite musical but of course they're not all there."

My mother nods distractedly; she looks around the room and meets the trapped, alerted eyes of the other women, but no decision is reached. There is nothing to be done. These children are going to play. Their playing is no worse—not much worse—than ours, but they seem to go so slowly, and then there is nowhere to look. For it is a matter of politeness surely not to look closely at such children, and yet where else can you look during a piano performance but at the performer? There is an atmosphere in the room of some freakish inescapable dream. My mother and the others are almost audible saying to themselves: *No, I know it is not right to be repelled by such children and I am not repelled, but nobody told me I was going to come here to listen to a procession of little— little idiots for that's what they are—*WHAT KIND OF A PARTY IS THIS? Their applause however has increased, becoming brisk, let-us-at-least-get-this-over-with. But the programme shows no signs of being over.

Miss Marsalles says each child's name as if it were a cause for celebration. Now she says, "Dolores Boyle!" A girl as big as I am, a long-legged, rather thin and plaintive-looking girl with blonde, almost white, hair uncoils herself and gets up off the floor. She sits down on the bench and after shifting around a bit and pushing her long hair back behind her ears she begins to play.

We are accustomed to notice performances, at Miss Marsalles' parties, but it cannot be said that anyone has ever expected music. Yet this time the music establishes itself so effortlessly, with so little demand for attention, that we are hardly even surprised. What she plays is not familiar. It is something fragile, courtly and gay, that carries with it the freedom of a great unemotional happiness. And all that this girl does—but this is something you would not think could ever be done—is to play it so that this can be felt, all this can be felt, even in Miss Marsalles' living-room on Bala Street on a preposterous afternoon. The children are all quiet, the ones from Greenhill School and the rest. The mothers sit, caught with a look of protest on their faces, a more profound anxiety than before, as if reminded of something that they had forgotten; the white-haired girl sits ungracefully at the piano with her head hanging down, and the music is carried through the open door and the windows to the cindery summer street.

Miss Marsalles sits beside the piano and smiles at everybody in her usual way. Her smile is not triumphant, or modest. She does not look like a magician who is watching people's faces to see the effect of a rather original revelation; nothing like that. You would think, now that at the

179

very end of her life she has found someone whom she can teach—whom she must teach—to play the piano, she would light up with the importance of this discovery. But it seems that the girl's playing like this is something she always expected, and she finds it natural and satisfying; people who believe in miracles do not make much fuss when they actually encounter one. Nor does it seem that she regards this girl with any more wonder than the other children from Greenhill School, who love her, or the rest of us, who do not. To her no gift is unexpected, no celebration will come as a surprise.

The girl is finished. The music is in the room and then it is gone and naturally enough no one knows what to say. For the moment she is finished it is plain that she is just the same as before, a girl from Greenhill School. Yet the music was not imaginary. The facts are not to be reconciled. And so after a few minutes the performance begins to seem, in spite of its innocence, like a trick—a very successful and diverting one, of course, but perhaps—how can it be said?—perhaps not altogether *in good taste*. For the girl's ability, which is undeniable but after all useless, out-of-place, is not really something that anybody wants to talk about. To Miss Marsalles such a thing is acceptable, but to other people, people who live in the world, it is not. Never mind, they must say something and so they speak gratefully of the music itself, saying how lovely, what a beautiful piece, what is it called?

"The Dance of the Happy Shades," says Miss Marsalles. *Danse des ombres heureuses*, she says, which leaves nobody any the wiser.

But then driving home, driving out of the hot red-brick streets and out of the city and leaving Miss Marsalles and her no longer possible parties behind, quite certainly forever, why is it that we are unable to say—as we must have expected to say—*Poor Miss Marsalles*? It is the Dance of the Happy Shades that prevents us, it is that one communiqué from the other country where she lives.

180

THE COLONEL'S HASH RESETTLED*

A Toronto critic, discussing the story "Images," said that the house in the ground—the roofed-over cellar that the hermit character lives in—symbolized death, of course, and burial, and that it was a heavy gloomy sort of story because there was nothing to symbolize resurrection. Typical of Canadian fiction, he went on to say, but I didn't follow him very far because I was feeling gloomy myself, about what he had said, and angry, and amazingly uneasy. Surely a roofed-over cellar doesn't mean any such thing, I thought, unless I want it to? Surely it's not that simple? I wrote the story, didn't I? If I hadn't sat down and written the story he wouldn't be able to talk about it, and come to all these interesting and perhaps profitable conclusions about Canadian Literature—well, he probably would have come to these conclusions all the same, but he would have had to dig up somebody else's story (I notice the choice of verb and never mind) to do it—so I get to say, don't I, whether a house in the ground is death and burial or whether it is, of all unlikely things, *a house in the ground*?

Well, the answer is no, I do not get to say, and I should have known that already. What you write is an offering; anybody can come and take what they like from it. Nevertheless I went stubbornly back to the real facts, as I saw them, the real house in the real world, and tried to discover what it was doing in the story and how the story was put together in the first place.

I grew up on the untidy, impoverished, wayward edge of a small town, where houses were casually patched and held together, and there was a man living in a house exactly like that—the roofed-over cellar of a house that had been burned down. Another man and his wife, I remember, lived in the kitchen of a burned-out house, whose blackened front walls still stood, around a roomful of nettles. (What is that going to symbolize, if I use it in a story some day?) Such a choice of living-quarters was thought only mildly eccentric. It was a cheap and practical way of getting shelter, for people with no means to build, or buy, or re-build. And when I think of the slanting, patched roof and the stove-pipe, the house as a marvellous, solid, made, final thing, I feel that I have somehow betrayed it, putting it in a story to be extracted this way, as a bloodless symbol. There is a sort of treachery to innocent objects—to houses, chairs, dresses,

---

*Alice Munro's essay was untitled. I entitled it "The Colonel's Hash Resettled" to echo the title of an essay by Mary McCarthy which explores the meaning of "symbol." That essay can be found in *The Humanist in the Bathtub*, Signet Books.—J.M.

dishes, and to roads, fields, landscapes—which a writer removes from their natural, dignified obscurity and sets down in print. There they lie, exposed, often shabbily treated, inadequately, badly, clumsily transformed. Once I've done that to things, I lose them from my private memory. There are primitive people who will not allow themselves to be photographed for fear the camera will steal their souls. That has always seemed to me a not unreasonable belief. And even as I most feverishly, desperately practise it, I am a little afraid that the work with words may turn out to be a questionable trick, an evasion (and never more so than when it is most dazzling, apt and striking), an unavoidable lie. So I could not go now and look at that house with a perfectly clear conscience, symbol or not.

I do think symbols exist, or rather, that things are symbolic, but I think that their symbolism is infinitely complex and never completely discovered. Are there really writers who sit down and say yes, well, now here I need a symbol, let's see what I have in the files? I don't know; you never know how other writers work. In the case of that house, I gave it to the character without thinking about it, just as I gave him the whisky-drinking cat that actually belonged to the father of a friend of mine. I don't remember deciding to do this. I do remember how the story started. It started with the picture in my mind of the man met in the woods, coming obliquely down the river-bank, carrying the hatchet, and the child watching him, and the father unaware, bending over his traps. For a long time I was carrying this picture in my mind, as I am carrying various pictures now which may or may not turn into stories. Of course the character did not spring from nowhere. His ancestors were a few old men, half hermits, half madmen, often paranoid, occasionally dangerous, living around the country where I grew up, not living in the woods but in old farm-houses, old family homes. I had always heard stories about them; they were established early as semi-legendary figures in my mind.

From this picture the story moved outward, in a dim uncertain way. When this was happening I was not so much making it as remembering it. I remembered the nurse-cousin, though she was not really there to remember; there was no one original for her. I remembered the trip along the river, to look at traps, with my father, although I had never gone. I remembered my mother's bed set up in the dining-room, although it was never there. It has actually become difficult to sort out the real memories —like the house—used in this story from those that are not 'real' at all. I think the others are real because I did not consciously plan, make, or arrange them; I found them. And it is all deeply, perfectly true to me, as a dream might be true, and all I can say, finally, about the making of a story like this is that it must be made in the same way our dreams are made, truth in them being cast, with what seems to us often a rather high-handed frivolity, in any kind of plausible, implausible, giddy, strange, humdrum terms at all. This is the given story (I hate to use that adjective because it calls to mind a writer in some sort of trance, and seems to wrap the whole subject in a lot of trashy notions, but it will have to do) and from that I work, getting no more help, doing the hard repetitive work of putting it in words that are hardly any good at all, then a little better, then quite a bit better, at times satisfactory.

The other story used here, "Dance of the Happy Shades," is done in the form of a memoir more or less as a matter of convenience. I have stories that come from inside and outside. This is a story that came from outside. But now that I write that, I wonder if it is a true distinction. When I get something from outside—in the form of an anecdote told at a family dinner-party, as this was—I have to see it in my own terms, at once, or it isn't going to be a story, however much in superficial points of interest it seems to be crying out to be made fiction. The *I* of the story is a masquerade, she is a little middle-class girl I never was, an attempt to see the story through the eyes of the relative who told it to me. But once I got used to being her I could, as in the other story, remember things—the house, the dresses, Mary Queen of Scots; I was not told any of that.

Writing or talking about writing makes me superstitiously uncomfortable. My explanations have a way of turning treacherous, half-untrue. Now I distrust the way I used the word *remember*, in the last paragraph. I could have said *invent*; the kind of remembering I mean is what fictional invention is; but I wanted to show, too, that it is not quite deliberate. I feel like a juggler trying to describe exactly how he catches the balls, and although he has trained to be a juggler for a long time and has worked hard, he still feels it may be luck, a good deal of the time, and luck is an unhappy thing to talk about, it is not reliable. Some people think it is best when doing any of these things—dancing, say, or making love—to follow very closely what you are about. Some people think differently. I do.

ALICE MUNRO

Ray Smith

Ray Smith was born in 1941 and is from Mabou, Cape Breton.
He lived most of his early years in Halifax, where he graduated
from Dalhousie University. He has been writing since 1964.
His stories have been published in Canadian and American
anthologies. (Smith has written a particularly interesting essay
on his work in *Sixteen by Twelve*, Ed. J. Metcalf. Ryerson
Press, Toronto, 1970) Evaluative remarks appear in *Great
Canadian Short Stories*. Ed. A. Lucas. Dell, New York, 1971.

Smith is currently working on a novel and a film script
and is teaching English in Montreal.

Bibliography

Cape Breton is the Thought Control Centre of Canada. House of Anansi,
Toronto, 1969. (Stories)

184

A Cynical Tale

Sweet William was a very successful fag couturier who lived in a reful-
gent fag apt. that had cost him five figures. He had a boyfriend named
George. Life was very good for Sweet William & indeed he had often
been heard to exclaim: 'Everything is George!' (one of his loudest
clangers). Sweet William was in his thirties.

But then there moved into the apt. next door to Sweet William's an
ultrafeminist of undeniable beauty named Barbary Ellen. Barbary Ellen
owned a string of health spas, a ritzy speed reading course for execs. &
a language school. Hardly a month had gone by when Babsi had insinuated
herself into the good graces of Sweet William. She did this by buying his
clothes and sending him cases of plum cordial which was his and George's
favorite drink. However, George did not like Barbary Ellen. Barbary
Ellen was herself in her thirties & George had made it to his twentieth yr.

One night Swt. Wlm. took George to a cocktail party and what happened was they didn't like it and went home for a plum cordial. (*It
should be noted here that Barbary Ellen in fact knew they were going
out.*)

When they got home again they found Barbary Ellen had insinuated
herself into their apt.

'I thaid she wath a nathty bitch!' This from Grg.

'Goodness gracious!' cried Sweet Wlm.

'Vithious prying creature!' He thereupon scurried off to protect his
protector's lingerie.

'Shit.' So saying, Babs E. proceeded to pull a neat little automatic
fromst out her garter holster.

(A NOTE OF EXPL.: *All was not what it might have seemed. Sweet
William was in fact a Russian spy—having been subverted whilst in
Moskva to view the spring collections ('All the sprightly charm of a pre-
war tractor')—and Barbary Ellen was in the employ of counter-
espionage.*)

Well!

(Note: *a frail swoon approacheth.*)

Sweet William sank to the Bokhara with a groan & all might have
transpired A-OK had it not been for George who came scampering in at
this moment and tried to strangle our lush Barbie Doll with a taupe
nylon. Of course she had to shoot him. (THE FATAL FLAW! THE
TURN OF THE SCREW! THE LAST TRUMP! *et al.: for B. E. was no*

less than a latent Lesbian & hated all fags & thus, stupidly, let old George have the full magazine of twelve rounds in the forehead. viz fitfitfitfitfit-fitfitfitfitfitfitfit! The 'fit' being caused by the silencer. So.) Then she put the corpse in the fridge and went on looking for the microfilm which was indeed the very object of her visit.

But! Sweetie W. was not so silly as some of us think fags to be. Not a bit of it! He had craftily secreted about his apt. various and sundry deadly devices of devious but innocent-seeming nature. Thusly, while Barbary Ellen's svelte St. Laurent suited back *(this being the final insult to Swt. W.)* was turned toward his supposedly swooned bod, Sweet William plucked a sprig of briar from a fag floral arrangement nearby and drove the stem *(previously dipped in a deadly poison by himself)* right the way through Bab's skirt, half-slip & chaste Lycra panty girdle into her right buttock.

'Fag creep!' screeched Barbary Eln. with somewhat less than her usual aplomb, then lamented as follows: 'Me, Barbary Ellen, beaten by a lousy fag creep: Arrgh!'

So saying, she plucked from the same floral arngmt. an equally poisoned rose clipping and this no-less deadly *fleur* she thrust through S. W.'s shot-silk fag trousers and through his Lycra panty girdle into his left buttock.

Ah! Irony!

Anyway, they both of them died and their cadavers just stayed there on the floor, one beside t'other. And by some shoddy admin. oversight on the part of their superiors in the spy game, and because the legal eagles conducting their businesses were straight folk thus in love with lucre, the persons of Barbary Ellen and Sweet William *(and of George on ice if it come to that)* were not missed. And they didn't live in France so there was no concierge to twig & rat.

The briar & the rose, strange though it seem to us of the routine, day-to-day world, took root in the bodies of Sweet Willie and Barbie E. & flowered & intertwined *(symbolic of the love which might have united them in life had not nature played a cruel jest upon their hormonal balances before birth)* & mingled, thus adding a piquant touch to this gruesome tableau, etc.

Peril

The rain poured down. It poured down upon the bare trees and the dead grass, upon the bushes and the gravestones. It splashed on the top of the coffin, it drummed on the umbrellas the mourners held, it trickled down Passquick's neck and over his forehead and down the sides of his nose. The rain fell cold out of cold clouds through the grey air: a perfect day for a funeral.

That one, said Passquick to himself, is the widow. Over there is the daughter; those will be friends and relations; that one standing off with the beard and sad eyes, that one is the enemy.

The minister said certain cue words. The mechanism was tripped and the coffin sank slowly into the pit. The minister threw a clod of earth in. The widow shredded flowers. Some of the other men threw clods in. Passquick thought he might do the same, but someone was sure to find he had never known the deceased. They would think him morbid. So Passquick moved away.

Then he noticed, off behind a clump of bushes, the gravediggers. They stood under a tree as if for protection, smoking for the same reason, knowing neither did much good. When the widow goes they will sidle over and cover the coffin. Will they pun together? Perhaps he should circle back and meet them. No, that would not do. . . .

At the lane where the cars were parked, Passquick turned and saw the mourners approaching. Near the end of the group was a red-faced man, middle-aged, chubby. That would be an uncle, a travelling salesman of, say, plumbing supplies. 'I travel in bathtubs,' he would be telling the man beside him. Yes, see, they were chuckling together.

Passquick wandered off through the cemetery, through the rain. Behind him doors slammed and the engines started up. A line of sight through the bushes and gravestones gave him a glimpse of the gravediggers hard at it; they had their work cut out for them.

It was some time later, as he rounded a clump of shrubs, that Passquick ran into the man in the black cape.

'Oh!' cried the man in the cape and leaped up and looked afraid.

Passquick mumbled an apology, bowed slightly (cemeteries bring out the formalities) and turned to go.

'Oh, I'm sorry,' said the man, 'I thought you were one of the sexton's men. You don't have to. . . . It's ruined anyway. . . .'

Passquick asked what was ruined.

'The spell, it's ruined now. I'll have to start over again tomorrow. . . . Oh, don't apologize; you couldn't help it. Really, it's my. . . .'

The man in the cape was middle-aged, thin and bony, the blue veins in his cheeks showing as they do sooner or later on people who use blade razors, and a great beak of a nose. He was dressed all in black, and the black cape hanging to his ankles had a hood which was tied tight around his face and came to a dull point at the crown.

'I'm always frightening away mourners and visitors. That's why the sexton is always after me and that's why I came today, there aren't many people here on rainy days. Most people have the sense to come in out of the . . . oh, sorry, of course you. . . .'

Passquick laughed.

'But so are you; so we're senseless together.'

The man in the cape didn't take that one at all well. He coughed meaningfully and began secreting his paraphernalia in a black bag.

'What I meant was, if I say we're both senseless and I know I'm not, then you can't be either . . . it was meant ironically. . . .'

'Straw for your irony!' said the man with unexpected vehemence. 'I've suffered from the irony of the fair-weather friends, of the hail-fellow-well-mets. Cruel, that's what it is, cruel I say, the way you all go on. Why. . . .'

'It wasn't meant to be unkind; it was meant in a friendly way. . . .'

'Yes, I'm sure . . . . Well. . . .'

They mumbled back and forth until the little man was mollified. Then Passquick asked timidly what the little man did . . . was . . . is . . . err. . . .

'Why, I'm a necromancer, of course.'

'A necromancer?'

'I conjure the dead.'

'Oh yes, of course.'

'I'm a journeyman, though I'm not working with a master these days. Journeymen usually work with one master or another.'

'It must be hard for you without a master's experience and wisdom to direct and guide your work. . . .'

'Well, yes. . . .'

The necromancer had all his bones and joss sticks and such in the black bag. As they walked away he explained that you had to be careful these days, many master necromancers were just frauds.

'Out for a quick buck, shysters, *no faith.* Sometimes you wonder. . . .'

As they strolled along he pointed out various graves he had worked: a good job on this one . . . this was the first . . . dropped a brick that night . . . . He explained that he no longer worked nights because he was afraid of the dark.

'It's silly, I know, but there are bats and owls twittering and hooting . . . awfully scary . . . and then you occasionally get graverobbers and body-snatchers. . . .'

'That right?'

'Oh yes, and they like to work completely in secret. Don't forget your average bodysnatcher is just a common thug; quite fierce when aroused. . . .'

Passquick admitted that necromancy wasn't the simple trade he might have thought it.

'But it isn't a trade,' cried the necromancer.

'Well, of course. . . .'

'Trade! How gross! The very idea! Why I'd . . . .' That petulance again.

'I mean, I meant it rather as a euphemism. As one minister would speak to another of their "trade"; it's. . . .'

'Then you're a necromancer too?'

There was no doubt about it; as dull-witted necromancers went, this one pretty well took the cake. After Passquick had explained it all and got things going again, the necromancer went on:

'No, you see, necromancy's an art. You must have heard it called "the art of necromancy" or "one of the black arts"? Yes, well, that's what it is, you see. Those poets and painters, they like to call themselves artists, but what do they create, eh, what, really?'

'Poems and paintings?'

'Yes, of course, any fool can see that. But what is a poem? Dead scratchings on dead paper. And a painting? Dead paint on a dead canvas. Dead: *no life*. But your necromancer, now, he's a different kettle of fish. Give him dead matter and he puts life into it, real guts, spirit. . . .'

Now there was an argument for you; Passquick accepted it as soon as decently possible. The necromancer went on:

'And what does society do? Eh? I'll tell you what society does, it rejects its necromancers. We have to skulk about graveyards, mortuaries and hospitals like . . . like common thugs. We have no artistic freedom: we are scoffed at, humiliated, hunted down . . . you just don't realize what it means to be forced to live outside society . . . most of us are warm human beings who need love, who want to love in return, to be accepted. . . .'

'But instead you have to live underground. . . .'

Fortunately the necromancer missed it and went on to talk about the younger necromancers he had met.

'Perhaps I'm growing older, perhaps I'm getting a bit conservative, but I think their work is pretty hollow. They've got no style, no elegance, no . . . beauty in their work. Rebels, that's what they are, rebels. And'— he grasped Passquick's sleeve for emphasis—'they don't even know what they're rebelling against, you know what I mean? This new stuff, it's all shallow . . . so shallow. . . .'

He shook his head to show the weight of his sorrow.

'Terrible,' murmured Passquick, 'terrible. . . .'

It was while the necromancer was explaining how he had gone as a clerk with a big brokerage house until one day . . . that he and Passquick came to the gate of the cemetery and found they had to separate. '. . . skinned my eyeballs,' the necromancer was saying.

'Well,' said Passquick, 'it's been a pleasure meeting you.'

'No, no, the pleasure was all mine. It's so rarely you meet someone who really appreciates the struggle and the sacrifice . . . . The world should make a place for necromancers. . . .'

And so they trudged down their separate ways through the cold rain. Amid the cars and the people and the buildings Passquick felt a great joy in his heart; he floated down the street. When he got home he had a bath and sipped hot lemonade as the steam rose about him. There's nothing like a graveyard, he said, to bring it out in people. But he couldn't think of a word for 'it.'

2

Period watched the carousel from a distance. Between him and the carousel stretched a green lawn with tree shadows like continents on a map. The lawn was so flat that Period had the impression (as had also many before him) that the lawn could be rolled up on a pole and carried away. (The carpet movers, stout, slow, their cloth caps. . . .) The month was May, a morning. The only people about were the women with their children and the pensioners on their benches.

Ump-tiddly music was piped out of the carousel. Period set off across the park toward a bench which was closer to the carousel but off to the right. A course tangential to a point on the radius. . . .

But really, he thought, why am I thinking about tangents when I am in the midst of this wonderful scene? Oh joyful! joyful! The mothers and children and pensioners, he saw as he moved slowly along, were arranged most artfully about. The scene was like a painting in its serenity; yet the figures were too small. It was like music in its harmony; but music was too demanding. Light hung everywhere; the shadows were blinding. The little toddlers toddled roly-poly short distances and their cries and laughs came lightly on the breeze, shattered, the sequence jumbled, random, like a volley of arrows shot by little painted soldiers.

So also the ump-tiddly music from the carousel.

The turf sprang underfoot, green and fresh and young. The melted frost moisture would still be inches from the surface, nourishing, full of rich goodness, plant food, the cycle of water, interlocking with other cycles, cloud, animal and plant remains, compost, smelling words. . . .

Period staggered. He was dizzy, a city man overwhelmed by nature. How can I know, I've never lived on a farm, never grown crops, my lungs dirty from soot and cigarettes, I can't smell the smells true, I can't . . . . Nature is also cruel . . . bad years, drought and flood, blight and locusts . . . . There's too much . . . I must . . . humility. . . .

The park had at least the advantage of being well-treed. Of course, one saw the lamp posts, the gravelled walks, flowerbeds and such, but the trees hid the buildings and streets and deadened the noise enough for a city man to call it almost silence.

But really, such a wonderful scene! And anyway, so what if a park is manmade? Think of it, he thought, as a park, a first-hand park, not second-hand countryside. A farmer would never be able to enjoy a park as much as I can. The birds, for e.g., are not imported, transplanted country birds, but real live original city park birds.

And the carousel! Four hundred and twenty three thousand bitter-sweet fantasies about Pierrot and Pierrette. That! for you Colin Clout and other such rude goatherds.

The bench Period had chosen sat beside a path and not far from a fountain (from which he took a drink of chlorinated water—well it wards off the bloody plague, doesn't it?) and gave a pleasant view of the carousel with a blooming lilac bush coyly obscuring it. Period sat down and stretched half a dozen limbs, yawned, groaned, hummed and whistled and finally sat still for at least twenty seconds. Then he enmeshed himself on purpose in the actions of smoking a cigarette—and the earth smells be damned—and decided to think about nothing. It was while he was failing at this that G. K. Chesterton came along and sat down beside him.

'I am G. K. Chesterton,' announced G. K. Chesterton.

'Are you really? I'm. . . .'

'Of course not. Chesterton has been dead for years.'

'That's what I thought. I'm. . . .'

'I'm his ghost.'

Period couldn't recall what Chesterton had looked like around the face (a beard?), but he knew he had been fat and that he sat in the park a lot.

'Yes, I ghost wrote all his stories, poems and essays.'

'Even Father Brown?'

'Especially Father Brown.'

'I didn't know Chesterton wrote essays.'

'Neither did I. I expect he did though, don't you. If a man wrote stories and poems, he surely must have written essays, don't you think? . . . Or do you?'

'It seems probable.'

'Yes . . . that's what I thought.'

'Um.'

'And who did you almost say you were?'

'Uhh . . . Pierrot.'

'That right? You meet the strangest people around a park in the morning. Pierrot, eh?'

'Yes, I live in that carousel over there.'

'That's not a carousel. That's a bandstand. A carousel is a merry-go-round. That's a bandstand.'

'I know, but it has the same shape as a carousel and "carousel" has a better sound to it.'

'Quite right. Of course. Yes.'

G. K. gazed off at the carousel and muttered to himself a while. Then he undid the neck of his tweed cape and turned to look at Period. There was so much fat about his neck that G. K. had to turn his shoulders too; a very elaborate and dignified movement.

'You're a bit happy for a Pierrot,' he said after a time. 'I thought Pierrots were supposed to be sad unless there was a Pierrette about. In which case the Pierrot (a) was allowed to be bitter-sweet and (b) would not have the time of day for anyone else. How d'ye explain that?'

'Well, it's true that I've lost my Pierrette, but the fact is, I've been trying to lose her for months.'

'That right?'

'Yeah.' They nodded at each other for some time. 'Not very bright, you know.' They nodded some more. 'In fact,' added Period after a full thirty seconds of nodding, 'I would say offhand that when the Pierrettes were lining up outside the brains department my Pierrette was pretty near the end of the line. When she got to the pot. . . .'

'Nothing but bone with the marrow sucked out, eh?'

'In other words, yes, a bonehead.'

'That was implied in my metaphor,' said G. K. stuffily.

'It was also implied in mine; and mine was before yours.'

G. K. Chesterton turned enthusiastically.

'Pierrot, I like you. You stand up for yourself. That's the way, meh boy, put 'em in their places; don't be afraid to swagger. Wave the fist. Shake the . . . err. . . .'

'Stick?'

'The very word. The . . . very . . . word.'

Period nodded and grinned and G. K. Chesterton nodded and grinned. Period stared across the park at the carousel and G. K. stared at him. This went on for a while.

'Tell me though,' said G. K. at length, 'tell me; your Pierrette, was she pretty at all? I mean. . . .'

Period stared.

'Pretty?! Pretty, you ask.'

'Uhh . . . yes, more or less, I guess I did. . . .'

Period extended his arms to indicate something which would require great imagination.

'My Pierrette was (is, I suppose you could say) was—is . . . well, even your massive brain cannot (I contend) project an image of a woman possessing half her beauty.'

'No shit?'

'Oh yes . . . yes. I tell you, she had a bust . . . well, you wouldn't believe it. Numbers alone couldn't express . . . I mean, I have a certain facility, with words, but I'm sorry, I'm afraid I couldn't begin to . . . .'

'Don't say you're sorry, meh boy. Sign of weakness.'

Period shook his head.

'You're right, of course, Mr. Chesterton. I apologize too much.'

'A terrible habit,' said Chesterton with terrible sincerity. 'A habit which you must . . . *smash*!'

G. K. illustrated this by bringing his fist down with crushing force upon his knee. 'Ow!'

'But there's another side to it,' said Period, brightening up. 'You see, I never mean my apologies.'

They went on about this for a while. Then Period went back to gazing at his carousel and G. K. Chesterton took from the folds of his cape a little volume of Hazlitt's essays bound in leather. He began to read one of the essays. Thus they sat for about half an hour.

'Must be off now,' said Chesterton at last.

'Going anywhere in particular?'

'Of course not.'

'Well, good day. It's been nice meeting you, Mr. Chesterton.'

'An honour, I assure you. I might have been Cecil Rhodes and then we'd never have gotten on, I'm sure.'

'And I might have been the young Goethe.'

'Heaven forbid.'

When Chesterton was some distance along the path he turned and called back: 'But then meh boy, you aren't such great shakes as a Pierrot.'

'No? Why is that? And how would you know anyway?'

'No. Because your feet are too big. And because I say so. Respect your elders and don't be so blasted impudent.' He turned and went. The words 'Young pup' floated back from him inside a balloon as green as your eye.

'It's a carousel,' said Period. 'And damn the consequences!'

He walked the opposite way along the tangent and not long after that the office workers began to arrive with their sandwiches and their little cartons of milk. Somewhere among them wandered a Pierrette, bone-headed, disconsolate and stacked.

3

Purlieu came out of the boulders at the south end of the beach and began walking north. The August sun hung high above his left shoulder and the water lapped and swished on his left. On his right, at the top of the beach, a cliff rose and the cliff was topped with twisted pines.

The day was a weekday so the beach was empty. Purlieu went along doing the various things people do while walking on beaches: he ran, he walked, he picked up driftwood, skipped stones, teased waves, etc. When he had gone a bit of a distance he took off his shoes because sand kept getting in them. Some time later he took off his shirt and undershirt so as to let the sun at his shoulders. Later still he rolled up his pantlegs so as to tease the waves without getting the cuffs wet. Purlieu was doing his usual mediocre job of relaxing.

When he had gone a mile, Purlieu was halfway along the beach. Here the cliff turned away and ran inland as far as the eye could see. Now, at the top of the beach, was a sand ridge as high as a man. This ridge marked a waterline of some sort (high water of storms, perhaps) and was topped with eel-grass. Behind the ridge (Purlieu scrambled up to see) lay a wasteland of sand dunes covered with waving eel-grass. The dunes rolled away for a mile or so until they stopped at the edge of a harbour. The cliff formed the southern edge of the dune waste and of the harbour.

The highest of the dunes was in the middle. It rose about twenty feet and had the appearance of a castle keep. Purlieu thought he would like to climb it; he considered this and kept considering it until at last he did not climb it, but slid back down and continued along the beach.

Purlieu had not gone much further when he became aware of the weight of clothing he was carrying. He had his shirt and undershirt, his shoes and socks in his hands. That was obviously pointless, he decided after five minutes thought, I will put them down on a driftwood log. This he did; and went on toward the north.

The north end of the beach was marked by two manmade structures. Shiny, black, low in the ocean lay the line of a breakwater. The breakwater ran through the surf and on up the beach and in past the ridge at the top of the beach. It kept the beach from sliding into the harbour mouth which flowed just beyond it. Some distance in from the top of the beach (and astride the breakwater) stood a little lighthouse to mark the harbour. On the far side of the harbour mouth rose a high treeless hill with grass of the peculiar grey-green which grass takes on when it has been blasted by gales and kissed by the fog.

It was when Purlieu was halfway along the north half of the beach that he decided to tease the waves again. With his cuffs rolled up and no excess baggage in his arms he became quite daring. So he fell; a wave had teased back.

After much complex deliberation Purlieu came to a decision about his situation: he would take off his wet pants and wet underpants and go for a swim while they dried. The point was that if anyone came onto the beach, Purlieu would have time to get out of the water and into his clothes. Purlieu put the things on a driftwood log and raced into the water.

Well known are the felicitations of a swim in the ocean: Purlieu had a whale of a time.

The first thing Purlieu felt when he came out of the water was the immensity about him. The beach swung off to the south in a crescent, one of those sumptuous curves only nature has the patience to bother with. The cliff, which had seemed so high at the time, was a pencil line. Then the sheer waste of dunes, wide as an epoch, and the pretty lighthouse, the hill, the sky and the sea . . . .

So, inadequately, the great landscape: Purlieu leaped for joy!

The second thing he felt when he came out of the water was that he was not alone. This for good reason, for he wasn't.

Not far from the pants and undershorts sat an old man in a wheelchair. Over the man's knees was draped a blanket; in his knobby right hand he held a cane and the cane was stuck in the sand. The old man wore a sleeveless grey pullover over a long-sleeved shirt. On his head he wore a tweed workman's cap. His lower lip jutted out, sunglasses covered his eyes and his head nodded forward and back slightly and continually. The old man did not seem to be looking at Purlieu; he seemed to be looking at the sea. But, of course, the sunglasses . . . .

About ten feet to the old man's right and back a bit stood a table. The table was of wood and Purlieu could see that the legs would fold and the top come down and it would thus be portable and like a small suitcase. It had been constructed, Purlieu guessed, in *fin de siècle* England for those elaborate picnics one reads about. Behind the table, preparing an elaborate picnic lunch, stood a young girl, naked.

Of course Purlieu felt certain things upon seeing the naked girl. But she seemed quite unconcerned with her nakedness, with his nakedness, with everything but preparing the lunch. She smiled at Purlieu and gestured did he want any. Of course he gestured yes.

'Wet,' said the old man to Purlieu without turning his head to look at him.

'Wet, sir?'

'Yes, sir, wet, sir.'

'Yes, sir, I've been in the water.'

'The ocean.'

'The sea,' said the girl and she looked up and smiled.

'How was the water?'

'Fine . . . just right.'

The old man's head kept nodding. He did not turn it at all to look at Purlieu and he said nothing else, so Purlieu, rather at a loss for words, turned and looked out to sea. He wished he had a towel to dry himself with. The sun had moved so that it was shining in almost straight across the water at the beach and Purlieu also wished he had sunglasses. He didn't have sunglasses and he didn't have a towel and he was still too wet to put his clothes on (which he probably wouldn't have done anyway because of the girl being naked) so he just stood looking out to sea.

'Did you see any eels, jellyfish, or other marine life whilst you were swimming?'

Purlieu, who hadn't, said he hadn't.

'Perhaps it's the wrong time of year,' said the girl.

'Poppycock,' said the old man.

Purlieu shifted his feet uncomfortably.

'I used to swim myself,' said the old man in a tough voice, as if he were angry at remembering something he could no longer enjoy. 'I won

196

races at it. We did a different stroke in those days. I think it was different; I don't suppose we thought much about the type of stroke we did.'

Purlieu went through the elaborate motions of sitting down on the log beside his clothes.

'Do you race, meh boy?'

'Err . . . no . . . . No, I don't . . . race.'

'Hunhh.'

'Neither do I,' added the girl.

And that was that for a while. The old man sat there nodding and staring at the sea; the girl took from little drawers in the picnic box sandwiches, radishes, hardboiled eggs and the like and went on preparing the lunch; and Purlieu went on in his usual way, looking and thinking and sooner or later ending up in much the same place he had started.

At last the girl asked if they would like the lemonade now.

'Why yes, thank you,' said Purlieu. 'Lemonade would be lovely just now.' The old man grunted a grunt which clearly articulated an affirmative answer. The girl brought them each a glass of lemonade with ice cubes tinkling.

'Thank you very much,' said Purlieu.

The old man grunted ditto.

'The air,' Purlieu ventured, 'is very bright, isn't it?' It was a brave venture; he realized this. But it worked out well enough:

'Yes,' replied the old man. 'It is very clean air, clear in a way, yet very full. That is a paradox: clean (or empty) yet full.'

'It's the light,' said the girl.

'Yes, the light.'

At this point the girl began to serve the picnic food. She carried a little tray each to the old man and to Purlieu. The old man's wheelchair had some ingenuity to hold the tray. The girl took a tray for herself and sat on a log on her side of the old man and as far forward as Purlieu so that the three formed an isosceles triangle, broad-based upon the sea.

They all ate with relish.

The little waves lapped and swished against the beach. Purlieu squinted at the blinding sun fragments splashed upon the water. Near to shore the water was a light blue (and light in weight, he remarked to himself) and darker blue farther out. But bright everywhere: the sea! the sea!

During the meal the old man gave a bit of a monologue starting with the smoked oysters the girl had served:

'The molluscs are fascinating creatures and little understood by man,' he began. 'I have made a particular study of the molluscs and have found out some very interesting things about them . . . .'

197

Purlieu noticed when he next turned to the sea that the sun was now obscured somewhat by high thin clouds which had come out of the west, quite suddenly, as clouds will do upon the ocean. The water darkened and a bit of a breeze sprang up.

'The tide is on the flow,' said the old man. 'The wind is freshening for the evening.'

'It looks like a storm this evening.'

'There's gold upon the sea,' said the girl.

'No. The storm won't begin till after midnight. But I grant you the sea *looks* like storm in an hour or so.'

'Peace,' whispered the girl, 'peace.'

It was about this time that some combination of the senses suggested to Purlieu that if he looked back over the dunes he would see something that hadn't been there the last time he looked. So he looked.

Apart from a band of light along the ridge at the top of the beach where the light gathered, the tops of the highest dunes with the castle keep off to the south rising high and stolid and the sky above, the dunes seemed much darker than they really were. At first Purlieu could see nothing that had not been there before; but very soon he saw the horseman.

'Why there's a horseman,' he said.

'Where . . . oh, there!' said the girl.

'Going to light the light in the lighthouse,' said the old man. 'Comes from over beyond,' and he gestured vaguely to over beyond.

'You can't hear the hooves,' said the girl.

'No you can't.'

And you couldn't. The sound was perhaps lost bouncing about the dunes. Neither were the horse's hooves visible, for the crest at the top of the beach hid them.

Purlieu and the girl stood and watched the silent horseman ride by. Once or twice he disappeared from view beyond high dunes. For a while he turned as he went to look at them and the light struck his face. After a time he disappeared beyond a dune far off toward the lighthouse and did not reappear on the other side.

Purlieu noticed suddenly that he was cold. But still the girl did not seem to want to get dressed; in fact, she seemed not to have any clothes about. So Purlieu stayed naked.

'Sailors,' said the old man, 'have a great feeling for lighthouses. Imagine what they feel. It is deep twilight and you are on watch on the starboard bridge wing. There is light in the wheel room but it is low enough to leave you with the dark. Overhead there has been a mackerel sky at sunset and now clouds are gathering in the southwest. It is chilly; the wind is stiffening; you shiver and you think about the rain that will be coming. You look down into the sea which is coursing by: the sea. Here I pause to let you imagine what the sailor feels about the sea.'

The old man paused. Purlieu and the girl glanced at one another, then out to sea. Purlieu felt uncomfortable and felt sure the girl did too. He felt certain things about the sea, but as he was not on a ship he felt he probably did not feel as the sailor would have felt.

'And then you look up and there, off the starboard bow, a pinpoint for a moment in the darkness is the light of the lighthouse you've been steering for all week. And now comes a great surge. You remember the peculiar sensation of stepping onto land after a week . . . of the warmth of your favorite waterfront bar . . . of the contrast between the enclosed spaces of land where you can walk for miles and the open spaces of the sea where you live in cramped tension . . . of land and home and love . . . .'

For a long time Purlieu and the girl stared at the sea and the sun darkened until at last it slid down into the thin band of clear sky just above the horizon leaving the clouds black and throwing a yellow path over the sea toward them, the yellow deepening to richest gold on the tops of the waves that lapped and swished against the shore.

'The sea . . . the sea. . . .' whispered the girl.

'Yes, the sea,' grunted the old man.

Then the same feeling came and Purlieu (and this time the girl) turned and saw the horseman riding back between the dunes. In the direct gold light of the sun, the horseman was gold now and he gleamed against the dark sky beyond. When he went briefly behind a dune his disappearances were sudden and surprising; and so his reappearances. And still the horse could not be heard, nor the horse's hooves be seen.

So the three waited; the old man in his wheelchair nodding his head at the sea and Purlieu and the girl, naked, watching the horseman ride by. When the horseman was near the cliff, he turned out of the dunes and continued down the beach to the boulders at the south end. Then the horseman was gone and Purlieu said he thought he would be getting on too.

'It's been a pleasure meeting you,' he said.

'And you too, meh boy.'

'You don't meet many people on the beach,' said the girl.

After other pleasantries, Purlieu began to walk off south. Then he paused and asked if he could help with the picnic box.

'No thank you,' replied the girl. 'It's very easy. It all fits together and folds up. There's a place for it on the wheelchair.'

'Very cunning appurtenance,' added the old man. 'Made to give pleasure.'

'Well . . .' and Purlieu walked on a way before turning to ask if perhaps they'd like him to wait and walk with them.

'No, that's all right. But thank you,' said the girl.

'We go the other way, you see.'

'Oh.'

He left them like that, the old man staring at the sea and nodding from his wheelchair and the lovely naked girl packing the picnic box. As he walked along he picked up the clothes he had dropped and when he reached the far end of the beach he put them on. It was only then that he turned and looked back.

The light from the lighthouse swung about. It swept the dunes and the beach; it disappeared over the sea, flashed across the hill. But Purlieu could not see the old man and the girl. It did not occur to him until much later to wonder what had been the other way.

DINOSAUR

1. What I do not write

Walter wanted to stay with her, he did not want to go outside again. Outside you were jostled by people, the eyes of strangers stared at you and hated you for being different from them. Down into the subway, bustle and push, sweat and rush, and up again into the street to those bloody big doors of Jaspers, VanDamme & Co. 'Have you finished the Commissions Post-Due Statement?' And you'd hardly finished your coffee . . . .

'Penny for them,' said Carol.

He squeezed her small body to him and looked desperately about him.

'The light on the ceiling,' he replied. 'I was wondering what you call that shape. A trapezium?'

'Funny man,' and nibbled his ear.

My God, if only she knew, and he squeezed her to him again, squeezing shut his eyes to keep out the terror and failing.

Who wrote that? When? Where? Obviously part of a novel. Twentieth century. English or North American. 'Subway' is American or Toronto. 'Penny for them' sounds rather English. Let's leave it for a while.

Call it the bone of a dinosaur and try to reconstruct the rest of the book. It began the previous Friday afternoon, inside Walter's head. He should have been working on Commissions Post-Due but was instead making bad metaphors on the slow passage of time. For a page or two he reflects on past injuries inflicted by the fat pig of a supervisor, daydreams of revenge. Miles, another clerk about Walter's age but better looking, a hotshot, owner of sportscar, with connections, slips a needle or two into him. Closing time, home for a weekend with Carol. He likes her, thinks he might marry her, but she's a bit dumb and he finds he's coming to hate that one stray strand of hair . . . . Rest of novel: Miles gets Carol, Walter makes fool of himself at office party, has several smoothly plotted perceptions about life and people (including another woman), Carol sees too late she was wrong and the novel ends with Walter coming to a largish symbolic, metaphoric and/or psychological perception about life. He acts upon this at about 3:06 a.m. on the dark night of his soul by attacking those bloody big doors at Jaspers, Van-Damme & Co. with a blow torch. We are left to guess if he goes insane, gets arrested, dies as the doors fall on him or writes a novel about the spiritual agonies of a Commissions Post-Due clerk.

Does your reconstruction look much different from mine? You included a couple of awful parents? A bit different, but not much. Right: the point is we both have dinosaurs on our hands. If we can reconstruct a novel from a fragment it is a dinosaur, extinct, and no damn use to a writer today. It was useful thirty, forty years ago: alive, flexible, adventurous, still growing, still discovering. In a word: healthy.

2. And why

The author? Me, of course. I wrote it an hour ago. It is part of a novel, a large pastiche novel floating about in my head, a novel I hope I never bother to write. Apart from a slight archness in tone which I think is understandable under the circumstances, it seems to me a reasonably convincing bit. It satisfies all the conventions of a standard twentieth century novel. The damnation of it is that I could whip it off in ten minutes. If a writer can do that with a style, with a form, it is dead.

The problem of the artist is to make a representation of the world. That seems general enough to be taken as acceptable by anyone. The question immediately following is how to make it.

I deliberately began the last paragraph with 'the problem of the *artist.*' Depending on his talents the artist can make his rep. in words, music, painting, dance whatever. Seen in this light, the hows of the artist extend through a very broad range and my little pastiche fragment is but one of an immense number of hows.

The style of my fragment has been widely used for at least a hundred years. Dickens didn't much use it, Tolstoy used it to a degree, so did Norman Mailer. I use aspects of it. But in the twentieth century almost all novels have used it exclusively. Like any other style it has its advantages and its limitations.

The most important characteristic of the style is that it allows a representation of human thought in words. Not symbols (like the big doors), not just figures of speech (having eyes hate), but a sober, prose account of a character's thought. The whole of the book will be contained inside Walter's head, the reader will see the world through his eyes. We find Walter lying in bed, presumably just having made love. He thinks of going to work tomorrow morning and we follow his mental journey. Certain aspects of the trip are selected so that the reader can fill in the feeling of the trip from his own experience. We are told what Carol says, Walter's reaction and words, we see him squeeze her, but we are not told what she is thinking or what is going on somewhere across town, although some novels allow this shift. In addition we can be sure that no character of importance will appear suddenly more than halfway through the book; that Carol's appearances will be carefully spaced through the story; so also Miles, the supervisor, the landlady. The novel will have a calm rhythm of event, conversation, reflection, action. Walter's problems will gradually mount; they won't fall like a load of bricks in the first or the second last chapter. But the defining point is that the book, or the world the book shows us, is filtered through Walter's mind.

The advantage of this approach is that it gives the writer a tool to represent the minds of any number of different people in any number of different situations. (One mind, twenty situations per novel.) The tool can be used in poetry but must be subordinated to the poet's other more important concerns. It can be used in movies, but awkwardly as voice-over narration. It can even be used in painting by lettering the words onto the ground. But it is most at home in prose fiction.

The limitations of the style are several. A lot of thought seems to be in words of a language. But a lot apparently is not. Over a normal day people will have a lot of repetitive thought: 'Christ, what a hangover . . . . where did I leave my wallet? . . . I wonder if she loves me . . . . Hope it's roast beef for supper . . . .' A lot of thought is specific to a profession. Novelists, being novelists, are not accountants or used-car salesmen or farmers in Uzbekistan. They do specialize in imaginatively constructing how other people think, and since young novelists rarely make living expenses from their writing, their biographies often include a sentence like this: 'MacSnurf has been a lumberjack, dishwasher, skip tracer, cabbie . . . .' Unfortunately these lists rarely include 'Uzbekistani goatherd, astronaut, banker, senator, ship's captain . . . .' Sometimes one of these more recherché types will take up writing as a second profession. If he is good at it, like Joseph Conrad, readers will have something truly unique on their hands. Doctors, lawyers, the odd soldier does this. But very few bankers or Uzbekistani (or Manitoban) farmers. Several generations of writers have tried their hands at creating the thoughts of these people. We have had bankers, bankers with dull wives, interesting wives, mistresses; bankers who hated their jobs, loved their jobs, who didn't care one way or the other; bankers who drank, took drugs or fondled little girls in parks. A notable feature of such books, though, is that one rarely sees the banker banking. Although I don't know of any books about Uzbekistani farmers, I expect the hero spends a lot of time philosophizing about sky and hills and grasslands; and damn little worrying about diseases of sheep or wheat.

This attempt to construct the mentality of various types became a major object of the novel. Books were touted with blurbs like this: 'Here is MacSnurf's brilliant and incisive probe of the corrupt world of high finance. Through the eyes of Payon Dumand, the dynamic and ruthless director of . . . .' This from MacSnurf who, without the aid of the Encyclopaedia, would have thought a kited cheque was a native of Prague aloft at the end of a string.

Not only is the imagination limited factually, but it runs out of new people. In his next book, MacSnurf will have to try harder. We have met a thousand Payon Dumands, we want someone with a few extra elements to his character. The end of the process is a hero who is the son of a Bombay brothel keeper and an Arizona cowgirl eight feet tall. Hero was brought up in the north woods of Finland and has had a career as a notary and white slaver in Beirut. Married to a gorgeous but insane Eskimo ballerina he has retired to Melanesia to catalogue butterflies. The novel relates his train of thought through the ten seconds it takes him to lace up his battered running shoes.

But perhaps the crux of the question lies in the phrase 'Through the eyes of . . . .' Point of view: once a useful tool, it has become an end in itself, and so a tyranny.

In a sense, of course, there is always point of view. But writers and readers have come to think that a single point of view is right, is the norm, the proper form. It is acceptable to get into Walter's mind for a chapter, then into Carol's in the next. But there will be an overall narrative point of view. Anything more extreme and the writer is being deliberately arty, is using artificial contrivance because he can't master the real thing.

But the only criterion for judging a how is: does it work? A normal beginning for an artist is: 'I wonder what would happen if . . . .' Right. I wonder what would happen if we said the hell with point of view. Let's try a ten page story with a hundred and twelve points of view. Explode it all over everywhere. Will it work? Yes. I have tried it and so have lots of other artists and it does work. The reader has to be willing to suspend his expectations, but any reader worth a damn should be ready for this from time to time.

Any style, then, has its limitations. Until those limits have been reached the style is alive. The writer says: 'I wonder what would happen if, in this style, I tried to represent children . . . love making . . . Marco Polo . . . green men from Mars . . . housewives with itchy crotches . . . turtles . . . .' And he struggles and finds that he can. To reread the book in which some previously un-tested limit has been tested is continually refreshing. We can go back to Henry James and watch as he explores the limits of point of view. We can read Hemingway or Cary or D. H. Lawrence for their original representations of the world as seen through the eyes of a man with no testicles, a whacky-wonderful painter or a horny English lady. But MacSnurf's novel using point of view as found in *The Ambassadors* and creating a horny English lady with the hots for her gamekeeper will be 300 pages of cliché, stereotype and unintentional parody.

As I said, I'm quite willing to use the style of Walter and Carol, but in limited bits, probably for intentional irony, hopefully in some new context. But to write entire works that way is to cheat the reader and oneself. The most obvious cheat involves the extensions of the world in the work. The implication of any work is: here is a way of seeing the world. Hemingway says: Life can be seen as a struggle to face death with honour. Lawrence says screwing is good. Any book written from a single point of view says the world can be seen this way. But to say: All good novels (or valid novels) show the world from one or a limited few points of view is tyranny and a cheat.

Another extension and another tyranny in the Walter and Carol book is the extension of plot. The statement of any sort of plot is: this is a way of seeing the relations between events; or, this kind of relation between events is a significant kind. Men have used all sorts of plots. The Greeks accepted *deus ex machina*; we call it a cheat. Dickens and Shakespeare both used lots of coincidence. Their imitators used coincidence as a crutch and a reaction took place. The twentieth century plot is, in this sense, a massive reaction against the plots of shameless junk like the Horatio Alger books. This sort of shift happens when a fresh writer says, 'Hold it a moment, it may look fine to you and your readers, but my world is not full of long lost brothers, millionaires in disguise and runaway horses bearing terrified virgins. In fact, my world hasn't included a coincidence since last Christmas when two of my gift books contained the word "Zeugma." And furthermore, I think it is far more interesting to look at a series of rather subtle, low key events to see if they will lead a character to some significant perception of the world.'

Right: and this attitude gave the world fifty to a hundred years of fine prose fiction. But again, this tool has been used to work just about every sort of material. Its use has become obsessive. Writers who use it without conviction can be seen hiding chance meetings inside pages of elaborate disguise: 'How long had it been since Walter had taken a stroll along the river? . . .' So we wade through half a chapter of desultory description of coal barges and used condoms before we come to:

'Dolores, what a surprise to run into you!' 'Oh, I often walk along the river. . . .' and a few bad metaphors about time passing.

The extension, then, is that there are no coincidences in life. But obviously there are and some of them are damn important and a whole literature which excludes them denies their existence and so misrepresents the world.

3. What I write

"A Cynical Tale" and "Peril" for your pleasure, gentle reader. In the hope that you see in them, in their extensions something of the world around you, perhaps even that you see the world in a new and fresh way. A pair of (hopefully new) 'I-wonder-what-would-happen-ifs.' Isn't that what it's all about?

I don't really consider them very odd or very new. You should be able to place them, but if you can't, here's a very brief and incomplete context.

They are part of a body of work called 'speculative fiction.' Generally ironic in tone. Aesthetic in approach; which means, I suppose, an indirect approach to the many social and political problems of the world around us. This is in clear contrast to the other rising body of writing which includes things like revolutionary writings, the new journalism, documentary novels and the like, all of which try to grapple directly with the aforementioned soc and pol problems. I should emphasize, or repeat, that spec fic doesn't ignore the world, but approaches it somewhat indirectly. The telling point is that both types have pretty much rejected the whole creaking apparatus of the Walter-Carol psychological-realism (or whatever it's called) form of writing.

Some big dogs in speculative fiction: Jorge Luis Borges, Vladimir Nabokov. Coming big dog: Kurt Vonnegut, Jr. Prominent younger dogs: Thomas Pynchon, John Barth, Donald Barthelme, Richard Brautigan. Incidentally, from considering these writers, their views, careers, antecedents and whatnot you can see spec fic as a continuing historical alternative, trace its ups and downs, off-shoots, roots and other such aspects as critical enquiry can profitably illuminate.

Some specific notes on:

A Cynical Tale. A modern fantasy re-write of the English ballad 'Barbara Allan' by the prolific and versatile lyricist, Anon. It is about italics, capital letters, parentheses, the semi-colon, a floating point of view, *non sequitors,* over-plotting, flat characters, spy thrillers, high rise apartments, lingerie, short stories, overstatement, understatement, drop-

206

ped endings and plum cordial. It is not, I swear, about homosexuality.
and:

Peril. Three incidents which each contain a hidden peril. Three youngish men, rather similar, rather different, take a walk. They meet a stranger or strangers and converse about one thing and another, then go on. In the graveyard walk the peril is in the necromancer's sanity. (His description of his introduction to the art is, incidentally, a loving parody of Gully Jimson explaining his conversion to painting.) The peril in the park is in the question: Is either of them sane? The peril of the beach is that, if everything is as it is presented, then Purlieu has lunched with a god and goddess.

I often use "Peril" to illustrate how I write. I began with a cluster of images, moods, words, people that took the shape of a line starting out in front of my eyes toward the right, but curving gracefully to the left and disappearing in the hazy distance. A very relaxing vision. Obviously the curve took shape as the beach in Part 3, but I hadn't thought of the beach when I began to write. It did come out, but the way I consciously tried to produce it in the reader's mind was by arranging and manipulating his expectations. When we read things, it seems to me, we are continually trying to guess what comes next. A long series of correct guesses, as in our reconstruction of the Carol-Walter Dinosaur would be a straight line. An ingenious and convincing thriller like *The Spy Who Came in from the Cold* would produce a jagged line with a jag for every time LeCarré caught you going in the wrong direction. I figured I could make the curve by fooling you just a little every paragraph or so. So if your expectation of outcome had been a straight line running out at thirty degrees on the starboard bow, and if each jolt brought the line a degree or so to port, then the completed line would be a long gentle curve.

But whether you saw the curve or not (and I don't suppose you did) the story should have left you in a gentle, curving mood. It should have given you some pictures you can't quite explain but which will stay with you for many years, pictures that will return when that sort of mood is upon you or which, returning, bring that mood on. If it did that, then the story worked, and I am happy. If it didn't work for you, then you can use the pages to make paper airplanes to fly in gentle curves and perhaps that will make you happy.

4. And why

Because they were there.

RAY SMITH

207

Kent Thompson

Kent Thompson was born in Waukegan, Illinois, in 1936.
He attended high school in Salem, Indiana, and received a
B.A. from Hanover College, an M.A. from the State University
of Iowa, and a Ph.D. from the University of Wales at Swansea.

He came to Canada as a landed immigrant in 1966 to teach
creative writing at the University of New Brunswick, where
he edited *The Fiddlehead* from 1966 through 1970.

He has published short stories in *Tamarack Review, Prism
International, Intercourse, Quarry, The Atlantic Advocate,
West Coast Review,* and the *University of Windsor Review.*
One of his stories was anthologized in *Best Little Magazine
Fiction 1971* (New York University Press). He has also
written radio plays, fiction and drama reviews, and comedy
sketches for the CBC.

He is currently working on a collection of stories and a novel.
He is married and has two children.

Bibliography

Hard Explanations. New Brunswick Chapbooks, Fredericton, 1968.
      (Poetry) Out of print.

The Problems of a Truancy

1. If I skip going to school again today, Miss Etheridge will be hurt. She will be hurt because I have betrayed her trust, and I don't want to do that. No, I don't. Miss Etheridge is harsh, but fair. If I fail to have my twenty-five lines of "Gaul is divided into three parts" prepared for her class, she will understand. She will think that there has been some upset with a girl, and she'll forgive me—for that day. The next day I had best be ready with fifty lines.

But if I do not go to school today, I will have missed two days in a row, and therefore will have skipped two classes of Latin I.

But Miss Etheridge would not admit that I am more ignorant than otherwise simply because I cut two days in a row. She knows better. She has been known to say: "You can't stop learning, and you can't retreat into ignorance. You may think you can, but you can't. You're gathering knowledge even as you walk around breathing because Knowledge is Experience." She shakes her blue-rinse white hair. "Even woolgathering is a kind of knowledge," she says. Her voice is laconic; the voice of experience. Every summer she takes a trip to Europe or South America all by herself. I suppose that she ought to be termed a spinster, but the fact is that we are so fond of her that it is our agreed-upon hope that she is not a virgin.

2. But right now I am concerned with the problem of "greyness." It is very difficult to explain "grey," because although one might say that it is a "light black" or even a "dark white," one hasn't got near *it*, of course —although it does have something to do with illumination. I would guess that "greyness" has something to do with "approach," and even more to do with "context." For example, right now I am trying to deal with the problem of "greyness" in Ralph's Restaurant, and the fact that it is dawn has relatively little to do with it. The dawn is slipping into the valley where this town is, of course, but it is slipping in over the white tiled front of Ralph's Restaurant. And although I have made it sound like a fog, it isn't. It's light. The light is picked up by Ralph's working tools—the stainless steel spatula he uses for turning the eggs and hamburgers, the blue-silver surface of the grill itself, where there are now three eggs glowing: white with yellow centers like daisies.

Ralph's Restaurant is right across from the High School. It is very early on a November morning. It is too early for school, of course, but without even looking over my shoulder I can know about the twisted bicycle rack beside the sidewalk leading up to the side door. There are never many bicycles in the rack any more. Last week mine was the only one. Mine is now in our garage. The other kids rode their new Whizzer Motor-bikes, and parked them in a row, nosed into the curb in front of the High School, just as if they were real Harley-Davidsons. Others drove cars—refurbished old cars with raccoon-tails on the radio aerials and green and blue lights on the back fender or bumper. Some drove their family pick-up trucks, shined up like new cars and adorned with white mud-flaps and Hollywood mufflers. A pick-up truck tricked out like that can function as a clever bit of costuming—like the clever idea of turning up the back of one's shirt-collar to make one more sinister and dashing. But mine was the only bicycle in the rack last week. Naturally I resent that.

It is too early for anyone connected with the school to be at Ralph's Restaurant. There is a large plate-glass window in the front of Ralph's which does *not* look out at the school. On it in large red letters is the title: RALPH'S RESTAURANT. I have just realized that Ralph has cleverly directed his attention to the town rather than the school by his careful decision about where that plate-glass window ought to go. He had a choice; he re-did this restaurant. It used to be a failure; we called it the "Bloody Bucket."

The window is fogged from the inside, just around the edges. There is a neon sign above the window, but I can't see any hint of its red glare.

There is no one here yet from the school. I have always thought that the teachers must come over here for a first cup of coffee when they come in in the morning, but I haven't seen any of them. It's still too early. The yellow school buses, in fact, are only just now starting out on their rounds of the stiff dirt roads of Washington County. I am imagining this, of course. There's no sign of a yellow school bus around Ralph's Restaurant yet. They won't be here before the sun is properly up; then they will arrive in a long line of yellow eminence. I like that phrase: the "yellow eminence" of school buses. It gives them a dignity which, I assure you, they do not possess.

But Ralph's has several customers, although I don't know any of them, and they don't know me, although all of us know Ralph and he knows all of us. He is at the grill, laughing at some unheard comment from one of the delivery men sitting at the counter. His back is to us; he is watching the eggs fry. He wears his hair cut very short; he's still a young man, only just out of the Army. He saved his money in Korea and opened Ralph's Restaurant. I think he saved it carefully because he runs a good restaurant. He'd like you to think he won it in a poker game, however. He's doing well here. Deserves to.

The men at the counter are the drivers of the delivery trucks and the hunters. The drivers are not quite in uniforms, but on the other hand, they are not quite not-wearing uniforms either. One has a matching grey work shirt and trousers. Another has a matching green work shirt and trousers. A third has a matching blue jacket and trousers and a white shirt with a black tie. Their trucks are parked outside: HoneyCrust Bread, Pepsi-Cola, Phillips 66 Oil. They drink their coffee, talk to one another because they meet here every morning, proud to be up in the grey dawn before other people have come out to invade the world.

It's too early for music from the juke-box, and besides I haven't the money to waste on it if I wanted to, although I'm tempted. I've read through the offering, and only Marty Robbins with "White Sport Coat and Pink Carnation" tempts me at all, and that not much. I like the near-silence, which fits with the greyness of the morning. There is the sound of the gas-fired grill, and the eggs frying. Ralph himself drinks a cup of coffee, and seeing that my cup is empty, re-fills it without looking at me. Will he charge me for it? I hope not, although I have enough to pay him for it even if he does.

The other men are hunters. They have on dark trousers and bright caps and red plaid shirts. Out in their cars they have their shotguns, broken open as required by law, perhaps, and they have already checked the actions of their guns, breaking the guns open and shutting them even in the dark silence of their kitchens. It's the first thing you do: even before you think about going out. Then they decide to slip down to Ralph's for a quick breakfast before going out to the fields. It is a kind of a treat.

The rabbits will be as grey as the dawn, kicking up from behind a clump of brush, sometimes as still as the dawn, hesitant and trembling. Then the morning is broken by the bright explosion of the gun, and the rabbit is dead.

Now the grey light has nearly taken command. The overhead lights are not really necessary although they are still on, and you can barely see their reflection in the hot grill. Sausage patties.

Should I have another cup of coffee? The day is nearly here. The thick white china cup in front of me has little dried drops right below where it has touched my lips. When I remove the cup from my mouth there is a small drop of coffee left adhering to the cup, and it starts to run down the side, but lacks the necessary weight to get to the bottom. It is a small dried brown drop. There is a chip in the rim of the cup, only a small one, stained brown. The automatic dish-washer cannot remove that stain, although the heat of the water sterilizes the cup. I only have a quarter. If I am charged for all the cups of coffee I am drinking (hunched over, looking down into the sepia brown liquid), I shall not be able to pay for them. Ralph, who knows me well by sight, who knows where I live, and who probably knows my father and mother by sight and name although not to speak to, would laugh it off. I would not. I've not been raised that way.

Someone has ordered French Toast. Ralph dips the bread into the prepared batter and slops the bread onto the grill. The sizzle is soft.

The light is gathering into day. The greyness is almost gone. I see that Ralph missed a spot when he wiped the black formica counter in front of me. I can see the beaded pattern where his rag went. Ralph's Restaurant is spotlessly clean, efficient, and fair-priced. When the big yellow buses pull in it will be boiling with people like me, raucous with concerns. When the bell rings (you can hear it from here), Ralph's will disgorge its occupants and fall silent again. The girls will go first. They are nearly women. At least three boys in the anonymous jackets of the countryside will hang back at the front door of Ralph's, finishing the cigarettes they are forbidden to smoke on school property.

What shall I do with myself until then? *And* then? Shall I have another cup of coffee?

3. How do you reply to a mother to keep her happy and yet give an honest answer? For example, when my mother asks me, "How is school going?" what am I to say? I know what I said. I said: "It's going very well." But then, in the interests of honesty I felt compelled to add: "Don't worry about me. At my worst I'm better than the rest of them at their best."

That shocked her. She threw my name at me (her choice) in an expletive of horror. I had said the unsayable: that I was *better* than someone else. It was not tactful; not good manners; just possibly it was Un-American.

Or when, in the midst of a tight and furious discussion about my girl, she said: "You know right from wrong, don't you?"

"No," I said. "Do you?"

Oh, no. Don't say that.

4. At the end of this brown street is the Farm Bureau, with its loading platform (and behind it, in the warehouse, rows and stacks of feed-sacks, both gunny and paper), its gas pumps, and beyond it, at the very end of the brown old street, the ice-house.

212

It is on this old brown street that I sometimes think I can hear horses. I have never seen a horse here, I think, although this part of town was once bright and jingling with horses when horses indicated prosperity.

The ice-house is large and grey, made of corrugated, galvanized metal sheets. There are canvas covers over the exits of the ice-chutes; the coin-operating apparatus is right beside the chutes. Behind the ice-house, I know, is the Monon Railroad.

I stand and listen. I hear neither a horse nor a train. Back there on that corner is a grey old brick building which was once a hardware store where even I can remember they once sold harness.

A green pick-up truck pulls up in front of the Farm Bureau, and creaks to a stop in front of the gas pumps. The driver gets out. His black trousers are held up over his blue-cambric workshirt by mustard-colored galluses like my grandfather wears. He is smaller than my grandfather, and even more bent. His hat is a crushed old stiff-straw farm-hat. My grandfather bought me a soft-straw hat every summer until I was too old. One summer he rented a pony for me. Mother worried that I would fall off. I did, but it was a slow, fat, and amiable old pony called Butterball.

There are no sounds of tall strong horses pulling wagons or buggies here. I hear somebody working on a car in the Oldsmobile Garage. The son of the owner of the Oldsmobile Garage is also in high school. He is as eager to play basketball as I have been, but he is even shorter. I am at least average height.

If I were to go up a block, onto the less fashionable end of Main Street (this granting that the *other* end is more "fashionable" because it is more prosperous), I would see the caramel-colored brick building where a great-uncle of mine once had the Buick Agency. At least he was called "Uncle."

How did they get the cars into the salesroom, I wondered. I could not see any door which was anywhere near big enough. Certainly I asked, and certainly I was told, but I do not remember what I was told.

Nor do I remember the cars themselves. They were always big, shiny, and smelled of rubber and newly-painted metal. They were strong and solid, complete. The doors went *thump* when you closed one of them in the confined and prosperous privacy of the show-room. Behind a counter at the back of the show-room there was a rack of fan-belts.

I remember only the advertising pamphlets which I was given to play with: thick, heavy, shiny paper which smelled deliciously of vanilla. It was almost sticky to the touch, but rich. The cars were scarlet.

What exactly was the relationship of Uncle Fons to me? Is he now dead? Did he die wealthy from the Buick dealership, or did he sell out cheap during the Depression or go broke? Who has the dealership now? *Is that still the Buick Garage?*

5. The town is at the bottom of a valley; it is in fact located at the drainage point of the valley. The valley is drained by the creek which runs through town, across from the Farm Bureau, down by the high school.

Grandfather's farm was up on the slope of the long valley. If you started down the hill in a car you did not need to use the motor until you got down to the creek. Of course, I cannot remember that happening, although sometimes Grandfather would let the old Model A pick-up truck roll out of the barn, out through the chipped stone gates, take a rolling right turn, and then drift down the hill until he kicked the motor into life. Perhaps I have not remembered correctly. I never saw him use the crank, however.

By the time I got out to the barn Grandfather would be finished milking. The stool he used (it was very low because—or although—he was very tall) was made out of chunks of two-by-fours, and it wasn't a proper stool at all, but something like a perch. You had to sit on it to keep it from falling over. However, it kept him out of the golden straw which, by now, was urine-sparkling, heavy-scented, ankle-deep in the brown/black manure. He put the milk-can which I could not lift into the back of the Model-A with a single swing of his strong arms, and I went around the back of the straw-smelling old black truck and got in.

The window was always down. You could grasp the door at waist level and pull it to with a sharp, solid, bang. It made me feel as if it were the door of a racing car. Then we rattled down the hill. The Model A smelled of Grandfather. Grandfather smelled of the barn, his age, and chewing tobacco.

We arrived at the Kraft Creamery. The most exciting feature of this brick-tile building by the side of the creek was its ramp of rollers. Grandfather would drive up alongside the ramp and stop the Model A. Then he would get out and swing the milk-can onto the ramp and give it a shove. It would rumble along the ramp, then bump against and then pass through the swinging doors. As the milk-can went in there was released the immense smell of warm milk and steam, heavy with the smell of milk.

Why did I love the Model A? I think it was because of the way the door slammed shut. It was solid; it felt good to shut it. And I also loved the sound of the milk-can scooting along the rollers and into the banging, clattering creamery.

214

6. There was a footstool in Grandfather and Grandmother's house which always fascinated me. Grandmother had made it out of old coffee tins, which she covered with green corduroy, and it looked like a four-leaf clover. It was almost never used. Grandmother was better at cooking. She made a dish of cooked apples dyed green which was delicious! Grandfather used an old Maxwell House coffee tin for a spittoon and he clung stubbornly to his right to it (right beside his rocking chair, by the Atwater Kent cathedral radio and his glasses) despite Grandmother's incessant chirpings.

In the evening Grandfather and I would sit on the front porch and look out over the town. Blackness and lightning bugs. In the distance the spire of the courthouse, the sound of it telling the Standard Time. They will not change it to Daylight Saving Time.

Grandfather said, "Well, sir, in those days it wasn't easy for a young doctor. And this one, well sir, he figured that for some reason or other he needed a corpse to work on. A corpse—a dead body. So one dark night he just slipped out to the cemetery and dug one up. . . .

". . . Well sir, one night they caught him . . . and do you know what they did? . . . Well sir, they fined him ten dollars, that's what they did."

Grandfather spat tobacco juice into the can.

"They fined him ten dollars."

Grandfather rocks in his rocking chair. Although the day has been very hot, the evening is suddenly cool. A breeze is drifting over the valley. I feel cold and lonely.

"Yessir, they fined him ten dollars. . . . 'course, it was worth more in those days."

7. ". . . they had crossed the river down there south of Corydon, and they were making a swing across southern Indiana and heading for Cincinnati. Colonel John Hunt Morgan and his Raiders. Yessir, they burned the town . . . headed east.

". . . but we were more concerned with an outfit called the Knights of the Golden Circle. They were southern sympathizers. Copperheads they were called."

"Which?"

"What?"

"What were they called—Copperheads or Knights of the Golden Circle?"

"They were called both. The group around here was called the Knights of the Golden Circle, and yessir, they'd ride around and if you were for the Northern side, why, they'd burn your barn. Come up in the night and burn your barn. Yessir. Well . . . you know that old muzzle-loader I got in there? You know that muzzle-loading rifle?"

"Yes."

"Well, my daddy got that rifle to hold off the Knights of the Golden Circle. We lay out in the wash-house waiting for them to come, but they never did."

"They didn't burn your barn?"

"No sir, they never showed up."

I shivered, imagining myself lying on my stomach in the old wash-house which smells of coal oil and old linoleum, lying there with the end-heavy old muzzle-loading rifle waiting for the silhouettes of the night riders on their huge shadowy horses to appear around the back of the barn with their flaring bright torches like flaming banners lighting up the night in the fire shadows. The bright torches.

Did they just fling the torches into the barn? And then did the hay catch, and then the walls of the old barn in a crackling flash? Did they get the cows out? And did we fire the old muzzle-loader because, if we did, wouldn't the night-riders know where we were and come riding down on the old wash-house to penetrate the thin yellow wood with fatal lead?

8. Grandfather's farm is a small farm, smaller now that the barn has been torn down (Grandfather is too old to drive a truck, although it took a wreck to convince him of that), smaller yet since Grandmother died. I am told that she died cursing my Grandfather. I do not know what for.

Across the road from where the barn was there is another field which also belongs to the farm. And at the end of the field (it slopes away) there is an oak grove, which we always referred to as "the woods." Before his eyesight went Grandfather used to go over there on a sunny afternoon and hunt squirrels with the muzzle-loading rifle.

A little squishy creek runs through the oak woods. It floods in the springtime and dries up in August. It goes under the road in a culvert, back to this side of the farm, and spreads out into a little swamp. The swamp was created when Grandfather had a pond dug there to catch the creek-water. He wanted it for the cows but also, I suspect, for fish.

Rabbits hide in the dried-out swamp. On a good day you can kick two or three out of there, but of course it's hard to get a good shot at them through the high grass and the old dry cat-tails.

The field rises back to where the old barn was. There's almost no trace of it now. If you didn't know it had been there, you'd never know where it was supposed to have been. There's a few old rusty nails in the

216

grass, and a lot of dangerous holes. Walk around on that spot and you're likely to break an ankle.

And the field itself has been neglected so long that it's dangerous. It hasn't been cut in years and it's probably full of copperheads. Wear high boots if you're going in there.

9. 3:30 and the town explodes. I am on one side of the square and I look over at the other, at the alley by the pool-hall, and here they come— the first rush of kids from the high school, my recent compatriots, not now my compatriots in crime. They spill over that corner of the square like colorful, flowerful insects, and sweep in a steady stream into the Candy Kitchen, known as "The Greek's," in an overwhelming display of triumph. But they are never in. In the fine weather there is a steady stream of cars zipping up along the square to squall to a stop in front of "The Greek's," and somebody jumps out to run in—or a girl shoots out, skirt and hair flying behind her—to jump into the car, or another girl— that one now, I can't make out exactly who it is—coming out ambling and proud, because she knows she is wanted. Or that one, who also knows that she is wanted, but can command so much less. They cluster around the door to the Candy Kitchen like bees—or flies. I see a violet sweater, a brown, a blue, a pink. I imagine the proud breasts of girls I cannot recognize from here.

Just this side of The Candy Kitchen is Berry's Drugs. My girl friend works at Berry's Drugs in the summer. It is considered a modern sort of place because Jim Berry had the old front of the building torn off and replaced with immense plate-glass windows. And he hires only pretty girls to work there, which makes everyone suspicious, not least of all the girls, who prefer to work for Jim Berry in pairs.

One hot day last summer my girl and her girl friend were working in the storeroom upstairs, counting and sorting stock, and "it was hot, you know?" She and her girl friend had stripped off their blouses to work in their bras. "No one could see us," she said. She said it to excite me and because, by saying it, she could excite herself.

I had my hand under her bra; her erect nipple was pressed into the exact center of my sweaty palm. I wanted to get her bra off, which seemed to me to offer a luxury of flesh.

"No, don't," she said.

"But if I stop you won't like it."

"How do you know?" she said.

"I know."

"You think you know too much," she said.

"I know as much as I can."

"You don't know all there *is* to know, you know," she said.

"I know that."

"The trouble with you," she told me, "is that you know too much for your own good." And by this she meant that after such a conversation she could not pretend to be "carried away," and therefore I would not get what I wanted after all. But I knew that she was angry also because she did not get what she wanted but did not want to admit wanting.

I also know what I do not know—which is much more dangerous.

10. Now I am missing basketball practice. On the last day of practice which I attended we were working on the three-man weave. It is still early enough in the season for us to dream of Tournament Time when the girls will explode with colorful laughter and screams and later give soft outrageous offers which will be taken up, trembling. That's tournament time in Indiana, which signals the growing season. But on the last day of my practice we were working on the three-man weave.

It is a simple manoeuver. You start with three men at the end of the floor. The man in the center starts with the ball. He passes it to the man on his right and cuts toward him, in front of him. The man who now has the ball uses the man coming toward him as a block and passes to the other man, runs toward him, sets a block, and then that man passes to the man who started it all.

Essentially the same procedure is used when one is working the ball in toward the basket against any kind of man-to-man defense. When it is played as a pattern it is called the Give-and-Go Offense. If you pass well and don't make mistakes, you can win the State Championship with it—as Milan did—and the lovely thing about it is that you don't need tall players. But you must not make a mistake. You must never lose the ball.

The squat little coach was trying to explain the principle to us, trying to show us that it was necessary to scrape the defense into confusion while pressing on toward the basket and the short shot, and he said: "You work in closer and closer and closer—and then POP! You cram it in."

Voice from the side of the group, subtle and knowing: "Just like last night." Laughter.

Until recently I was working on the jump shot. You don't see many people using the jump shot yet. It's difficult. The Jasper team uses it. I saw it illustrated in *Sport*. The coach says that we are not to shoot *any* shot until we can make five out of eight consistently.

In the jump shot you simply leap into the air, poise there, and shoot

218

the ball at the basket. The pitfalls are many, however. The leap may throw you off balance. You may put so much energy into leaping that you lose control of the ball and merely throw it at the basket.

And, although it is a difficult shot to stop, it can be done. For example, the defensive man may time his jump to coincide with yours and consequently when you go up to shoot he goes up to stop you, and his hand is on the ball as well as yours. You are nullified.

Therefore you must learn to fake before leaping. Then you have your opponent off-balance and while he is recovering you rise into the air, sighting in on the basket, and flick the ball off your fingertips, and POP, as the coach says, and it's "in for a couple."

Yet, if your opponent is taller than you are, even a fake may be of little use. Even a partial recovery will have you blocked. And therefore you must learn to shoot when you go up, shoot at the top, shoot on the way down, shoot falling backwards—which is the least satisfactory of all because, when you shoot falling backwards, you tend to fling the ball and, perhaps worse, you throw yourself out of a rebound position. And in most games most points are scored by picking up a short rebound and cramming it in.

But I have skipped my second basketball practice in a row, and that's it. The coach says: "Now listen to me—I'm serious about this. Sulk and off you go. Cut a practice without my permission and you cut yourself off the squad. If you want to play for fun, go somewhere else." This is Indiana, remember?

11. On the first day of practice the coach said: "How tall's your father?" I whipped in the jump shot which I had perfected during the summer. "5-7," I said, and he walked away, nodding that he had heard. I wanted to call out that my Grandfather had been 6-5 when he was a young man, but I didn't.

12. One of the sweetest experiences I know is scissoring your man away on a block at the top of the keyhole and then cutting in through the melee for the basket, protecting the ball with your body, going up past the stretching lout who is playing their center, and flicking the ball in— just flicking it in with a sweet, neat touch of understated skill. And then hearing the girls' flowering cheers falling over you like water.

13. Aunt Bessie now lives in a little house on Maple Street, after a lifetime spent on a farm. I approach it up two little steps which are tilted by the roots of the maple tree, across a broken, grassy walk. The house

is a little four-room thing—two rooms in front and two rooms behind. However, it has a porch (with lathe-turned posts) and two front doors—one for each of the front rooms. One door is nailed shut.

Aunt Bessie is half asleep when I knock on the screen door which is never removed. I can see her sitting in her wicker rocking chair by the table. When she hears my knock she starts, doesn't know where—or when—she is, and then slowly turns her head toward the door in something like fear. She rises with effort, hobbles to the door to let me in. I could have opened the door and shouted, "It's me, Aunt Bessie," and come on in. But I do not feel like it.

I haven't been home for two days, and I'm tired.

Aunt Bessie recognizes me and lets me in. I smell the house: linoleum, coal oil, old papers, old stuffed furniture, oil-cloth. Aunt Bessie says that she should be doing her ironing, but she just doesn't feel up to it right now. Come on in.

Aunt Bessie is thin and ropey although once, I believe, she was fat. She moves like a heavy woman—as if she had a heavy silhouette still with her, a fat, young shadow which now she must drag along with her thick old legs. She is wearing house-slippers. Her stockings are heavy, a cocoa-brown, and baggy.

I do not know why I am here except that I am tired of walking.

Aunt Bessie asks me how my folks are ("fine") and how's school going ("fine"). I do not tell her I have not been home since yesterday and that my parents are probably looking for me, and I shall not know how to face them or what explanation I can possibly give. No explanation would ever suffice. This one I shall have to endure.

"Set a spell," she says, and settles herself back into her wicker rocker. She has thrown an old limp pillow in it: the pillow is black and covered with large white flowers. My father painted her wicker rocker that black color last year; before that it was a muddy brown and sat on her porch out at the old place.

"I ain't got much ambition today," she says. The room we are in seems to be crowded with calendars and calendar pictures: Jesus is on the wall in several poses, blessing the children, distributing the loaves and fishes, looking out over us in benediction with a golden halo flashing over his head. A Gideon Bible is on the oilcloth-covered round dining-room table which is too big for this room and which prevents this room from being a proper sitting room. The room is too hot. The little green coal-oil heater in the corner sucks up the air, leaves a faint oily touch in what is left to breathe. Aunt Bessie repeats: "I ain't got no ambition at all today."

She doesn't want to look at me because she has gotten out of the habit of looking at her younger relatives, who are of no help to her. She knows she is going into a nursing home shortly, and so do I, although only I have heard of it directly, having overheard my parents planning it. Aunt Bessie's life has been used up raising children, raising chickens (going out to gather the eggs, hobbling across the shit-slippery yard), cooking, sewing, and slopping the hogs from the foul-smelling stone crock which used to be by the back door, with green flies buzzing near. I pity her most the number of walks she must have made to the out-house at the old place—in the cold, rainy mornings, ashamed of the indignity of going out in the cold rain for such a monotonous purpose. The smell was disguised with the smell of disinfectant when I was there, and Aunt Bessie herself had insisted on planting hollyhocks around the building, but nothing would erase the smell of years, nor the flies, bees, or spiders.

There is nothing left for Aunt Bessie to be ambitious about. She would never understand my urge to "get out" which is screaming right through my seventeen years. She is eighty, at least.

"Preacher was here today," she says. Her eyes are like raisins. "He read to me for a spell."

Should I offer to read to her? I hate to read the Bible. It is all unction and prohibition.

"Seems like a right nice sort," she says. "School all right?" she repeats.

"Fine," I say.

She rocks. The chair squeaks lightly on the linoleum, which once had a pattern of lilies.

"My grandfather used to tell me about Morgan's Raiders," I say. "About the Knights of the Golden Circle and how they terrorized the country for miles around."

"Yes," she says. "I hear tell they did that."

"Do you know anything about it?"

"No. No, can't say that I do," she says. "Your Grandfather still poorly?"

"Yes," I say. "Do you know any of the old songs?"

"The old songs?"

"Yes."

"No, I used to know some. I don't know any now. Maybe a hymn or two. I don't know. Don't seem to remember."

Because I am Drunk

Because I am drunk.

Hear me, O Israel! Hear the voice of the Fallen. Hear the voice of Jonathan Seeg, your lost lad, drunk on Fredericton Queen Street in the middle of the afternoon. Because I am drunk I step very slowly.

I am not falling down drunk.

I am upright, careful—yea, very thoughtfully drunk. I am aware-drunk. I would not speak aloud. Yes, I've learned from experience. Have seen the grey-whiskered rummies upright in the government store. I would not speak aloud, but I will think. I will think, ponder—yea, O Israel,—even *taste* because everything is slowed down. Even the rain falls slowly. I can feel my eyes move. Like when you're very, very tired.

It is raining, and our lost lad Jonathan Seeg, last of the lost lads and tardy spenders, is downtown in Fredericton, N.B., capital city of New Brunswick, and it is raining very hard. Seeg, however, your watchful Seeg, avoids people and therefore is pleased that it is raining.

Verily, Lord, it pisseth down.

Queen Street is being pissed on, by God, and Queen Street is sweating. The royal street giveth off a fragrant steam. I catch glimpses of myself in passing shop windows, perceive that I am huddled up in my raincoat purchased in Britain years ago, my cap down over one eye, my Napoleonic spit-curl wet with perspiration rather than rain-water. Napoleonic spit-curl; I should be bald as Yul Brynner. In Shute's Jewelry there is green Wedgwood to attract the American tourists. Little bit of the great Britain. I am myself looking at it, at me, and give all a wary eye. Shy eye. Wary Seeg, happily drunk this late afternoon. The rain falls in torrents. Cars splash by, fogged windows. Occupants look out to see silly fellow Seeg walking along Queen Street stoned out of his mind.

No. My mind is solid as stone. Solid as stone to be rolled away. The Seeg is wary in his principles.

Seeg, of course, is free at last. After all these years of trying to deal with Greta (Greta's the wife, good wife these three years, met her in London, humped her there, fell in love with her—admit, admit—and immigrated to Canada, both Americans, both compromise, both lose). After all these years of trying to deal with Greta and her pathetic illnesses she one day in the long life of Jonathan Seeg turned her ugly face, once beautiful when she loved, turned her ugly face to Seeg and said:

"I hate you, Jonathan Seeg."

He, quick of eye and wary as a cornered animal, turned blackmail on her. "That's all very well and good, but I love you." That tied it. My mother used to pull that trick. I'd threaten to leave home, shout: "I hate you," and she would go on baking, stop only to slip a plump arm around my shoulders, say, "But I love *you*, Jonathan." And that would be that. One trades tears of rage for tears of humiliation (go bury head in familiar pillow already damp and full of own particular smells). Tears of humiliation give way to tears of relief: I shall not have to run away from home. I can stay here. I return to the sweating kitchen and tell mother that I'm sorry, that I won't say that again. She tells me there will be hot apple pie ready in a few minutes. Truly love has no morals.

Greta's mouth was blubbery and ugly with rage. Her cheeks shiny with tears. "I hate you, Jonathan Seeg," she said. My name is part of the curse. When I'm lucky I'm only "Seeg," the quick mark, quick smile in the grey rainy world.

Consider that the traffic on Queen Street is nearly nil and that Seeg has ensconced himself in the foyer of the Gaiety Cinema (*Thoroughly Modern Millie* is playing, with Julie Andrews and Mary Tyler Moore, who plays loving wife to hilarious Dick Van Dyke on the Dick Van Dyke Daytime Show: 12:30 in the Maritimes.) Consider that the afore-mentioned Seeg fully realizes that his breath reeks of the rye whiskey drunk straight out of the bottle.

Greta returned to the pale pink bedroom to her considered weeping and Seeg took up the harsh amber bottle and drank in gulps from it. It did not bring the tears to his eyes that he had thought it would. He considered—sniff—that his entire system had gone numb from shock.

To drink like that was the only recourse of a civilized man.

Today Greta had taken him, Seeg, aside in the quiet afternoon and she had sat him in the large brown chair which he loved and loves still and she had prepared tea for him and she had said that if he loved her he would have to let her go. Love, she said, involves respect for the beloved and her freedom.

Seeg had then hit Greta. The blow caught her on her left eye and knocked her off her feet and she splashed askew into the sofa.

Now, across the street from the Gaiety Theatre where I am now standing to be out of the rain—or rather, to be accurate, catty-cornered from the Gaiety Theatre, there is Officers Square.

Officers Square is symbolic for the Seeg. He admits it. To his left as he stands sheltered in the Gaiety Cinema foyer there is the barracks where the officers were quartered. You can go through it for a nominal fee: it is now a museum. There were British officers garrisoned here 'way

223

back when. When the Americans here were United Empire Loyalists, *i.e.*, they backed the wrong horse. There is a tunnel from the officers' barracks to the enlisted men's quarters on Carleton Street. Why? Communications, of course. Why?

What do you think you are gaining by this shilly-shallying away from the central agony. Tears begin to roll down the cheeks of Seeg, but it is raining. They are hardly noticeable.

Greta is a lovely woman, if somewhat flighty. She was attending an art school in London when she met the handsome dog, Seeg, and she was taken by his insouciance, by the way he wore his cap and his duffel coat and the great laugh he wore like an Elizabethan come back to life. She, in her turn, was dark, ripe, mysterious. Lately, of course, Seeg had grown older and fatter; had laughed rather less often; had found himself asserting a certain sense of dignity and kept secrets from her. Oh, God, he had come to *care*.

And Greta's mysterious illness had become more evident. At first she had wept when her illness doubled her up and he came to her in bed with his laughter up like a stallion. Then she had been ill for a week at a time. Already she had been in the hospital three times for two weeks each time.

In Officers Square also, of course, there is a fine lawn, where once the ladies who were the fine colonial ladies of the garrison's fine English gentlemen played gentle tennis. Seeg imagined the photo he had once seen of the ladies playing tennis in their demure skirts.

In those days when you ran a hand up a lady's skirt she knew it was no accident. She had, positively, to acquiesce. Positive acquiescence. The lady pulls up her skirt in the gentleman's carriage. Unthinkable.

Seeg, admit it, you are remembering, exactly, the taste of Greta's tits.

"Don't call them tits."

"What shall I call them?"

"Breasts."

"I like to play with your tits."

"Oh, please."

Lately he had come to call them breasts and found himself a beaten dog.

Greta had wept in a corner, and Seeg felt good in the flush of anger that had finally been released.

The rain was slack. It flopped unevenly on Queen Street.

He had apologised and helped Greta to her feet. He had said, "I'm sorry," when he meant—and she knew he meant—"I'm scared, and please don't leave me because I've come to love you." He hadn't said that.

He had then prepared her another cup of tea and poured it for her, walked over to the window, gazed out on rained-upon Fredericton where everyone was indoors, and said: "Is there someone else?"

She had been bitter in her reply. He of course knew there was. He, Seeg, knew HIM, *Jeremy,* very well. It was Jeremy who had welcomed them to Fredericton's harsh civilisation, and tucked them away from the coarse world. Jeremy had laughed when he told them how savage life was in the Maritimes. Jonathan Seeg imagined Jeremy savage upon a motorcycle. Greta had deliberately dropped clues, hints, ideas. Her idea was that Jonathan Seeg should gradually acquire the idea that Jeremy was his wife's lover and do the gentlemanly thing and step aside. He wouldn't be so nasty as to demand a flat statement. Seeg demanded.

"Who do you want in my bed?"

"Please," she said. He could see the pain rising from her stomach to her eyes. Perhaps he should have kicked her in the stomach while she was falling from his blow: she would have remembered him that way, right into her death. Hemorrhage flashing like roses through her.

"Whom do you wish to have hump you in the future?" Seeg had by-the-by pointed out to her the politeness of the euphemism. He counted on her shyness; she would not scream "You mean *fuck*" at him simply to win the point. How nasty manners are. It was worse then than when I hit her. Surely you realize that?

She wiped the word from her mouth. "Jeremy."

He understood, of course. "Who?" he demanded. "I didn't hear."

"Jeremy."

"Yes. Well." Seeg at that point considered himself a civilised man. He took the bottle of Acadia 400 rye by the neck and swilled it down. Shortly, with luck, he would be drunk.

I was drunk. Now I am sober.

The rain is slight, sporadic. It mists like memory. Heads begin to appear at windows, checking the outdoors to see if it is safe to go outdoors. I examine the sky for signs of light or late sun slipping through. There is a greyness over all, and a blackness is slipping down the river from Woodstock. It is a tight summer.

When did I first realize that I loved Greta, who was later my wife, later still Jeremy's mistress, will yet be my ex-wife; perhaps his wife. O certainly. They will marry. For Greta love is a fact of forever, and therefore marriage is imperative to seal the fact in plastic.

When I married Greta I did not love her, although, of course, I said I did. One follows the customs. Indeed, one observes more customs in private than elsewhere. In the bathroom, for example, or even in bed.

225

She: "That was lovely, darling." She was lying and I knew it. I had miscalculated a certain sketching of her hands on my back as a signal. We did not know one another well, then. We had been lovers for only perhaps a few weeks, on a side street of a side street—a retreat—in red-brick London. She gave up her friends for me; I gave up my friends and mistresses for her. Surely such sacrifice had to be named love. I said: "I love you." I admired her good manners in lying to me about her enjoyment in bed. I said: "I love you." At a restaurant in Soho that first week I leaned over to her and said, *apropos* of no particuar circumstance, "I love you." We looked so well, so vital together. I said: "I love you."

Then for one horrible long month she thought she was pregnant, and we debated the matter. I suggested nothing until she volunteered to have an abortion. I said no, and I said I was being selfish, but I wanted my child to live. Love, I said, is not only an artistic exercise. I volunteered to marry her. Don't be foolish, she said. That wasn't necessary. She would have the baby and put it (him, her) up for adoption. We were just at that point one evening and she had made up her mind to have the baby and I had made up mine to seek out an abortionist and somehow borrow the money to pay him. The next morning she woke me with a cup of tea (usually I brought it to her) and kissed me. "All our worries are blood," she announced.

"What?" I said.

"Blood. Beautiful bright blood."

I ran my hand up under her gown and, sure enough, she was riding the cotton pony. That day was lovely. We went for a walk in St. James Park, and clowned at one another and mimicked nurse-maids and civil servants, and followed two Americans and played at being crasser than they. I said loudly: "These backward people ought to have some real American know-how. *Then* they'd know what to do with the Queen." We succeeded in embarrassing the couple we were following and when he turned around (they were from Texas) to tell us loudly to mind our manners and to remember that we were guests in Great Britain, we broke into whoops of laughter. Then we let them in on the joke, and we all went to dinner at a Wimpy Bar where we complained at great length about British cooking. After the Texans had left to return to their hotel, Greta and I decided to get married. We felt very good about the decision and held hands all the way back to her flat, where we had been living.

But I didn't love her then.

We suited one another perfectly. Like me, Greta has a marvellously obscene imagination, although she is shy about words. Our wedding night, our honeymoon to Scotland, our first years of married life were occasions for us to have orgies with one another. She used me; I used her. There was no sexual game we didn't play between us. We broke right through the games. We ate all the forbidden fruit and laughed, and we had quiet Sunday breakfasts in bed together over the Sunday papers. She painted; I read and I designed impossible buildings which flashed across the landscape or swirled on the city street-corner like the flick of a woman's skirt. After a particularly good night she would leave a note, "I love you," in the drawer among my underwear. Once we painted one another with watercolors, and then bathed together, and then made love in the tub.

But I did not love her. I loved her, of course, when it became apparent that I was going to lose her, when I saw how fat I had become and how, if I lost her, I would never again have such a dazzling woman, and I imagined her in bed with Jeremy and her legs around his neck.

But I loved her one night after a party here in Fredericton. It was a good party with drinking and laughter and wild Scottish dancing. Out in the wilderness in an ancient white house we danced and thumped away at the bright brown floor. She had been flirting with Jeremy; but she flirted with other men as well. I confess that I had not been inactive.

But when we got home she said, "I'm sick," and I helped her to the toilet and she knelt over the bowl and vomited and I held her hair out of the cat-colored vomit. We went to bed; we did not make love. And I did not tell her I loved her. I loved her.

I have left her weeping in our apartment on University Avenue and she will have a black eye. I hit her very hard. The rain has begun to fall heavily again.

II

The rain is washing down Queen Street in great swaths. I am cozy in the foyer of the Gaiety cinema, and almost content: I am soft and warm. I smoke a snug cigarette, safe from rain. Those brave ones who, a few moments ago, took a chance with the storm, have scurried again to cover.

But one of these is Lila, and she takes cover with me. She is a bright colorful girl: she wears a raincoat which is an electric pink. Her eyes are grey and quick as a cat. She has met Seeg once or twice in her quick young life, enough to give him a warm smile. She is adventurous, and her opening comment—"Oh, it's *pouring* out there"—is an invitation. She hops into the foyer. She says to Seeg: any port in a storm. Seeg smiles: welcome to harbour. They stand in silence. Where were you headed in this mess? Nowhere in particular. You?

Seeg: "I was getting drunk."

Are you drunk? Lila looks closely at him. Are you? No, she decides. You are not drunk.

I am not drunk so as you would notice. I'm feeling very sober.

Well now, that's another matter. One needn't be drunk, she admits laughing, but one needn't be sober, need one?

No.

Silence.

Careful looks. She makes mention of the film. Has he seen it. Neither has she. Does he want to see it. No. Neither does she. I suppose it's going on now. Yes. I haven't been to a matinee in years. Nor I.

She is pleased that Seeg thinks of her as a woman rather than a girl. Careful looks. The looks raise a question. At the fourth or fifth look Seeg says, It's very hot isn't it? Yes. Seeg says: my wife is at home. Yes. Do you feel adventurous? Yes. Your move.

Would you like to come to my place for a cup of coffee?

Yes. Heart beating rapidly at the thought of sin. Balls tightening in anticipation.

They run through the rain, and at her flat, cover themselves with laughter. She dries her face with a towel and gives it to him. He dries his. They are in the living room, wary, careful.

There is an agreement that everything must be agreed upon. There are rules of conduct to be observed.

She goes to her tiny kitchen to prepare the coffee. Seeg follows to watch. He tells her when she asks that he likes both cream and sugar. She says he will get fat. I am fat, he says. No you're not, she says. *You're* not fat he says to her. Yes I am she says, and she puts down the cups and comes over to be wrapped in his arms as they kiss formally and then deeply and greedily, with tongues slopping in and out. Her breath is fast; his cock is rising in a hard knot.

How far do we go?

I don't know.

Honestly?

Honestly. I don't know. Do you?

No. Then we'd better have coffee.

They sit to talk. She stretches. I'm hot, she says. I know, he says. Should we hop into bed? No. Not yet. Wait until it is unbearable. It's better then. Her laugh is sad. You're right.

228

She tells him about her love affair. She has never told anyone else. It was a Lesbian affair. With a painter. She's left town long since. You didn't know her. She was in love with a man who went mad with love for another woman. Dignity is shed when secrets are revealed. But Seeg does not tell her this.

Crazy, isn't it. The coffee cups are dry in dry brown rings in their clanking saucers. Cigarettes are butted.

Goes round and round.

You can't get off.

No.

There have been men as well. I prefer men in bed. But I haven't loved them.

When she takes off her clothes Seeg tells her she is beautiful and she is pleased. Please say that again, she says. You are beautiful. You are beautiful nude.

Naked?

Naked and nude. Your eyes are naked.

I want you.

While she is bathing Seegs watches and tells her that Greta wants to destroy him, wants to crush him altogether so she can be free.

He soaps Lila's breasts and she bends over and he laughs and soaps her perfect rump. Perfect, he says. I know, she laughs.

My wife wants ultimate freedom, and you have to kill to have that.

Why?

No answer.

Why?

No answer.

And Seeg dries her off well and does not kiss the offered body, and is brisk with the towel even between her legs.

And she is already beginning to cry because he will not take her to bed. She cries while he apologizes for being such a shit, and when she hits him he can only deserve it, and allows her to hit him until she scratches his cheek and the blood crawls down his chin.

Better?

She cries, but says yes, it is better. As he leaves she calls after him, "You shit. You miserable shit."

Outside her apartment the street is shiny still from the rain. A heavy summer breeze has come down the river. It has stopped raining. The evening is loose and out of control. To this there is only one solution, I realize, and that solution is suicide. Kill self. Hang self. But I do not want to kill myself. I want to live. Even in a garbage dump I want to live. I wish I could laugh.

III

There is no thought of consequence. There is no thought of sequence. What have we come to that we think and act so abstractly with nothing but thought, and thoughts, and thoughts. And nothing adds up. Random sampling.

I realize that I must eat, and therefore choose to eat at the Lord Beaverbrook Hotel Coffee Shop. I surge toward it, eager for all its fakery, because, of course, if all comes to nothing then I am nothing and nothing means nothing, and there need be only the slight act: pills, razor, rope. I wonder if Lila will ever commit suicide. Will she ever throw away that perfectly rounded ass, will she ever decide that all her bright cat-eyes, her rosy nipples and curly hair, her muscular arms and thighs, her lips on the lips of the woman whose name she did not tell me—will she decide that someday they are nothing and cancel them out? Living alone like that, with only the occasional man to fuck her or leave her unfucked, the man who is vaguely hated in either case. I hurry toward the fake coffee shop, with its bright colours, its quick, butterfly waitresses, smiles flashing professionally as if from posters. I shall even now undress them all in my mind.

Lila left alone.

Greta left alone.

Greta will by this time have gone to the hospital. Jeremy was to come by to take her. Won't there be awkward questions?, I said. Won't you need your legal husband for your Blue Cross/Blue Shield. Give me the card, then, she says. I do. I'm going there to die anyway, she says. All right. Die then. I'm sick of it all. I want the warm brown coffee at the Lord Beaverbrook Hotel Coffee Shop. Yes, and Muzak and fake-leather-upholstered chairs, and cheap, shiny maple furniture hardened in plastic, and cheap wood-panelling, and this modern decor of an air terminal. Let me settle in over the paper place-mat, printed with the great LB for Lord Beaverbrook; I want to hear the Air Canada flights announced. Because, Greta, when you are dead I shall step on a plane and be gone. The air hostess will smile at me; I shall be able to afford good clothes, rich fantasies. The flashy fantasies of the great world far from Fredericton await me. And I know, of course, that they are fantasies, that they are as air, that they are juvenile and childish. But they don't cost the price of love, which is to have your insides hung up on a cross in your gut. That's the price I have to pay for your freedom.

230

Because your freedom consists not only in having Jeremy to bed; it consists also in having me cease to exist. Love, you admit, is everything. Love is a real thing, we agree, although it is real as a dream is real, an experience which cannot be bottled and sold. But because it is real, it is a fact. Because it is a fact and I am an opposing fact, I must be destroyed for the argument to be won. For you to love Jeremy, I must be destroyed; for your love to be forever, I must never have been. I am the price to be paid. You cut off my laugh with the razor of your pure love. Grrrrk. Emasculate the man of his laugh.

Because you are dying, you love so that you will forget you are dying, and I am going to run away to die more slowly. I leave you to the growl of Jeremy's motorcycle. Have him at your corner.

But, in this moral algebra game, there is a remainder: R. Me. I am free.

The future for the Remainder is infinite. Therefore I count my money. I count the last chuckles of my lost laugh. I tot it all up and head for the Lord Beaverbrook Hotel Coffee Shop, where there is always an atmosphere of raspberries and cream, and there I shall settle down to a steak sandwich. My mouth waters to get at it. Love gone, there is gluttony to feed the fat heart.

Let me walk along Queen Street now in the fading light, the sun breaking through the brief interstice at the horizon; between purple clouds and earth, and the oil-slick on the puddles in front of the Beaverbrook Hotel breaking into rainbows. The Playhouse, across from the Beaverbrook, is so terrible architecturally that I am ashamed for it. But it is firm as rock. In front of it there is the bright red London bus for tourists. The smell of London diesel will raise a guilt forever.

Of Greta's cheek shiny from rain, on the upper deck, looking out over rainy London.

The wandering Seeg, wanderer of women, finds a seat at the Lord Beaverbrook Coffee Shop, and feels for the plastic-coated masonite counter before him. He is very quick in his movements. Too quick. The Seeg wishes to have his steak sandwich and eat it quickly. He drinks his coffee in a gulp. The glutton is forever frightened, he realizes, and he goes at the food too quickly. His stomach hurts already. He chomps on his steak sandwich. He looks neither left nor right, although the restaurant is crowded with men who look like Mitchell Sharp or Paul Hellyer. He does not look at the waitresses, and they, who do not know him, do not smile.

He hurries out, and rushes into the street, and down Queen Street. The hospital is at the other end, and he hurries toward it. His lungs ache because he is walking so fast. It is dark and hot. Hurry. He dashes across Carleton Street against the lights, and at York, and at Westmoreland Street.

What will the nurse say? What will she think? She will think that here is the man whose wife was brought in by another man. She will blame Seeg; think him heartless, that a friend must bring the wife to the hospital to die.

He rushes toward the hospital, and when he is there, he is afraid to go in. No, he *won't* go in. He stands outside like a suitor.

Inside, the doctors will be going at Greta. Does that hurt? And that? And she will say, "A little." How about there? Yes. A little pain there. What happened to your eye. I tripped. Have you been having fainting spells? Yes. Finally she will scream.

They will delve into her cavities and smell the sweat of Greta, and know all the secret smells in their clinical abstraction. Cunt will smell of cunt. *Her* cunt. She will scream.

Seeg does not go in. He walks faster than before back to the apartment. He walks down Brunswick Street. As he passes the graveyard he breaks into a run and hopes that no one sees him because he is weeping.

He rushes into the apartment, and throws off his raincoat and his British cap. He does not turn on the lights. He is crawling across the floor in the silver light from the streetlight, and he is grabbing at the furniture, grabbing at the chair and burying his head in the hollow that he and Greta have shared, and tearing at it with his teeth, ripping into the dirty upholstery, and he is crawling over a footstool, and slobbering on all fours across the kitchen floor which she has not washed nor waxed for weeks, and he tips over the garbage can which has her used Kleenex and his used Kleenex, and he will not turn on the lights, and he crawls about the apartment on all fours, grunting and hitting his head against table legs and knocking over chairs and a lamp falls and smashes, and he refuses to turn on a light to light these savage lumps and he smashes his head against the sofa and then again and again and he refuses to say a word. He refuses to say: Greta.

ACADEMY STUFF

I

Like most "literary theories," my ideas on the short story form are less "theories" than they are simple reactions—on the one hand—and "working principles"—on the other. And although they may have some relationship to that great grey Thing known as "Literature," they are first and foremost (as far as I am concerned) the tools of my own individual trade. If I am called upon to justify them in the Grand Arena of Criticism (as I am here doing) I think that I can do so, but I must issue the warning that I am doing something "after the fact." That is, having committed the crime of passion (as it were), I am now trying to explain how rational I was all the time.

But most theories, I believe, are developed in reaction to something or other—perhaps something even so vague as "the way things are." But the fact is that in the past ten years, as writer, teacher, and editor (of *The Fiddlehead,* for four years), I have found myself growing more and more dissatisfied with the stories I have been reading.

This does not mean that I have much sympathy with what passes for *"avant-garde."* What is usually meant by that term is the use of typographical techniques which were developed fifty years ago (half a century!) and are now used in an attempt to finesse the writer into the future courses of the "Development of Literature," or whatever. Most *"avant-garde"* is all flash and no substance. Worse, it is ridiculously easy to imitate and fake. Worse yet, it is imitative of the fresh fashion of the 1920's. Nothing could be more provincial than the apeing of a fashion of fifty years ago, nothing is more futile, and nothing is done more often. (It might be worth reminding oneself that the real *avant-garde* writer rarely thinks of himself as such, and that we have blithely forgotten most of the so-called *"avant-garde."* Who has read Wyndham Lewis lately? Tried him myself once. Got bored; quit.)

In another way, however, I have reacted against some of the writing which was submitted to me when I was the editor of *The Fiddlehead.* This was quite often the symbol-sodden maundering parable of the beginning writer, and when I worked my way through it I thought to myself, "Oho, somebody's been reading Coleridge and Kafka on the same afternoon." Mind you, I was less dissatisfied with this kind of attempt than I might have been. I began writing symbol-sodden parables when I was young and reading Coleridge and Kafka on the same afternoon. My friends said it was "pretty impressive stuff," although somehow it was never accepted for publication. Yes, and it was pretty pretentious stuff, too—a papering-over of an insufficient conception with a flowered wall-paper of prose. One thinks one can disguise one's weakness—or one's youth—with great gobs of obscure prose. Its chief characteristic is that it is only obscure, and not worth the effort of dis-entangling it.

But I think that the writing which I have reacted most strongly against is what I call the "Academy" work—that is, the successful story of fifty years ago which I now teach three or four days a week, and the contemporary imitation of it. When this work is done by one of the masters, I am full of admiration for it. When it is a lesser imitation, it seems like pretty weak stuff.

This is the kind of story developed to an incredible degree by the skills of Chekhov, Hemingway, Fitzgerald, or James Joyce. It was a grand era for the short story, and the results were so astonishing that their conventions have hardened into something very like rules. We study the masters in literature classes; we study them in creative writing courses. It is not difficult to see what has happened.

But I can hear myself standing in front of my English 2010 class and intoning: "The chief characteristic of the short story in the 20th century is the use of *implication.*" Then, while my minions are writing that down in their dubious spellings, I go on to explain how James Joyce, *et al,* worked by *patterns of implication.* They get that down; underline it, too. I continue: "The writer implies; you infer." (I follow this with a brief two minutes on the different meanings of the two words.) And in a moment I am launched into an explanation of the "epiphany." The writer is God showing the truth to Saul on the Road to Damascus. We the readers, or the characters in the short story, or all of us, infer a certain *truth* about a character's entire life from the circumstances of the story. We discover that Mr. Duffy of "A Painful Case" was a moral coward because he was afraid of sin. The boy in "Araby" deluded himself about the nature of Romance. In other words, we "work it out," we "solve the problem," we "see the point."

It is neat and intellectually satisfying. We academics have been making a living out of it for years. But I think we have been less than kind toward that great grey Animal of Literature.

First of all, is anyone's entire life revealed in one moment or one set of circumstances? This is the basic tenet of the short story as we commonly know it. It throws a man's life into focus, as it were. But I am uneasy about this. I know too well that human life is more complex than that, and that one moment, however dramatic, does not sum up a person's life nor does it even throw it into focus. It seems to me to be too arbitrary: a rough handling of humanity for a quick effect which is not fair to the multiplicity of mankind. I realize that it is a useful convention, but I am not too sure that it has not outlived its usefulness.

Then there is the more fundamental matter of the Joycean "epiphany." The writer *makes his point* by throwing the character's life into focus. But I would argue that by making us "see the point" the author has turned his story into an intellectual exercise. And worse, the moment we "see the point" the characters themselves are erased from our consciousness. We put the point down in our copious notebooks and forget the humans at the core of the story. Mr. Duffy disappears in our comment about his moral cowardice. Mrs. Sinico is only the means of revealing his moral cowardice; she has ceased entirely to be a person.

And indeed, this may not have been what Joyce intended at all, but this is what we have done by our methods of criticism. We tend to read all stories as parables—and this is not surprising because the parable is one of the basic forms of the short story in our culture—but I think that such a reading is unfair to the art of writing, which I see as the business of invoking humanity. (One of my favorite poets is Browning; one of my favorite poems is "Fra Lippo Lippi.")

But because we read stories in this way, it is inevitable that we should write them in the same way. And consequently writers—some very *good* writers—are still using the convention of the epiphany. The lesser writers are being used by it, and their characters have become algebraic symbols by which the reader is driven toward a "solution to the problem."

The result of the pervasive use of the epiphany, then, is an "Academy" technique: what were once techniques have become conventions, and the conventions show every indication of hardening into rules. The result of writing by the rules is usually academically respectable, but the work produced is imitative, conventional writing. It is "Academy Stuff."

And perhaps because of this discovery, I have come to see the bones of dead structures everywhere. I find the syllogistic form of the Shakespearean sonnet concealed among free verse forms: Point A (image) is contrasted with Point B (image) and results in Synthesis C (image). A small image serves as the concluding couplet. Worse, I have found the same thing in the work of some short-story writers. Dramatic conflict is constructed from Points A and B through C, and zippered up by the final imagistic paragraphs of the short story. The intellectual point is not only *made*—it is made *neatly*.

So, I have come to the conclusion that the fine old techniques have become conventions, and have become worn-out.

These "reactions" of course, are not and have never been quite as rational as perhaps I have made them sound. There have been vague feelings of uneasiness which I have here attempted to codify into something resembling coherence. And it is quite possible that in what follows I shall simply drag in techniques under new names which I think I have thrown out under old ones. But my reactions against the current forms of the short story have been sufficient, at any rate, to set me off on what I hope is my own direction, and as a result I have been forced to develop what I call, grandly, my "working principles."

But the starting point is essentially negative. I know only what I do *not* want. I do not want the reader of my stories to clap his hands and say, "I see the point." I do not want the intellectual progress toward an epiphany.

What do I want then? I think I want to control an emotional experience. That is, I want to send the reader through a set of circumstances which will alter the reader's emotional awareness. I do not want to "change the reader's mind." I want to "change his emotions." (I am well aware that this might be a Romantic—and false—dichotomy.) In other words, I want to induce an emotional attitude, and to do this I try to take the reader through a number of attitudes and circumstances. The total accumulation of these experiences is to be the effect of the short story. Inevitably, I think, my way of writing a short story throws the emphasis of the short story away from the dramatic point or the intellectual insight and onto the immediate *experiencing* of the character.

For example, I find that I am particularly drawn to the first-person point of view. It gets me out of myself, for one thing, and of course it invokes the immediately human dimension of the human voice. The reader is told something directly in the words of the central character. The relationship between the reader and the character is therefore one-to-one; there is no mediating author to judge or analyse for the reader. The reader has to judge or know the character as he might a close friend—with all the restrictions of "knowing" that that entails, but with all the humanity of it, too. The reader knows the narrator in a human dimension—not in the god-like omniscience of the third-person point of view. And of course, with this approach, the teller of the story is at least as important as the story itself. Quite often he *is* the story. In "Because I Am Drunk," for example, I wanted Seeg to speak directly and also to see himself as a character, and consequently I moved back and forth from the first-person to the third-person. It is not an uncharacteristic feature of a drunk: he sees himself doing strange things and wonders at himself for doing them, but does them anyway because something within him makes it impossible for him to stop. (Think about F. Scott Fitzgerald, for example, drunk and dancing on a table with Zelda, and taking mental notes about himself, his behavior, and the party.) The narrator of "The Problems of a Truancy," on the other hand, is very much aware of his physical and historical surroundings, but he is not aware of the despair he feels at his failure to "connect" with them—the despair of the alienation of his knowledge. If the torn-up Seeg is a man of violent love who is trying to be civilized, then the narrator of "The Problems of a Truancy" is more suicidal than he recognizes. (Incidentally, "The Problems of a Truancy" is much less autobiographical than it might appear; most importantly—I am *not* the narrator.)

But if I want to *induce* a particular emotional effect, the trick is to *control* it. I have tried to do this by inducing attitudes, and one of the qualifications of the inducement is that it must go unnoticed—and yet it must be *felt*. To this end I have tried to utilize certain literary techniques to perhaps an uncommon degree.

For example, I think of my stories as consisting of a series of "weights." I even use the term as a verb. I think to myself: "I'll weight this section 'heavy,' and that next one 'light,' 'quick,' or 'sharp,' and that last one 'very heavy.'" This is the structure of "Because I Am Drunk." In other words, I am attempting to structure the story by means of emotional "weights." I want the story to "weigh on one."

But I very seldom plan the "weighting" in any formal sense. I try to catch the tone I want, the voice of my narrator, and then hope that the story will generate its own energy.

And in fact it occurs to me that my so-called "working principles" are really little more than metaphoric descriptions of things which I feel while I am working. The terms are drawn chiefly from the art of painting (about which I know almost nothing—but a number of my friends are painters), and in fact the term "weight" might best be thought of as something analogous to the painter's or sculptor's use of *mass*.

But the "weight" of a section can be controlled by several means. For example, an incident told from a long perspective (the view from across the Square in "The Problems of a Truancy") is, to my feeling at any rate, much lighter than the "heavy" density of details in the close perspective. The reader (and narrator) are simply farther away. But *very* close perspective (as in the last paragraph of "Because I Am

Drunk") is very heavy. If you are close to a person, you are weighed down by him. The narrator of "The Problems of a Truancy" is weighed down by the consciousness which notices the infinity of details in the restaurant. The mass of them oppresses him, although he tries to control them by his carefully ordered thought.

Pace and syntax, therefore, also contribute to "weight." The reader of "The Problems of a Truancy" may not realize it intellectually (and perhaps I prefer him not to), but he feels the narrator trying to order his consciousness; the reader feels this because of the pace and the sentence structure. Then in the last paragraph of "Because I Am Drunk" the release of emotion is indicated by the turned-loose sentence structure. Or again, in the same story, the sharp moral debate which takes place in Section II is indicated less by what is said than it is (I hope) by the quickness of the dialogue, the brevity of the sentences. It is a moral battle, and the moral knives are quick and sharp.

Diction contributes as well. Abstract words are heavy, I think. (See what Faulkner does with a carefully placed Latinate word.) And metaphors are heavy because they slow the pace; a mass of metaphors bundled into a paragraph is very heavy indeed.

The rhythm of the story (which is probably my substitute for the intellectual or confrontational dramatic structure) is achieved by playing the weight of one section against another. The design of the story is the relationship of the parts to one another.

But in addition to all of these "principles of composition," there are other factors which do not fit into anything so coherent as a theory, and yet may be more important in the production of the story. For example, I write myself little notes which gradually accumulate across my desk until they are either filed away or composed into a short story. Whatever it is that is behind the notes is probably responsible for the short story, although it might not appear in the story itself. But why do I write the notes?

Usually the notes are simply phrases (this is how "Because I Am Drunk" began) or a scrap of dialogue or an image. I know I do not begin with an idea or a character, much less a "theory of fiction." And it is also true that a story which one has read, or has been told by a friend, can have much more influence on the story at hand than any literary theory, however sincerely or strongly held.

In other words, it seems to me that there are other factors which contribute to a story which are perhaps more important than the "theory," but which are too incoherent to fit into any kind of rationally explicable pattern. These are the individual, personal offerings of the individual writer, and these are the things which indicate his style—perhaps more accurately than his literary philosophy.

At any rate, I know that I think a short story is finished when all of these factors seem somehow contained; when I can no longer separate the thinking about the short story from the doing of it.

KENT THOMPSON

Rudy Wiebe

Rudy Wiebe was born in Saskatchewan in 1934. He graduated
from the University of Alberta in 1956 and then continued
his studies at the University of Tubingen in West Germany,
the University of Manitoba, and Iowa.

He has worked as a carpenter, beet-hoer, research officer,
civil servant, high school teacher, and editor of a weekly
magazine. He is presently an associate professor of English
at the University of Alberta in Edmonton.

His stories have been published in such magazines as
*The Fiddlehead, The Mennonite, Tamarack Review, Der Bote,
Pluck* etc. and have been broadcast on the CBC. He is working
now on a long novel, his fourth, which is set on the Canadian
prairies.

Bibliography

Peace Shall Destroy Many. McClelland and Stewart, Toronto, 1962. (Novel)

First and Vital Candle. McClelland and Stewart, Toronto, 1966. (Novel)

The Blue Mountains of China. McClelland and Stewart, Toronto, 1970. (Novel)

The Story-Makers. Macmillan Co. of Canada, Toronto, 1970. (A short story text book edited by Wiebe.)

Millstone for the Sun's Day

Most of the people seemed to be already on the docks when the boy and his parents arrived, but the press parted swiftly for them. Without hesitation the boy passed down the long dock, the ladies smiling and the men reaching to pat his head, to where the boats lifted easily in the quick morning sunlight. Turning on the last quay, he saw the Yacht. Its white with imperial black piping burned under the solstice sun and, not quite able to believe it, he turned with a laugh to his mother just behind him.

"Mom, can I really ride on it?"

And his father's hand came down on his shoulder with his deep voice, the people all about them quiet and looking, "Joey, just go ahead— over there. We can't be late."

But the boy was looking at his mother still. Usually when he asked her a question his father did not answer. When the boy had come into the kitchen that morning to find the porridge steaming in his bowl but with the unexpected delight of brown sugar beside it, his father had been saying,

"Mary, it's better now than maybe later. You've never said anything against it until—"

But his mother, usually so gentle and quiet, her back stiffly turned and her hands slicing bananas—brown sugar and bananas both on porridge in one day, hey, this was really a holiday—interrupting fiercely, "We don't *have* to let them!"

His father stood rigid as at a blasphemy. "What—Mary—what in all the almighty world—not *have* to?" his voice hanging on incredible pitch, the sunlight in the big-windowed kitchen gleaming on the hair of his half-lifted, abruptly paralysed arm. Then he saw the boy in the doorway. "Joey! We didn't even hear you. And dressed already! Ready to go."

"Uh-huh—we better hurry, huh, for the ride?"

His father was smiling, bending to him, swinging him aloft so his head almost touched the ceiling, his father was so tall. The boy cried with delight as he swung up and over, and then he was plopped down facing the steaming porridge. He turned to his mother, laughing. "Mom, we can all ride the Yacht 'cause it was me drew the Lottery. At the meeting-house, eh Mom?"

But his mother did not turn or speak. When she moved at last, placing the tiny bowl of sliced bananas beside his porridge, she sat down beside him, her features tight and stiff, as now on the dock, but her eyes, now bunched against the direct sun, distorting even more her lovely face. The boy did not like her frown. She was always too happy for frowning; rather, singing in the kitchen, shaping towers and boats with his building blocks, walking in the Windy Woods and naming the birds flicking high on the tips of the ferns. Now, suddenly, the boy twisted from under his father's hand and tugged at her dress. "Mom, don't you *want* to ride in the Capitular's Yacht?"

She bent swiftly, her summer skirt flaring out like a dark blot and she was hugging him tight against her breast, silently. Over her shoulder he saw the dark lanes of the people up the lift of the dock, their pale faces turned stiff in their smiles against the dead-blue sky. His mother shivered, and he pushed back.

"Mom, shouldn't I of pulled the Lottery yesterday?" It was incomprehensible. He could remember the disappointment of his friend, Eric, behind him in the line and all the people in the meeting-house waving and clapping for him, the Capitular's hand holding his high to show the mark, the clapping hands flickering everywhere so that he could not see his parents though he knew exactly where they were from watching them as he inched forward in the long line. For an instant only he saw his father's black onyx ring flash in the sunlight from the great arched window in the rhythmic clapping at his winning draw. He was looking at his mother's face now, but her eyes avoided him. And then between the people beyond the sheen of her hair he caught a flash of white and he looked up. A slim white figure came down the dock, floating without sound or seeming motion, the gold-and-crimson ribbon across its breast merging with the crimson of the cantors he knew were following.

"Mom!" The boy jogged her shoulder, "Look—look! It looks—just about, all dressed up, like—" he stopped, his recognition shimmering away, then, "isn't it—like Miss Grierson? Look!"

His father's hand fell on his shoulder. "Joey, stand over here, where we belong," and he was hustled to the very edge of the quay where the Yacht waited, motionless as a castle in the water. Past his father's black trouser-leg the boy saw the long bent line of red figures and hats ebbing down between the people and heard the gentle sound that wavered, rising and falling, in the still air, a sound as he had never heard from them before though he had gone since before he could remember, as everyone once a week, and heard them chant in the rood-loft.

"Dad," the boy tugged at the trouser-leg. "What're they singing?"

His father's hand slid over his mouth, the wide ring clicking against his teeth, and he could only look as the flaring baldachin of the Capitular emerged at the head of the dock, flashing red-gold, and the procession stopped and parted, and at long last, in the rising sound, the Capitular at the head of the Lesser Capitulars moved down through the dividing ranks of the cantors to stand beside Miss Grierson in the middle of the dock before the boy and his parents.

The Capitular's benign smile broadened. "Joey." His voice was rich in the motionless air. "Come forward please." The boy had no time to look to his mother. His father's hand was at his back and he was under the Capitular's raised palm. "Joey. You won the Lottery last evening. Therefore you are our special guest today. We will ride in the Yacht together to Sun Rock, and then perhaps around the island. Will you like that?"

Directly facing the Capitular, the question of what every child on the island dreamed of doing stirred a vague apprehension in the boy, for there was something—and then he forgot not only the correct words but also the bow for suddenly he knew and he spoke without thinking, "Sir, your Highest—but—but there aren't my friends here."

From the low gasp of the people he knew his breach of whatever was correct and shrank back even as the laugh rumbled above him.

"Of course. But all your little friends *know* you are going with us. On the Yacht. They have all gone to the picnic at the Garden in the Valley, like you did on this day last year. But you are the special one, the only boy," the hand was on his head now, the great form bending over him, "that can come on the Yacht. Because you drew the Lottery. Now, don't you like that?"

This time he remembered, and bowed. "Yes. Your Highest."

The hand lifted his head and the sound of the cantors belled. The boy stood motionless, as they all did, eyes on the gold slashing of the Capitular's robe, hearing,

The shepherd heard the sheep alway
High hummocked humitry
The day of wrath to scath shall pass
High seared in scarify.

The diagonal gold and crimson on white of the other figure before him drew the boy's eye. So very close now, he could recognize Miss Grierson even less than from far away. Her face was immobile, as if caked in something not her own skin, and her eyes, which had laughed only days before with him and Eric building sand-castles in the schoolyard now stared away as through all the people and over the water and through the very sun itself. He stared at her in turn, the Capitular's long intoning above his head not moving him from his amazement. Then abruptly he

244

was wheeled about and, as he twisted for one more look, his father's voice said, "Joey," and he had to turn.

Wonder of wonders to the boy, he walked up the short gang plank first, followed by his parents. And at the head of the gang plank, beard almost brushed into order, stood the old man who sunned himself day after day in the park across the street from the school. No child knew his name, or ever talked about him; no child had ever seen him do anything, but his standing there at rigid attention was merely a minor amazement as the boy and his parents, followed by the Capitular under his baldachin, stepped aboard. In a moment the deck was filled, the motors vibrated, and they were out on the water, smoothly, as if unmoving in their dignity.

No one said a word; motionless their faces sat upon their bodies like blocks. The boy squirmed, trying to look between, around them.

"Joey." The Capitular's voice stung him to stiffness. "You want to explore the Yacht?" He could not say it but the Capitular, seated in the circle of the Lesser Capitulars and the cantors, seemed to pluck out his thought and the gentle voice continued, "Yes. They always do. You are our guest—go."

The boy's mother, the only other person seated, was holding the boy's hand tightly. But when he looked at her, she nodded hastily. "Yes. I—I'll stay here—now." For an instant he was disappointed. But how often had he dreamed of exploring the largest, the most beautiful vessel on the island! He was gone, slipping between the people. The tall masts where the flags curled and stiffened in the breeze of their motion; the black-bronze railing; the polished wall of the wheel-house where high above through the window glinted the skipper's glasses; the coiled ropes like barrels; the boy saw it all, and all was wonder. Finally he shouldered back, through the cluster of cantors and for a moment a press of skirts stopped him. And voices.

"—but I'm askin' yuh, why her? You'd think, of all the—" said a young feminine voice, but another interrupted,

"Look kiddo, don't bother. It never makes no difference. None. Just do what you're told."

"Well, it's a shame. And don't it make yuh think, huh?" the other insisted.

"I don't think. It never—" but the boy was pushing between them and the voice shifted, "Oh—it's Joey."

As the boy moved to avoid them the first girl stepped suddenly into his path. "Say, you're seeing the big Yacht. That's nice. Look at the view, over here," and her long bare arm was pulling him and he reluctantly ducked his head below the railing to look as she bent to him. "See the town. Looks nice, don't it, with all the nice tall buildings. And look, over there, there's the boat factory." She was pointing in what he vaguely sensed was a kind of flurry, keeping his eyes away from the Yacht. "And doesn't your father work—ain't he a director at the factory—see, over there—"

He had not followed her finger for the flotilla of small boats following had held him. All the boats of the island seemed spread behind the Yacht, bumped full of tiny people, cutting through the water in their wake, but he looked then at the tall chimneys of the factory. "Uh-huh," he said. "Sometimes he takes me along to his office or we look at the motors—" his voice trailed away. "Where's the smoke?"

"There's never no smoke today. See, everybody's here, coming with us." She was erect, gesturing vaguely, pushing him ahead between several girls, and then he was behind an air-funnel, momentarily alone. From deep within the ship rose a muffled throb and he could imagine the great motors running easily, motionless as rocks in their unseeable spinning. With a twist he pried himself between the people again.

And then he saw Miss Grierson. She was sitting, clustered about by girls all dressed, as he suddenly understood the girl talking to him had been, in white but without the band of gold and crimson over their breasts. He wanted to step forward, to tell her—but he saw that she looked even more strange and rigid, sitting so motionless. His mother, now Miss Grierson. A pennant snapped high on the mast above him; he wished suddenly, overwhelmingly, that Eric was there.

He did not want to explore any more. But pushing to find his way back he came upon the old bearded man in a little gap away from everyone leaning over a great block of iron by the railing. The boy looked at it, for it seemed very familiar, but he could not quite decide what it was while the old man muttered to one of the Lesser Capitulars who was hunched down trying to work a rope through one of the innumerable holes in the iron.

"—ain't nothin' what it usta be. Naw sur. In the old days. Usta climb up there, before the sun come up, spend all night climbing, up the trail, through the dark with damn few torches. Just climb. And gettin' them up there was a job. Ha! But everything's gone soft, new stuff, and floating along in boats! Not like we usta climb, *before sunrise.*"

The younger man looked up, face flushed. "Is that well tied, sir? This new rope—"

"It's gotta be new rope!" The old man bent over, not touching the knot. "Yeah," he said grudgingly. "I guess. And you take this platform contraption—" he struck the boards under the iron lightly with his scuffed boot. "One more o' the Cap's new ideas—" he snorted and the boy jumped a little. "Usta be tough, man. None o' this soft psychology stuff. Carried it up right. We done it right then, but now—" the old man glared with a fierce brilliance at the other, his chin bristling over the mass of iron as the crest of Sun Rock emerged out of the mass of the island beyond the wide water. The boy turned frantically, slid between the people, not stopping until he felt his mother's arm about his shoulder.

He stood, panting a little. He said nothing and she did not ask. The peak of Sun Rock grew above the people's heads and the boy understood that they were approaching much closer to the highest point of the island than they ever did in their family boat-picnics. He looked to his father, but his head was high, eyes distant as if he saw nothing. The Capitular's voice was saying, "We hope you had a nice exploration tour, Joey. We were just beginning to wonder where you might be." His Highest was not looking at him as he spoke, but rather at what seemed to the boy was a watch one of the lesser Capitulars was holding before him. Everyone stood silent, grim as if they had never smiled. The Capitular's face was the only friendly one; and suddenly the boy stepped forward.

"Sir, Your Highest, I saw Miss Grierson. But she didn't—look at me. At school we always played in the sand, Eric and me, and she—is something—" The Capitular, still smiling, threw a swift glance at the sky and stood up. The cantors began, their sound lifting unintelligibly into the warm morning, united, plaintive, strangely harrowing. The boy turned sharply for his mother but the Capitular's soft hand was on his shoulder, his voice in his ear.

"Come, my boy. I want you to do one thing, something just for me. For this you were chosen yesterday when you drew the Lottery." The boy gazed wide-eyed at him. The Lottery was for the ride. He twisted, one glance finding his mother now standing. Her eyes were dilated and her face pulled out of shape, but she was nodding soundlessly to him. He could not but obey and he walked forward, the heavy hand on his shoulder, through the lane opening between the people, hearing the chant merge to words as the motors throbbed and died under his feet. And then over the cantors, the high voice of the Capitular lifting and they were standing before the riddled bulk of iron on its little platform, the people all about and sounding now also, the morning sun just visible over the high thrust of the Rock.

"—the-evergoodness-of-the-undying-and-golden—" but the boy did not hear, his eyes shifting from the water where there was now no bronze railing to interrupt his view of the wedge of boats sitting like gulls along the edge of the Rock's shadow on the blue-black water. In the hesitance of silence the Capitular bent to the boy, voice now almost sorrowful.

"Joey, do exactly as I say. This is the handle." The thick fingers pointed to a lever on a raised panel. "When I nod my head at you, pull it back. Just one little pull. It is very easy. But don't," the fingers closed on the boy's hand lifting, "don't touch it till I nod. Exactly then. That's my fine boy. Now, watch me. Exactly. When I nod."

The mesmerizing smile on the broad face, so close, held the boy watching the great arm lift as they did each week in the ambo, the sound of the cantors rising, rising to the top of comprehension and the world flaming with their incredible sound as the boy had never heard it in the rood-loft. He stood erect, swaying slightly to the sway of the people. Then the Capitular bowed to him, his hand found the handle and, standing all alone, facing the water now and the sun flush in his eyes over the peak of the Rock, he pulled.

The sound of the cantors was now the sound of all the people, swaying beyond the water's lift of the Yacht. The boy was the only one who saw the little platform stir and tilt at his feet and the iron slide from the deck like a living thing. Amazed, he stepped to the edge. The splattered circles of its falling fled away from the very apex of the Rock's shadow on the water and he saw the mass of it sink into blackness and the white rope snake along the waterline, his eyes following, and seeing suddenly, beyond the people tight to the rail, the rope ending in a white form falling from the Yacht in one smooth motion. The form hesitated, flat, spread-eagled on the water like a great headed T crossed with a golden-and-crimson slash, before it smudged, then vanished in the black water. The boy stood, staring, remembering only the gaping hole in the mask-like face.

Under the sound of the people floating over the water, the old man was leaning over the railing, cursing softly. "—goddam motor block—so goddam many holes, gurgling to hear it above the chant! In the old days we used millstones. Clean, sure. Damn new-fangled stuff—"

The boy's fingers dug through his mother's thin black dress as she crouched down, clutching him to her.

"Mommie—Mommie—"

"Hush," said his mother. She shuddered in the sunlight. "Hush. Just hush."

Where is the Voice Coming From?

The problem is to make the story.

A difficulty of this making may have been excellently stated by Teilhard de Chardin: 'We are continually inclined to isolate ourselves from the things and events which surround us . . . as though we were spectators, not elements, in what goes on.' Arnold Toynbee does venture, 'For all that we know, Reality is the undifferentiated unity of the mystical experience,' but that need not here be considered. This story ended long ago; it is one of finite acts, of orders, of elemental feelings and reactions, of obvious legal restrictions and requirements.

Presumably all the parts of the story are themselves available. A difficulty is that they are, as always, available only in bits and pieces. Though the acts themselves seem quite clear, some written reports of the acts contradict each other. As if these acts were, at one time, too well known; as if the original nodule of each particular fact had from somewhere received non-factual accretions; or even more, as if, since the basic facts were so clear perhaps there were a larger number of facts than any one reporter, or several, or even any reporter had ever attempted to record. About facts that are still simply told by this mouth to that ear, of course, even less can be expected.

An affair seventy-five years old should acquire some of the shiny transparency of an old man's skin. It should.

Sometimes it would seem that it would be enough—perhaps more than enough—to hear the names only. The grandfather One Arrow; the mother Spotted Calf; the father Sounding Sky; the wife (wives rather, but only one of them seems to have a name, though their fathers are Napaise, Kapahoo, Old Dust, The Rump)—the one wife named, of all things, Pale Face; the cousin Going-Up-To-Sky; the brother-in-law (again, of all things) Dublin. The names of the police sound very much alike; they all begin with Constable or Corporal or Sergeant, but here and there an Inspector, then a Superintendent and eventually all the resonance of an Assistant Commissioner echoes down. More. Herself: Victoria, by the Grace of God etc. etc. QUEEN, Defender of the Faith, etc. etc.; and witness 'Our Right Trusty and Right Well-beloved Cousin and Councillor the Right Honorable Sir John Campbell Hamilton-Gordon, Earl of Aberdeen; Viscount Formartine, Baron Haddo, Methlic, Tarves and Kellie, in the Peerage of Scotland; Viscount Gordon of Aberdeen, County of Aberdeen, in the Peerage of the United Kingdom; Baronet of Nova Scotia, Knight Grand Cross of Our Most Distinguished

249

Order of Saint Michael and Saint George etc. Governor General of Canada'. And of course himself: in the award proclamation named 'Jean-Baptiste' but otherwise known only as Almighty Voice.

But hearing cannot be enough; not even hearing all the thunder of A Proclamation: 'Now Hear Ye that a reward of FIVE HUNDRED DOLLARS will be paid to any person or persons who will give such information as will lead . . . (etc. etc.) this Twentieth day of April, in the year of Our Lord one thousand eight hundred and ninety-six, and the Fifty-nineth year of Our Reign. . .' etc. and etc.

Such hearing cannot be enough. The first item to be seen is the piece of white bone. It is almost triangular, slightly convex—concave actually as it is positioned at this moment with its corners slightly raised—graduating from perhaps a strong eighth to a weak quarter of an inch in thickness, its scattered pore structure varying between larger and smaller on its perhaps polished, certainly shiny surface. Precision is difficult since the glass showcase is at least thirteen inches deep and therefore an eye cannot be brought as close as the minute inspection of such a small, though certainly quite adequate, sample of skull would normally require. Also, because of the position it cannot be determined whether the several hairs, well over a foot long, are still in some manner attached or not.

The seven-pounder cannon can be seen standing almost shyly between the showcase and the interior wall. Officially it is known as a gun, not a cannon, and clearly its bore is not large enough to admit a large man's fist. Even if it can be believed that this gun was used in the 1885 Rebellion and that on the evening of Saturday May 29, 1897 (while the nine-pounder, now unidentified, was in the process of arriving with the police on the special train from Regina), seven shells (all that were available in Prince Albert at that time) from it were sent shrieking into the poplar bluff as night fell, clearly such shelling could not and would not disembowel the whole earth. Its carriage is now nicely lacquered, the perhaps oak spokes of its petite wheels (little higher than a knee) have been recently scraped, puttied and varnished; the brilliant burnish of its brass breeching testifies with what meticulous care charmen and women have used nationally advertised cleaners and restorers.

Though it can also be seen, even a careless glance reveals that the same concern has not been expended on the one (of two) 44 calibre 1866 model Winchesters apparently found at the last in the pit with Almighty Voice. It also is preserved in a glass case; the number 1536735 is still, though barely, distinguishable on the brass cartridge section just below the brass saddle ring. However, perhaps because the case was imperfectly sealed at one time (though sealed enough not to warrant disturbance now), or because of simple neglect, the rifle is obviously spotted here and there with blotches of rust and the brass itself reveals discolorations almost like mildew. The rifle bore, the three long strands of hair themselves, actually bristle with clots of dust. It may be that this museum cannot afford to be as concerned as the other; conversely, the disfiguration may be something inherent in the items themselves.

The small building which was the police guardroom at Duck Lake, Saskatchewan Territory, in 1895 may also be seen. It had subsequently been moved from its original place and used to house small animals, chickens perhaps, or pigs—such as a woman might be expected to have under her responsibility. It is, of course, now perfectly empty, and clean so that the public may enter with no more discomfort than a bend under the doorway and a heavy encounter with disinfectant. The door-jamb has obviously been replaced; the bar network at one window is, however, said to be original; smooth still, very smooth. The logs inside have been smeared again and again with whitewash, perhaps paint, to an insistent point of identity-defying characterlessness. Within the small rectangular box of these logs not a sound can be heard from the streets of the probably dead town.

> *Hey Injun you'll get hung for stealing that steer*
> *Hey Injun for killing that government cow you'll get*
> *three weeks on the woodpile Hey Injun*

The place named Kinistino has disappeared from the map but the Minnechinass Hills have not. Whether they have ever been on a map is doubtful but they will, of course, not disappear from the landscape as long as the grass grows and the rivers run. Contrary to general report and belief, the Canadian prairies are rarely, if ever, flat and the Minnechinass (spelled five different ways and translated sometimes as 'The Outside Hill,' sometimes as 'Beautiful Bare Hills') are dissimilar from any other of the numberless hills that everywhere block out the prairie horizon. They are not bare; poplars lie tattered along their tops, almost black against the straw-pale grass and sharp green against the grey soil of the plowing laid in half-mile rectangular blocks upon their western slopes. Poles holding various wires stick out of the fields, back down the bend of the valley; what was once a farmhouse is weathering into the cultivated earth. The poplar bluff where Almighty Voice made his stand has, of course, disappeared.

The policemen he shot and killed (not the ones he wounded, of course) are easily located. Six miles east, thirty-nine miles north in Prince Albert, the English Cemetery. Sergeant Colin Campbell Colebrook, North West

Mounted Police Registration Number 605, lies presumably under a gravestone there. His name is seventeenth in a very long 'list of non-commissioned officers and men who have died in the service since the inception of the force.' The date is October 29, 1895, and the cause of death is anonymous: 'Shot by escaping Indian prisoner near Prince Albert.' At the foot of this grave are two others: Constable John R. Kerr, No. 3040, and Corporal C. H. S. Hockin, No. 3106. Their cause of death on May 28, 1897 is even more anonymous, but the place is relatively precise: 'Shot by Indians at Min-etch-inass Hills, Prince Albert District.'

The gravestone, if he has one, of the fourth man Almighty Voice killed is more difficult to locate. Mr. Ernest Grundy, postmaster at Duck Lake in 1897, apparently shut his window the afternoon of Friday, May 28, armed himself, rode east twenty miles, participated in the second charge into the bluff at about 6:30 p.m., and on the third sweep of that charge was shot dead at the edge of the pit. It would seem that he thereby contributed substantially not only to the Indians' bullet supply, but his clothing warmed them as well.

The burial place of Dublin and Going-Up-To-Sky is unknown, as is the grave of Almighty Voice. It is said that a Metis named Henry Smith lifted the latter's body from the pit in the bluff and gave it to Spotted Calf. The place of burial is not, of course, of ultimate significance. A gravestone is always less evidence than a triangular piece of skull, provided it is large enough.

Whatever further evidence there is to be gathered may rest on pictures. There are, presumably, almost numberless pictures of the policemen in the case, but the only one with direct bearing is one of Sergeant Colebrook who apparently insisted on advancing to complete an arrest after being warned three times that if he took another step he would be shot. The picture must have been taken before he joined the force; it reveals him a large-eared young man, hair brush-cut and ascot tie, his eyelids slightly drooping, almost hooded under thick brows. Unfortunately a picture of Constable R. C. Dickson, into whose charge Almighty Voice was apparently placed in that guardroom and who after Colebrook's death was convicted of negligence, sentenced to two months hard labor and discharged, does not seem to be available.

There are no pictures to be found of either Dublin (killed early by rifle fire) or Going-Up-To-Sky (killed in the pit), the two teenage boys who gave their ultimate fealty to Almighty Voice. There is, however, one said to be of Almighty Voice, Junior. He may have been born to Pale Face during the year, two hundred and twenty-one days that his father was a fugitive. In the picture he is kneeling before what could be a tent, he wears striped denim overalls and displays twin babies whose sex cannot be determined from the double-laced dark bonnets they wear. In the supposed picture of Spotted Calf and Sounding Sky, Sounding Sky stands slightly before his wife; he wears a white shirt and a striped blanket folded over his left shoulder in such a manner that the arm in which he cradles a long rifle cannot be seen. His head is thrown back; the rim of his hat appears as a black half-moon above eyes that are pressed shut in, as it were, profound concentration above a mouth clenched thin in a downward curve. Spotted Calf wears a long dress, a sweater which could also be a man's dress coat, and a large fringed and embroidered shawl which would appear distinctly Doukhobor in origin if the scroll patterns on it were more irregular. Her head is small and turned slightly towards her husband so as to reveal her right ear. There is what can only be called a quizzical expression on her crumpled face; it may be she does not understand what is happening and that she would have asked a question, perhaps of her husband, perhaps of the photographer, perhaps even of anyone, anywhere in the world if such questioning were possible for an Indian lady.

There is one final picture. That is one of Almighty Voice himself. At least it is purported to be of Almighty Voice himself. In the Royal Canadian Mounted Police Museum on the Barracks Grounds just off Dewdney Avenue in Regina, Saskatchewan it lies in the same showcase, as a matter of fact immediately beside, that triangular piece of skull. Both are unequivocally labeled, and it must be assumed that a police force with a world-wide reputation would not label *such* evidence incorrectly. But here emerges an ultimate problem in making the story.

There are two official descriptions of Almighty Voice. The first reads: 'Height about five feet, ten inches, slight build, rather good looking, a sharp hooked nose with a remarkably flat point. Has a bullet scar on the left side of his face about 1½ inches long running from near corner of mouth towards ear. The scar cannot be noticed when his face is painted but otherwise is plain. Skin fair for an Indian.' The second description is on the Award Proclamation: 'About twenty-two years old, five feet ten inches in height, weight about eleven stone, slightly erect, neat small feet and hands; complexion inclined to be fair, wavy dark hair to shoulders, large dark eyes, broad forehead, sharp features and parrot nose with flat tip, scar on left cheek running from mouth towards ear, feminine appearance.'

So run the descriptions that were, presumably, to identify a well-known fugitive in so precise a manner that an informant could collect five hundred dollars—a considerable sum when a police constable earned between one and two dollars a day. The nexus of the problems appears when these supposed official descriptions are compared to the supposed official picture. The man in the picture is standing on a small rug. The fingers of his left hand touch a curved Victorian settee, behind him a photographer's backdrop of scrolled patterns merges to vaguely paradisaic trees and perhaps a sky. The mocassins he wears make it impossible to deduce whether his feet are 'neat small.' He may be five feet, ten inches tall, may weigh eleven stone, he certainly is 'rather good looking' and, though it is a frontal view, it may be that the point of his long and flaring nose could be 'remarkably flat.' The photograph is slightly over-illuminated and so the unpainted complexion could be 'inclined to be fair'; however, nothing can be seen of a scar, the hair is not wavy and shoulder-length but hangs almost to the waist in two thick straight braids worked through with beads, fur, ribbons and cords. The right hand that holds the corner of the blanket-like coat in position is large and, even in the high illumination, heavily veined. The neck is concealed under coiled beads and the forehead seems more low than 'broad.'

Perhaps, somehow, these picture details could be reconciled with the official description if the face as a whole were not so devastating.

On a cloth-backed sheet two feet by two and one-half feet in size, under the Great Seal of the Lion and the Unicorn, dignified by the names of the Deputy of the Minister of Justice, the Secretary of State, the Queen herself and all the heaped detail of her 'Right Trusty and Right Well Beloved Cousin,' this description concludes: 'feminine appearance.' But the picture: any face of history, any believed face that the world acknowledges as *man*—Socrates, Jesus, Attila, Genghis Khan, Mahatma Gandhi, Joseph Stalin—no believed face is more *man* than this face. The mouth, the nose, the clenched brows, the eyes—the eyes are large, yes, and dark, but even in this watered-down reproduction of unending reproductions of that original, a steady look into those eyes cannot be endured. It is a face like an axe.

It is now evident that the de Chardin statement quoted at the beginning has relevance only as it proves itself inadequate to explain what has happened. At the same time, the inadequacy of Aristotle's much more famous statement becomes evident: 'The true difference [between the historian and the poet] is that one relates what *has* happened, the other what *may* happen.' These statements cannot explain the storyteller's activity since, despite the most rigid application of impersonal investigation, the elements of the story have now run me aground. If ever I could, I can no longer pretend to objective, omnipotent disinterestedness. I am no longer

254

spectator of what *has* happened or what *may* happen: I am become *element* in what is happening at this very moment.

For it is, of course, I myself who cannot endure the shadows on that paper which are those eyes. It is I who stand beside this broken veranda post where two corner shingles have been torn away, where barbed wire tangles the dead weeds on the edge of this field. The bluff that sheltered Almighty Voice and his two friends has not disappeared from the slope of the Minnechinass, no more than the sound of Constable Dickson's voice in that guardhouse is silent. The sound of his speaking is there even if it has never been recorded in an official report:

> *hey injun you'll get*
> *hung*
> *for stealing that steer*
> *hey injun for killing that government*
> *cow you'll get three*
> *weeks on the woodpile hey injun*

The unknown contradictory words about an unprovable act that move a boy to defiance, an implacable Cree warrior long after the three-hundred-and-fifty-year war is ended, a war already lost the day the Cree watch Cartier hoist his gun ashore at Hochelaga and they begin the retreat west; these words of incomprehension, of threatened incomprehensible law are there to be heard, like the unmoving tableau of the three-day siege is there to be seen on the slopes of the Minnechinass. Sounding Sky is somewhere not there, under arrest, but Spotted Calf stands on a shoulder of the Hills a little to the left, her arms upraised to the setting sun. Her mouth is open. A horse rears, riderless, above the scrub willow at the edge of the bluff, smoke puffs, screams tangle in rifle barrage, there are wounds, somewhere. The bluff is green this spring, it will not burn and the ragged line of seven police and two civilians is staggering through, faces twisted in rage, terror, and rifles sputter. Nothing moves. There is no sound of frogs in the night; twenty-seven policemen and five civilians stand in cordon at thirty-yard intervals and a body also lies in the shelter of a gully. Only a voice rises from the bluff:

> *We have fought well*
> *You have died like braves*
> *I have worked hard and am hungry*
> *Give me food*

but nothing moves. The bluff lies, a bright green island on the grassy slope surrounded by men hunched forward rigid over their long rifles, men clumped out of rifle-range, thirty-five men dressed as for fall hunting on a sharp spring day, a small gun positioned on a ridge above. A crow

255

is falling out of the sky into the bluff, its feathers sprayed as by an explosion. The first gun and the second gun are in position, the beginning and end of the bristling surround of thirty-five Prince Albert Volunteers, thirteen civilians and fifty-six policemen in position relative to the bluff and relative to the unnumbered whites astride their horses, standing up in their carts, staring and pointing across the valley, in position relative to the bluff and the unnumbered Indians squatting silent along the higher ridges of the Hills, motionless mounds, faceless against the Sunday morning sunlight edging between and over them down along the tree tips, down into the shadows of the bluff. Nothing moves. Beside the second gun the red-coated officer has flung a handful of grass into the motionless air, almost to the rim of the red sun.

And there is a voice. It is an incredible voice that rises from among the young poplars ripped of their spring bark, from among the dead somewhere lying there, out of the arm-deep pit shorter than a man; a voice rises over the exploding smoke and thunder of guns that reel back in their positions, worked over, serviced by the grimed motionless men in bright coats and glinting buttons, a voice so high and clear, so unbelievably high and strong in its unending wordless cry.

The voice of 'Gitchie-Manitou Wayo'—interpreted as 'voice of the Great Spirit'—that is, Almighty Voice. His death chant no less incredible in its beauty than in its incomprehensible happiness.

I say 'wordless cry' because that is the way it sounds to me. I could be more accurate if I had a reliable interpreter who would make a reliable interpretation. For I do not, of course, understand the Cree myself.

PASSAGE BY LAND

I have heard people say they can never tell one end of a poem from another and, what's more, they don't intend to bother finding out how to do it; I've never heard anyone say that about stories. There may not be anyone on earth who doesn't like stories. Certainly everyone at some time or another tells one, and the people who are most insistent that a story must actually have happened (i.e., be *true*) often care least about whether it has happened physically (ie., is true in the sense of *fact*) or largely in the mind (ie., is true in the sense of *fiction*).

When one thinks about it, it's soon clear that the best stories always emerge mostly as fiction; *Of a Fire on the Moon* is immeasurably better than the voice of Houston Control. Perhaps that's because the facts come to us through an organizing, imaginative, sometimes almost a transcendental intelligence. Who of us, unaided, can marshall all that overwhelming data; condense it; hammer it up to meaning?

All of which is general theorizing and, though I find it exciting, all the theorizing I wish to do about *why* people like stories has been done in another place.* Here it is enough to give some of my specific apprehensions about story writing. It would be useful to accept the whole of what follows as true even though I myself on any given day find it impossible at certain points to separate the layers of fact (the thing done) from the prisms of fiction (the thing made).

I never saw a mountain or a plain until I was twelve, almost thirteen. The world was poplar and birch covered; muskeg hollows and stony hills; great hay sloughs with the spruce on their far shores shimmering in summer heat, and swamps with wild patterns burned three and four, sometimes five feet into their moss by some fire decades before, filled with water in spring but dry in summer and sometimes smoking faintly still in the morning light where, if you slid from your horse and pushed your hand into the moss, you could feel the strange heat of it lurking.

In such a world, a city of houses with brick chimneys, telephones, was less real than Grimms' folk tales or Greek myths. I was born in what would become, when my father and older brother chopped down enough trees for the house, our chicken barn; and did not speak English until I went to school, though I can't remember learning it. Perhaps I never have (as one former professor insists when he reads my novels); certainly it wasn't until years later I discovered that the three miles my sister and I had meandered to school, sniffing and poking at pussywillows and ant hills,

*Introduction to *The Story-Makers*, Macmillan, 1970.

lay somewhere in the territory Big Bear and Wandering Spirit had roamed with their warriors always just ahead of General Strange in May and June, 1885. As a child, however, I was for years the official flag raiser (Union Jack) in our one-room school and during the war I remember wondering what it would be like if one day, just as I turned the corner of the pasture with the cows, a huge car would wheel into our yard, Joseph Stalin emerge into the Saskatchewan air and from under his mustache tell my father he could have his farm back in Russia, if he wanted it. Then I would stand still on the cow path trodden into the thin bush soil and listen, listen for our cowbells; hear a dog bark some miles away, and a boy call; and wonder what an immense world of people—I could not quite imagine how many—was now doing chores, and if it wasn't for the trees and the curvature of the earth (as the teacher said) I could easily see Mount Everest somewhere a little south of east. Or west?

My first sight of the prairie itself I do not remember. We were moving south, leaving the rocks and bush of northern Saskatchewan forever, my parents said, and I was hanging my head out of the rear window of the hired car, vomiting. I had a weak stomach from having been stepped on by a horse, which sounds funny though I cannot remember it ever being so. Consequently, our first day in south Alberta the driver had me wash his car and so I cannot remember my first glimpse of the Rocky Mountains either. It was long after that that anyone explained to me the only mountain we could see plainly from there was in the United States.

But sometimes a fall morning mirage will lift the line of Rockies over the level plain and there they will be, streaked black in crevices under their new snow with wheat stubble for base and the sky over you; you can bend back forever and not see its edge. Both on foot and from the air I have since seen some plains, some mountains on several continents; jungles; the Danube, the Mississippi, even the Amazon. But it was north of Old Man River one summer Sunday when I was driving my father (he had stopped trying to farm and he never learned to drive a car) to his week's work pouring concrete in a new irrigation town, that we got lost in broad daylight on the prairie. Somewhere we had missed something; the tracks we were following at last faded and were gone like grass. My father said in Lowgerman,

"Boy, now you turn around."

I got out. The grass crunched dry as crumbs and in every direction the earth so flat another two steps would place me at the horizon, looking into the abyss of the universe. There is too much here, the line of sky and grass rolls in upon you and silences you thin, too impossibly thin to remain in any part recognizably yourself. The space must be broken somehow, or it uses you up, and my father muttered in the car,

"If you go so far and get lost at least there's room to go back. Now turn around."

A few moments thereafter we came upon a rail line stretched in a wrinkle of the land—the prairie in Alberta is not at all flat, it only looks like that at any given point—white crosses beside rails that disappeared straight as far in either direction as could be seen. We had not crossed a railroad before but the tracks could no more be avoided here than anything else and some connecting road to the new town must be eventually somewhere beyond.

In that wandering to find it is rooted, I believe, the feeling I articulated much later; the feeling that to touch this land with words requires an architectural structure; to break into the space of the reader's mind with the space of this western landscape and the people in it you must build a structure of fiction like an engineer builds a bridge or a skyscraper over and into space. A poem, a lyric, will not do. You must lay great black steel lines of fiction, break up that space with huge design and, like the fiction of the Russian steppes, build giant artifact. No song can do that; it must be giant fiction.

The way a man feels with and lives with that living earth with which he is always laboring to live. Farmer or writer.

To be specific about my two stories in this book: writing a story is much like rappelling up a mountain whose top may not exist because it can never be known by anyone but yourself. For me, the climbing—that is, the writing itself—rarely takes as long as deciding that this is the particular mountain on which I want to spend my energy. I have not written many stories; not one has ever confronted me in the same way as any other and so I live always with the possibility that whatever happens, whatever I see or think, suddenly there it will be—the true base of a story mountain.

Forget that crazy analogy; it's too much work to construct for what it's worth.

Anyway, 'Millstone' I wrote in 1965 from an idea that came to me while I was sitting in a church and not listening to the sermon. I always make sure I have a Bible in church, to read when whatever else is happening isn't worth attention. On this occasion I read again some hard words spoken by the usually considerate Jesus; they seemed excessively hard, cruel, perhaps almost sadistic and my imagination started spinning around this vortex: what would happen to a person who believed those words literally? What, through the centuries, would have happened to such a group of literalists? In my files are three pages of doodlings and details: 'age of boy,' a scrap of conversation, several attempts at chants, something about 'flowers' and '6-7 pages.' There are four versions, the last two getting successively shorter; the title mutates from 'Day of the Rood' to 'Day of the Sun' to 'Millstone for the Sun's Day.'

Almighty Voice has been in my awareness for at least a decade; somewhere the sound of names, somewhere a shadow of violence. About three years ago I came across (libraries and used bookstores are great places for 'coming across' immensities) the name again in an old RCMP history and suddenly I knew: here is a story I must write. The many accounts of it, the official reports, the pictures of places slowly accumulated, but it was the bone and the picture in the RCMP Regina museum that forced me out of any head-on realism in telling the story. I found I couldn't face the usual writer problems: shall I tell it from the viewpoint of a policeman or Spotted Calf or a district farmer or—if I dare—Almighty Voice; how much historical time will the story itself cover; where will it take place and how much can I move the scene around; how shall I begin?

For four months, then, I had been thinking intensely about the story when in October 1970, by some minor miracle of timetable in perfect conjunction with administrative class cancellations I found almost ten days for myself. I had not written a word, and for two more days I wrote none. There were times when I almost suspected I never would. But then it emerged; in random words, phrases; a feeling and a memory; a landscape seen. Pulled together suddenly by a vaguely remembered tableau of the Battle of Cut Knife Hill in the *Illustrated War News*, 1885; by glancing up one day while leaning in half-despair against one of the Cameron Library stacks and my hand going up to pull out the one book in the library's million that my eyes might have focussed upon: Toynbee's *A Study of History*, volume 12: *Reconsiderations*.

Not that all of the story as it now stands actually happened to me. Far from it. But I want to make you feel that it did; and it *did*, to some story-maker who, if I had perfect wishfulfillment at the moment of writing, I would be.

RUDY WIEBE

Harry Bruce

Harry Bruce, 37, is an editorial gypsy among Canadian
newspapers and consumer magazines. He has worked for
Saturday Night magazine, *The Canadian* magazine, *The Star
Weekly* magazine, the *Toronto Daily Star,* the *Ottawa Journal*
(twice), *Maclean's* magazine (twice), and the privy council's
task force on federal government information services (once,
which was enough). Mr. Bruce has sold freelance work to
virtually all of his former employers, to other magazines and
newspapers in Canada and the United States, to various
governments and, from time to time, to private industrial
concerns. He is the author of one hardcover book, a collection
of newspaper columns entitled *The Short Happy Walks of Max
MacPherson,* and of a few short pieces of popular history
that have turned up in anthologies of one sort or another.

In 1956-57, Mr. Bruce lived with his wife in London,
England, while studying under the benefits of a Lord

261

Beaverbrook overseas scholarship. (He is a graduate of Mount Allison University, Sackville, N.B.) In 1970-71, he lived with his wife and three children in Newcastle (population 1,500), southern Ontario, while studying environmental issues at the University of Toronto under the benefits of a Southam Fellowship for journalists. At the moment, he has established himself and family on the shores of Prospect Bay, which is 12 miles from central Halifax. He performs editorial services for the Nova Scotia Light and Power Company Limited, and continues to dabble at free-lance writing. A native of Toronto, he thinks he has settled down in Nova Scotia for good.

The Courtship of Edith Long

I've no way of knowing for sure but I suspect late February and early March are a time of many suicides in Toronto; a time when men quit good Canadian jobs to run away to the hot heavens of the southern states; a time when drama critics are far more cruel than they ever are in July; a time when upright and unadventurous businessmen suddenly find themselves wondering how long they're going to last, and turn to thoughts of embezzlement and adultery. This is a time of harder drinking than usual, and harder words, of bewilderment and meanness. It is the Season of Despair.

The Season has struck me a little early this year. I sit here, refusing to shave, scratching my hairy stomach, drinking canned beer, staring numbly out the front window at the snow pointlessly blowing by.

I look like the hero of a movie about unemployment and, after a while, my wife allows a kindly old relative to enter the room. He places his hand on my shoulder (which twitches) and says, 'Max, you can't go on like this. You can't just sit here, hour after hour, rotting, brooding, festering, guzzling, hating the things you can never change, feeding the evil that lurks in us all. There's a lot of use left in you, son, and the world spins on, you know. There's work enough to challenge every man with a strong back and two hands. Come, I'll drive you out to Collectors' Corner (1633 Kingston Road), and you can take a Therapeutic Walk in the flea market they've got going out there. Maybe, just maybe, you'll find a magical old beach parasol, or some other golden bargain that will restore the summer in your soul.'

'All right, all right, I'll come,' snap I. 'I'll come if you'll only shut your avuncular yap.'

The Season of Despair has slowed my mind somewhat and the real reason I agreed to walk around Collectors' Corner is that I've confused the flea market with a flea *circus*. I'm not yet so far gone that I don't want to see a bunch of fleas pulling chariots, swinging on trapezes, and imitating Emmett Kelly.

But, as soon as I enter the place, I know I've made a hideous mistake. I've allowed myself to be dragged out to this distant and homely corner of distant and homely Scarborough to observe, not a team of brilliant bugs, but a supermarket of antiques. Collectors' Corner is an old Canadian Tire building that's been turned into a grab-bag of cultural activity. It's got folk music, classical music, smelly old books, a lot of Centennial stuff, and a couple of dozen dealers in antiques, stamps, coins, swords, guns, and artsy-craftsy conversation and effort.

The proprietors describe the adventures in their basement as a 'Paris (France) type flea market' to distinguish it from a 'Paris (Ontario) type flea market', and, partly because the prices upstairs are enough to bring on a Season of Despair all by themselves, I clump sourly down to look at the cheap stuff.

The flea market is a gigantic version of those basement sales we downtown Toronto kids used to hold periodically to unload stolen goods, marbles, and limp comic books. It is a miracle of Camp; a beautiful explosion of fascinating crap; a triumphant harvest of old, beady, stringy, shiny, brassy, dusty, silvery, corny, and cheesy things.

I've no hope of describing the range of stuff that's on sale at the flea market but, as entertainment, it's at least as good as bugs on a tightrope. It is full of things—like rusty tin Players' cigarette boxes, *Boys' Own Annuals*, naked-girl letter-openers, and toy soldiers from the Second World War—that I haven't seen for years, or even considered. They throw off real smells of the past.

And then, just around the corner from a table that displays soft, ornate, silver-backed dressing-table tools for ladies—hand mirrors, things to tailor one's dainty fingers, yellow-bristled hairbrushes—I discover a batch of grubby postcards and, among them, the record of a sixty-year-old love affair.

The postcards are almost all addressed to a Miss Edith Long. She lived on Manning Avenue in 1906. She was young and pretty and popular. She was alive, and moving around, and being wooed in that great time— the sleepy, innocent, quiet, slow, happy years of horses, stylish picnics, white wooden houses, clean air, and lilacs that bloomed in every backyard. I have always thought of the North America of 1900-10 as one of the Classic Eras of serious walking, and Miss Long's postcards carry me out of the Season of Despair and into the aroma of her fine times.

The postmarks on her cards from the States show a curly U.S. flag with only thirteen stars; the green one-cent stamps all boast a double-chinned Benjamin Franklin. Edward VII stares blandly off the Canadian stamps at the affectionate words various friends, relatives, and lovers have sent to Miss Long.

The faded photographs on the fronts of the cards confirm my irrational affection for this time before I was born: The Union Jacks are flying on the dirt road that passes for Main Street in Renfrew, Ontario, and a brass band is swinging past the straw hats, fluffy white blouses, and long dark skirts . . . more flags in Welland, and a couple of kids are sitting on a veranda on an impossibly shady street that slides off into the distance to meet another impossibly shady street . . . ships nudge at the quaint little skyscrapers of lower New York . . . sunlight beams through the churchy avenues and low trees of Indianapolis . . . the women, even on a beach in New Jersey, are cheerful, quiet, and fully dressed . . . and all the streets, even in the biggest cities of the continent, are strangely empty.

On May 8, 1906, a man who cannot bring himself to write anything so personal as 'Dear Edith' sends Miss Long a postcard from Cobourg. 'You can look for me when the weather gets warmer,' he says. 'Cannot say how long that will be. A.D.S.' All that summer and fall he continues to send her these terse, non-committal little messages. They follow her even to the Uneeda Rest Hotel at Sparrow Lake, Muskoka, where she spends some holidays, and by September he feels he knows her well enough to sign his cards 'Ad' and to write from Welland, 'Town is crowded, no place to sleep, send me a bed at once.'

For a couple of years, breezy notes from a married sister named Win dominate Miss Long's postcards. Win travels endlessly all over the eastern United States. She worries a lot about her weight, sticks 'ha ha' in the middle of sentences, and sounds as though she might be in show business.

Then, suddenly, on July 26, 1909, someone named Ruby writes to Miss Long from Connecticut. 'Dear Edith,' she writes, 'We are anxious to know if Ad has accepted the position at Cobalt. If he has, I am sorry you are disturbed so soon, but hope it will turn out all right. Lots of love to you.' The card is addressed to *Mrs.* A. D. Smith and it is clear that, by 1909, Ad's 'see you when the weather gets warmer' has turned into a proposal that he see her as long as they both should live. Adam and Edith.

I don't quite know why, but my singlehanded discovery of the Romance of Edith Long turns the Season of Despair into the Season of Expectation. I leave the flea market with the cards in my overcoat pocket. The snow blasts stupidly against my face, but it doesn't hurt. I wonder, 'Where have you gone, Edith Long?' and calculate that only five more weeks of my life have to go by before spring comes back to Toronto.

The Bad Samaritan
Down at the Railroad Station

I am comfortable enough, financially, to rent or purchase from among many thousands of pleasing things but none strikes me as more profoundly gratifying than a bedroom on a train. Not a mere berth, in which only a coarse brown curtain separates one from the commerce in the aisle. Not one of those ghastly "roomettes," in which one must raise the entire blooming bed in order to relieve oneself, while the train is not standing in the station. But a real little bedroom. Here, assuming one is traveling alone, one can stand up or lie down in comfort and dignity. One can study one's profiles in the many mirrors over the gleaming sink. One can fiddle with the buttons and switches that control the temperature, the fan, and the elaborate complex of lights for the bed, the ceiling, the dresser and the annex (where one's toilet bowl resides, as it should, in a chamber of its own).

On the outskirts of town, the train picks up speed and the lights of the common public cease to flash against the black window pane. I take off my clothes and arrange them on the polished wooden hangers in the clothes closet. I cleanse my teeth and limbs. I pass water. I don clean pyjamas. I open my briefcase, and pour myself a Scotch-and-water. I light up a small, mellow Dutch cigar of the better sort. I climb under the snowy sheets and the heavy railroad blankets, and I sip and read, sip and read. I read a yachting magazine, history by Alan Moorehead, stories by O'Hara, or perhaps a gourmet cookbook. I read anything that cannot possibly contain real unpleasantness. If more infants died today in Vietnam, I'd rather not read about them. If Black Panthers, rabid young radicals and Quebec separatists are all frothing at the mouth and shooting up the city I've just left, I do not want to know about them. Thank you all the same but, no, I do not want tomorrow morning's newspaper. You may stuff it somewhere else. I paid six dollars over the price of a roomette for this bedroom, and I'm not about to allow the disorders of the day to intrude upon its perfect luxury.

I move through the black and rolling nighttime, never knowing exactly where I am on the land. The speed is great and rhythmic. This small place of mine consists entirely of hard, heavy metal, the softest linen, and supreme security. The solitude is matchless. I turn out all the lights, even the frosty blue night light. Tomorrow will be soon enough to read about the bad news, and maybe about an airline crash, too. Clackety-clack. Clackety-clack. I'm going home.

Well, for some time, that was the way it was for me, overnight travel, and I wish it had remained that way, but it did not. Something happened one ugly night a year or so ago and, though I have certainly not abandoned the small investment in personal pampering that bedrooms on trains represent, the incident of that night continues to discomfort me and to sap me of the old slumberous contentment.

I had been in Toronto a week, and I had found the place even more demanding and nerve-jangling than usual. Everybody wanted things I was not prepared to give. Mere acquaintances asked to borrow money. My university alumni fund caught up with me once more. Two insurance salesmen and one mutual-fund salesman phoned me, all on the same day, and they forced me to be rude to them. People kept wanting me to *do* things: for the local Liberals; for the ratepayers against the corrupt land-developers; for those who oppose sonic booms; for polar bears and orangutans, and other creatures who were in peril of extinction; for an alcoholic friend; for the wife of the alcoholic friend; for the lover of the wife of the alcoholic friend; for a radical theatre group; and, for God's sake, for women's liberation; and so on, and on, and on. Adopt a child in the Philippines. Help the retarded. Give to the Heart Fund. Fight the population explosion. Fight cancer, cerebral palsy, the police pigs, the pinko kids, and fight City Hall, too. Buddy, can you spare a fin? Come on, commit yourself. Sign right here. Where do you stand? Do you *care*? What are you *doing* about it?

I suppose we all experience weeks like that (about 52 of them a year), but this one depressed me in a peculiarly tense and irrational way. Even the casual greetings of working associates, the stupid ringing of the telephone, and the blatancy of the traffic in the streets, everything seemed to harbor some nameless demand on me. Like a stranger's smile, they forced me to decide how to respond, and by what bloody right did they think they could get away with that? You will understand then that, all through the last day of that visit to Toronto, I yearned for a certain moment. The porter would say, "And what time should I wake you, sir?", and I would say, "Oh, about 7.30 will be all right, and would you bring me a coffee with cream and sugar at that time?" Then, I'd close the door on him, and on everyone else.

A little while before midnight, I got off the Toronto subway system at Union Station, and walked briskly toward the ramp that leads from the subway to the railroad trains. The walls were hard, shiny and very yellow tile, with vivid-red trim . . . kitchen walls for some immense and imaginary home for the criminally insane. The glare of the lights was merciless, there wasn't a soul in sight to ask me to do or give anything, and then I rounded a corner and I saw a rangy, goofy, awkward youth and, exactly at that split second, he smashed a middle-aged drunk square in the mouth. The boy was wearing gloves, and his fist was big enough to blot out the man's entire face. The back of the man's head struck the glassy yellow tile a horrid thunk. He slumped, he leaned forward, and then I heard a light, clicking sound and, though I had never heard the sound before, I knew it was human teeth falling on the terrazzo floor.

The boy had two shorter friends. I was just standing there for a second, two seconds, and in my right hand there was a rich, brown brief-case, with the good Scotch in it. The three boys looked foolish, scared, and high on their thrill. They giggled, and then they ran crazily all the way down the long, yellow tunnel and up the escalator at the end, and I never saw them again. The man was down on all fours, looking for teeth. Maybe the teeth were false. He was wearing a dirty, black overcoat, and I had a train to catch.

I closed the sliding door on the porter, and sat on the edge of the berth, and the train gave a tiny jolt and drifted out of the station, out of the city, out into the long, obscure countryside. It was a while before I took off even my overcoat. I had not helped the man look for his teeth. I had not asked him if he were all right. I had not chased the boys. I had not looked for a police officer. I had not given my name to anyone. I had not even shouted out, to declare to the world for one instant that I had witnessed an act that was purely wrong. I had not done a goddamn thing, and the time will not come round again.

The Last Walk

It is hot for early April, beautifully hot, and I am sitting on my front steps, drinking a cold beer from the bottle . . . watching the black dog who belongs to the nice, old, one-armed lady across the street . . . watching the convertibles and the red motor-bikes go by, and the girls who please, and the hippie kids carrying hippie clothes down to the laundromat in plastic bags . . . watching the last of the snow as it dies on the small lawns, shrivels up and disappears the way those Invaders from another planet disintegrate when they're killed on television. The television is on now and, behind me, I can hear Bugs Bunny yakking at my children in the darkness of the living-room. The spring of the year is so sure today that, for the first time since October, I've propped the front door open. The insects that grow among the leaves of MacPherson Avenue are still weeks away.

This ritual, beer-drinking on the steps of my house, is one I enjoy. There is something about it that's old and sleepy and beyond the terrors of the year. It is as though, in some summer before my memory begins, I envied men who drank beer on their front porches. The knife-sharpener will be walking along here in a few weeks, and his swinging bell speaks of the time in Toronto that's hanging here in my mind. So does the pop-cornman, with his whistle and his flowing butter. So do the door-to-door hawkers of fresh strawberries, and, this coming summer, they'll very likely all be back under the trees of MacPherson Avenue. This coming summer anyway. The junkman used to drive his horse and cart square in the middle of these streets, and he yelled something that sounded like 'Hardy-boo, hardy-boooo.' He, too, seems to have had something to do with drinking beer on front porches, but I don't think any of us will be seeing him again.

He did his business only about twenty years ago—along with Mackenzie King, and Harry S. Truman, and Syl Apps, and Jack Benny on Sunday nights—but, even so, that has been long enough to bury not only him but a million other Toronto things that, for a time, belonged here as surely as the pyramids belong on the Nile.

This beer, like Frank Sinatra, goes on for ever; but the great, decadent, and gracefully ugly wooden mansions that stared across the lake from the Toronto islands for more than half a century, they're all gone now. And the main drag at Centre Island—with its two beer-halls, its movie house, its smell of sin and shoddiness and romance in the heat of July —it's gone too, and with it, the background for several hundred thousand hot and real flirtations. And Sunnyside. You may catch some of its flavour in a dozen old American film musicals—the kind that star Dan Dailey and Betty Grable—but can anyone remember the exact conformation of its fantastic roller coaster? Or the feeling that it would leave the rails at its high south-eastern corner and fling us up under the flashing moon and far out into the black lake? Oakwood Stadium— where, as the world's skinniest and pimpliest football player, I once fell on a fumble—disappeared a long time ago, and so did the privately operated swimming-pool out there, and the pool at Hogg's Hollow. And the radial streetcars, on north Yonge, that used to hurtle gangs of wildly carousing skiers all the way up to Richmond Hill. We won't be hearing them again.

There were more streetcars in Toronto then than there are now, wooden ones with black stoves in them, and more trees. The streets

269

were skinnier, the ravines were wider, the zoo was dirtier, the Canadian National Exhibition was hickier, and the teen-agers were chippier. Their fashion inspiration was not the hippies but the Mob, the junior Mob. Their vision of a place for sexual discovery was not a pad in Yorkville but, if they could get their hands on one, a Naughty Nash. Often, they couldn't get their hands on any car, but in that time which, as I say, was not very long ago, they still had a good chance of finding utter seclusion on certain Toronto beaches and in certain Toronto parks. Even in the afternoon. It was a time of softball without fielders' gloves, hockey without pads, love without the Pill. How quaint that birth control was the boy's responsibility.

I move in my mind to the parts of the city that have not changed a great deal—over to next summer's heavy shade on the bending streets of Rosedale, east to the boardwalk and sand of the beaches, west to the sultry edges of the Humber River. And then, back there in the living-room somewhere, I hear my son, who is seven now, reading one of his handwritten pronouncements on the solar system to my daughter, who is five. She is already very female about his lectures; she knows that a respectful silence makes him feel good. 'The sun is our thing,' he says, 'that gives us light and heat. We don't all know how big the sun is. But we can *think* how big the sun is. The sun is so big that it seems like it can break the whole universe. But it can't. The universe goes on for ever.'

He draws rockets. I drew Spitfires, and, in 1941, Rudolf Hess parachuted into Scotland; the Germans reached Moscow; the Japanese hit Pearl Harbor; and George Bernard Shaw, H. G. Wells, Lloyd George, Richard Strauss, Gandhi, Al Capone, Sir Frederick Banting, and Henry Ford were all still alive. Trotsky had been dead only one year; Freud, two; Marconi, four; and Alfred Dreyfus, six. I was seven that year, as my son is seven now, but even though I know he'll never see the junkman and the junkman's horse come down his street, I still wonder: Can I really be *that* much older than he is?

None of these reflections sadden me deeply, but in some way they leave me restless. My beer is gone, and I consider disrupting my son's lecture on the sun long enough to fetch another one from the kitchen. I'll get it later. Right now, I must move off down the street. I must explore yet another April among the uncertain ration of Aprils that each one of us receives.

I'm going for a walk.

GRUB STREET?

It is at least possible that in North America some of the most beautiful, evocative and highly crafted English prose of the past few years has not been fiction at all but, rather, rich new offshoots of journalism in print. Call it advocacy journalism, personal journalism, subjective journalism, the New Journalism or, just to make sure we're not leaving anything out, contemporary topical non-fiction.

Whatever you want to call it, it has not flourished in Canada. The stuff I mean appeared first in *Esquire, Harper's, The Atlantic, The Village Voice, Ramparts, New York* magazine, to a certain extent in the *New Yorker,* in quite a few other sometimes hot American periodicals for people who wanted to know what was going on in the world, and in a handful of daily American newspapers.

Later, it spread a bit, and its influence began to humanise corners of even such historically impersonal organs as the great newsmagazines, and *Saturday Evening Post, Life,* and *Look.* At the opposite end of the periodical business, at the distant other end—out among the underground, college and "opposition" press—the movement may have been one inspiration for some embarrassing excesses in first-person writing. That is, if any outside inspiration were needed. Personal journalism is irresistible to undergraduate newspapers. It seems to permit hunch to replace research, emotion to stand in for talent, and a ready flow of creative juice to drown the effort that clarity and conciseness demand. The result can be blush-making.

Among Canadian newspapers and mass magazines, personal journalism or, if you like, introspective journalism has flared up occasionally in such publications as *Maclean's, The Star Weekly,* the *Globe Magazine* but, as a rule, it has not survived the suspicion and mild contempt that publishers seem to feel towards it.

In the Winter of '68, the *Toronto Daily Star* banned from its pages virtually all first-person writing but, not too long before that, it had tolerated more than a year of weekly columns by a man who, although writing under a phony name, used the word "I" to describe various walks he'd taken around downtown Toronto. I mention this not only because I happen to be the man who wrote the walks but also because they now help to make a point.

Some time after the walks appeared, I discovered *Flying a Red Kite* by Hugh Hood and, immediately, I thought that this guy Hood was stealing his whole approach to writing and even some of his subject matter from me. He must have some uncanny pipeline that extends all the way from Montreal and down into my very soul in Toronto. Later, when I finally met Hugh, he beat me to the punch; he cheerfully told me he'd read some of my *Star Weekly* stuff and thought that I was a pretty obvious imitator of him. He's a bit older that I am, and he has the better case.

Well the point is that, although my pieces were lightweight and lumpy beside Hugh's "Recollections of the Works Department" and his "Silver Bugles, Cymbals, Golden Silks," his stuff and mine were nevertheless two of a kind. His appeared first in such publications as the *Tamarack Review* and the *Queen's Quarterly* and, from the first, it has been regarded as part of a body of fiction. Mine appeared first in the *Toronto Daily Star, The Star Weekly* and *Maclean's* and, from the first, it has been regarded as journalism. Off-beat journalism, but still journalism. There are times when such labels as Fiction and Journalism are more confusing than they are convenient, but more about that in a moment.

The best of the new journalism includes Norman Mailer's political and street-scene reporting of the late Sixties and, most recently, his amazing and gorgeous description for *Life* of the night Joe Frazier beat Muhammed Ali; Jimmy Breslin, the newspaper columnist, as he told us, among many other things, about the soldiers' coffins on their way home from Vietnam; the crazy effrontery and style in Tom Wolfe's work for *Esquire*; the grace, authority and drama of Gay Talese, both in his *Esquire* profiles and in his book on *The New York Times*; Willie Morris, the young editor of *Harper's,* on his unsentimental journey home to Mississippi; Loudon Wainwright and Shana Alexander for a while, in *Life*; and perhaps a couple of dozen others. Most of them are Americans, and fairly young. My own favorite is a woman in her mid-thirties named Joan Didion.

Miss Didion never writes a bum sentence. She is a journalist and a novelist, and I quote from the introduction to her book of essays and reports, *Slouching Towards Bethlehem,* only to indicate that the journalist in her may work as desperately hard at her prose as the novelist in her ever does:

"I am not sure what more I could tell you about these pieces. I could tell you that I liked doing some of them more than others, but that all of them were hard for me to do, and took more time than perhaps they were worth; that there is always a point in the writing of a piece when I sit in a room literally papered with false starts and cannot put one word after another and imagine that I suffered a small stroke, leaving me apparently undamaged but actually aphasic. I was in fact as sick as I ever have been when I was writing 'Slouching Towards Bethlehem'; the pain kept me awake at night and so for twenty and twenty-one hours a day I drank gin-and-hot-water to blunt the pain and took Dexedrine to blunt the gin and wrote the piece. (I would like you to believe that I kept working out of some real professionalism, to meet the deadline, but that would not be entirely true; I did have a deadline, but it was also a troubled time, and working did to the trouble what gin did to the pain.) . . ."

Miss Didion's effort is an insight into what certain kinds of journalism *are*. Most people keep in their minds a handy distinction between fiction, which is a great and difficult artistic creation; and mere journalism, which is a comparatively easy and somewhat automatic recording of events. And yet Miss Didion's title piece, "Slouching Towards Bethlehem," was just an article for the *Saturday Evening Post* about hippies in San Francisco, so why did she endure such agonies to set it down?

The answer is that the handy distinction between fiction and journalism is often very wrong and that, in recent years, it has been wrong more often than ever before. Miss Didion, like a great many other magazine journalists, had to shape her piece. She did not just write down the things that she saw and heard. She made something. Her work is always *wrought*.

She, and some of the other writers I've mentioned, have brought such style, and quality of language, and imagination, and personality and terrible effort to their writing about the supposedly real events of the day that they've begun to mash the old distinction between fiction and journalism into meaninglessness. Is Norman Mailer, the sportswriter, less creative than Norman Mailer, the novelist? If you think so, you should probably read more of his sportswriting.

Moreover, you can approach the fuzziness of the distinction from the other side as well. I can think of no more fascinating literary investigation than research into the novelist as a reporter, pop historian, and social commentator. Charles Dickens, Marcel Proust, Theodore Dreiser, John O'Hara, James Jones, Philip Roth, John Cheever spring to mind. Dozens of others would undoubtedly occur to more serious students of the novel.

In the case of Jimmy Breslin, the newspaper columnist, the distinction between fact and fiction became so obscure that one critic championed him on the grounds that it takes so much more courage to put fiction into the mouths of living people than it does to put fiction into the mouths of fictional people. You have all those lawsuits and punches in the nose to contend with. Moreover I gather that Breslin, having written his superb columns, had no great difficulty creating his first novel. Breslin, the newspaperman, just strung some of the columns together and called them a novel; and at last his journalism was formally presented as the fiction that his devotees had always suspected it had been. Norman Mailer, the novelist, went to the Pentagon, and then to Miami and the siege of Chicago for *Harper's* magazine; and some might argue that at last his fiction was formally presented as the journalism it had always been.

In his journalism, Mailer often refers to himself in the third person, as "Mailer," or as "the reporter." He does this even when he's discussing something so intimate as the substance of his own terror. Breslin would introduce himself into his stories in a sly, secret way, as though he were Alfred Hitchcock sneaking into his own movie. He would be the fat guy at the end of the bar, or over at the table in the corner. This practise may be some sort of tribute to the conventional newspaper-man's revulsion for that sissy pronoun "I."

Editors of newspapers have good reason to detest first-person writing. It can get out of hand. It can sound collegiate. If the supremely sensitive writer that could just be lurking in the heart of every hard-boiled newspaper reporter were ever to get the upper hand, if the whole reporting staff were suddenly to start substituting their feelings for facts, the newspaper would instantly become uninformative, boring, and probably rather nauseating as well.

The truth is, however, that the old distinction between fact and fiction was never as neat as it appeared anyway. Even in the driest and cleanest and supposedly most objective presentation of the daily news there is never any such thing as purely *im*personal journalism. Before you get the news, people have handled it, ruled on its importance, and chosen the words to express it. They have also made a whole lot of decisions about the stuff you would *not* be interested in knowing about. (Novelists make such decisions for you, too, though I would not care to push the comparison very far.)

Cold objectivity in the presentation of the news is an essential ideal but an impossible achievement. Good old boys in the newspaper business keep it in mind the way they keep the goal of fairness in mind, and the knowledge that if they do not try to hear both sides of a controversy they're liable to get in trouble. Nowadays, however, it is frequently not even fair for a news report to just give us the facts, ma'am, just

274

the facts, because the facts may not mean anything at all without interpretation and, indeed, they can sometimes add up to a lie.

Some people argue that nothing obscures truth like a mass of facts, but whether or not you want to go that far, it's clear that we must have interpretation, punditry, news analysis or, to use a favorite cliché of the times, depth reporting. Most of these shapings, these squeezings and filterings of the raw facts involve at least a superficial effort at cool, rational judgment by the journalist who's doing the work. He tries to keep his own warts from showing.

A brilliant early flowering of this kind of journalism was *Picture,* Lillian Ross's book-length history of the production in the early Fifties of a Hollywood movie called *The Red Badge of Courage.* The book appeared first as a series in the *New Yorker.* "Miss Lillian Ross names names," said the *New York Herald-Tribune,* "and at the same time she uses all the selectivity of a good novelist. Hers, indeed, is what might be called the technique of the candid typewriter, which is no more truly candid than the candid camera, since neither clicks unless and until the operator chooses." In *In Cold Blood,* Truman Capote is as apparently remote from the action as, say, the voice of Walter Cronkite; and he *fashions* his book from above, manipulating real events and real people just as the God-like novelist manipulates fictional events and fictional people. (Which, by the way, is the greater work of "art"? *Breakfast at Tiffany's,* which is supposed to be pure creation; or *In Cold Blood,* which is supposed to be mere journalism?)

Picture and *In Cold Blood* seem to impose on contemporary events the novelist's discipline, creative influence, and narrative power. As far back as the Forties, Rebecca West was doing something the same sort of thing in her superb book of essay-reports on *The Meaning of Treason*; and, in the years since, this kind of effort has resulted in such crops of excellent work (as well as bad work) that hard-cover journalism now takes its honorable place beside biography and history.

In all these cases however the author, somewhat like the news analyst, takes pains to prevent his own personality and feelings from obtruding on the content. The writers I set out to describe, the Mailers and the Didions, do almost the exact opposite. They are difficult to capture in a generalization. They are often wildly individualistic prose stylists. But if they have a common ground it is their impulse openly and self-consciously to force themselves and often their spiritual agonies on the real events of their times. They want their warts to show. They jump right into the story, tell the reader clearly that that is what they

275

are doing, and present themselves and their feelings as a piece of the progressing event.

In Norman Mailer's description of *The Siege of Chicago*, we learn a great deal about Norman Mailer's fears, his drinking habits, his dreams for the future. We watch his soul as he overcomes the things that have been torturing him. And these revelations are slight compared to what we learn about Norman Mailer when Norman Mailer writes about the Women's Liberation movement.

In *Paper Lion*, a very funny book by George Plimpton about his experiences while "training" with a pro football team, we learn quite a bit about pro football but we learn just as much about George Plimpton.

When Joan Didion writes about the movie star John Wayne we end up knowing Joan Didion better than we'll ever know John Wayne:

"In the summer of 1943 I was eight, and my father and mother and small brother and I were at Peterson Field in Colorado Springs . . . .We went three and four afternoons a week, sat on folding chairs in the darkened Quonset hut which served as a theatre, and it was there, that summer of 1943 while the hot wind blew outside, that I first saw John Wayne. Saw the walk, heard the voice. Heard him tell the girl in a picture called *War of the Wildcats* that he would build her a house, 'at the bend in the river where the cottonwoods grow.' As it happened I did not grow up to be the kind of woman who is the heroine in a Western, and although the men I have known have had many virtues and have taken me to live in many places I have come to love, they have never been John Wayne, and they have never taken me to that bend in the river where the cottonwoods grow. Deep in that part of my heart where the artificial rain forever falls, that is still the line I wait to hear."

Still, in the end, all of this leads me only to a bunch of fat questions. Why is it that in most university English departments *The Naked and The Dead* may be part of a course but *Miami* and *The Siege of Chicago* may not? Since university English departments formally pursue the novel from its beginnings right up to Roth and Bellow and Updike, why is it that their courses in topical non-fiction may include the prose of Milton, Swift, Defoe, Addison and Steele but virtually nothing from the supreme "journalism" of our own century? Must modern "Literature" exclude everything that any fool can plainly see is not a Novel, a Short Story, or a Poem? What then are we going to do with people like James Thurber? Was Leacock a literary craftsman (aside, of course, from being a pretty good journalist)? And finally—the fattest and busiest question of all—what are the relationships among the rise of what I'll

276

call the New Journalism, the decline of fiction in mass magazines, the arrival of the age of television, and the possibility that actual events have become so fantastic and fiendishly gripping that they cry out as never before for the literary treatment that the Norman Mailers are giving them? Is it fair to ask: with writers of this calibre tackling the breaking events of our peculiar and terrible times, who needs fiction?

HARRY BRUCE